The Regulation of Natural Gas

The Regulation of Natural Gas
Policy and Politics, 1938–1978

M. Elizabeth Sanders

Temple University Press

Philadelphia

Temple University Press, Philadelphia 19122
© 1981 by Temple University. All rights reserved
Published 1981
Printed in the United States of America

Library of Congress Cataloging in Publication Data

Sanders, M. Elizabeth, 1943–
  The regulation of natural gas.

  Includes bibliographical references and index.
    1. Gas industry—Government policy—United
States. 2. Gas—Law and legislation—United States.
3. Trade regulation—Economic aspects—United
States. I. Title.
HD9581.U5S26   333.8′23317′0973   81-9239
ISBN 0-87722-221-5   AACR2

For Richard

Contents

Figures

Tables

Preface

Mention natural gas regulation and you will probably produce a shudder in the average congressman or presidential aide, as he or she recalls the monumental battles that have been fought since the 1940s over federal control of the industry. The combatants tend to view their opponents in exaggerated terms: they are either the minions of the devilish oil lobby or northern socialists bent on pillaging southwestern colonies of their natural resources. The regulation of natural gas is, in the words of a House committee staffer, "a theological issue."

Such conflicts have an irresistible appeal for political scientists. Here is a national debate that calls forth broad and varied participation from the public. The Cleveland City Council sends representatives to Congress when changes are proposed in natural gas law; their testimony is recorded alongside that of Standard Oil, the AFL-CIO, the mayor of Tulsa, the Consumer Federation of America, the Texas Independent Producers and Royalty Owners Association, and a contingent of economists from MIT. This is an issue on which presidents and party leaders meet to plan strategies, bureaucrats brace themselves for an immediate outcry when a pricing decision is handed down, and coalitions are marshalled on the floor of Congress to rewrite committee recommendations. Even the federal courts have been politicized. Lawyers for producers and consumers race to file their appeals in Washington or New Orleans, expecting quite different outcomes from the two circuits. Given the breadth, intensity, and long duration of this conflict, an analysis of the politics of natural gas regulation may provide the student of American politics with important insights into the determinants of congressional, presidential, bureaucratic, and even judicial behavior on economic issues.

In dealing with case studies, the question that must be addressed at the beginning is, "What is this a case *of*?" The first tasks are to make explicit the underlying assumptions and to specify the boundary conditions within which the propositions put forth in the investigation should hold. The following is a case of national economic regulation, specifically, in the energy sector (even more specifically, to make a bad pun, in the natural gas field). It undertakes to analyze and explain the political conflict that has accompanied four decades of the administration of the Natural Gas Act. The primary focus is on Congress because that is where the law is made. However, since regulatory law is generally quite ambiguous, leaving it to administrators and judges to say what the law *means*, agency and judicial decisions are also central to the policy-making process. It is assumed, nevertheless, that regulatory agencies and the courts to which their decisions may be appealed operate within the constraints provided by the two elected branches. The congressional constraints are found in statutes, in oversight of the bureaucracy, in appropriations, and in confirmation of appointments to both agencies and courts; the presidential role involves making those appointments and recommending (and vetoing) regulatory legislation.

It is assumed here that political actors are rational, goal-directed, and self-interested individuals. Although politicians and ordinary citizens often behave in ways that seem to contradict that premise, the rationality assumption is more useful for theory building than alternative assumptions, and there is a substantial body of evidence that both voters and elected officials do adopt goal-directed, utility-maximizing strategies on questions of economic policy. If the government's economic decisions have immediate, differential, and measurable impacts on the incomes of their constituents, then, in a representative democracy, congressmen and presidents will act in the interest of income-maximization (over a fairly short term) for those constituents. It is not claimed that political behavior on the variety of foreign policy or "social" issues (dealing with definitions of moral and criminal conduct, for example) that come before the government has similar determinants, although arguments can be made that opposing positions on these issues also have roots that may be traced back to different regional economic systems.

The opening chapter reviews leading theories of regulatory behavior and explains why each of them fails to account for the political processes characteristic of natural gas regulation. A "political economy" approach is developed as an alternative interpretative framework within which the behavior of congressmen, regulatory commissioners, and presidents on the natural gas issue can be analyzed.

Chapters 2 and 3 describe the economic and political environment surrounding passage of the first Natural Gas Act in 1938. An analysis of the political and market forces operating in the Depression period explains the consensus reached by consumer, producer, and pipeline interests on the need for federal regulation of the gas industry.

Chapter 4 covers the early history of gas regulation under the Federal Power Commission and the impact of statutory interpretation on the ensuing four decades of political competition between consumer and producer interests. The ambiguity and broad discretionary power that distinguished the 1938 act ensured a dominant role for the regulatory agency and the courts. The latitude inherent in the statutory mandate allowed the meaning of the law to evolve and adapt to both a changing economic environment and a shift in the balance of political power in Congress.

The middle period of natural gas regulation, from 1954 to 1968, is covered in Chapter 5. When the jurisdiction of the agency was extended to producer prices by a 1954 Supreme Court decision, the political process was transformed from a relatively non-controversial example of utility regulation into a much more conflictual redistributive policy. As a result, the Federal Power Commission was forced to redefine its role in an increasingly polarized political environment.

Chapter 6 explores the long-term economic consequences of redistributive regulation and describes the reemergence of demands for amendment of the organic statute. Advocates of regulatory reform proposed two diametrically opposed solutions to regulatory failure: one group urged an extension of federal controls over intrastate gas pricing and industrial fuel use in order to correct the unanticipated and undesirable consequences of FPC regulation; an opposing coalition advocated that regulation of gas producer prices be eliminated altogether.

Throughout the 1970s supporters of these conflicting policy alternatives clashed while the FPC, besieged from both sides, pursued an unpopular and ultimately untenable middle course. The study concludes with a discussion of the contest over the Carter administration's consumer-oriented energy program and explains how "spectator" interests with no immediate stake in the outcome came to play a decisive role in the passage of the 1978 Natural Gas Policy Act. The penultimate chapter also highlights the political instability that characterizes the 1978 compromise.

The intellectual debt that this study owes to the work of Theodore Lowi will be apparent to readers; he is, of course, not responsible for the uses made of his policy typology or its integration into an "economic" perspective. I would also like to gratefully acknowledge the helpful criticism and encouragement offered by Alan Stone and Edward J. Harpham of the University of Houston and Michael Miller of Syracuse University. They are absolved from any responsibility for remaining errors or deficiencies. The Stanford University business and government documents libraries granted me access to their excellent collections during the preparation of this study. Rice University provided essential research funds. I would also like to thank the following people for their assistance: Margaret Greenwood and Gayle De Gregori for typing the manuscript; Michael Ames, Dianne Sigler, and Nanette Bendyna at

Temple University Press for supervising, encouraging, and editing this work, and my mother, Mildred Rowe Sanders, for cheerfully devoting a year of her life to the care of her grandson, Seth.

My greatest and most varied debt is to my husband, Richard F. Bensel. His constant encouragement, thoroughgoing criticism, and help with editing and computations were invaluable. In recognition of his generous and thoughtful support, this book is dedicated to him.

The Regulation of
Natural Gas

FIGURE 1
Major Natural Gas Pipelines, March 31, 1980

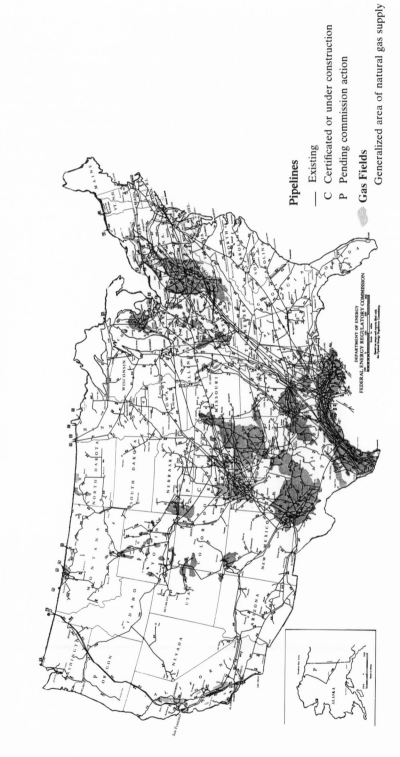

Pipelines
— Existing
C Certificated or under construction
P Pending commission action

Gas Fields
Generalized area of natural gas supply

DEPARTMENT OF ENERGY
FEDERAL ENERGY REGULATORY COMMISSION

1 | Introduction

In the 1970s, it became apparent to most economists and political scientists concerned with the subject that federal economic regulation had, in most cases, failed to achieve its ostensible goals. Prominent among examples of regulatory failure was the case of natural gas. Forty years of natural gas regulation by the Federal Power Commission was said to have produced a shortage of natural gas in interstate pipelines, given advantages to some regions at the expense of others, encouraged the wasteful consumption of a high quality fuel, caused severe harm to a competing fuel industry, and increased the nation's dependence on expensive foreign oil. While particular actions of the FPC could be associated with each of these maladies, there was no satisfactory explanation for why the commissioners should have behaved in such a manner. Were they merely shortsighted and incompetent? Some economists seem to imply that they were, although it is often granted that the regulatory endeavor itself is impossible to perform competently, even for men and women of intelligence and good will.

Political scientists naturally seek explanations for regulatory failure that emphasize "political" motives and processes—that is, behavior that is concerned ultimately with the distribution of power in society ("power" being defined as legitimate, or publicly sanctioned, control over the allocation of scarce resources). Unfortunately it has proved impossible to find, in the large body of literature dealing with political bureaucracy, a theory that accounts for the historical behavior of the Federal Power Commission.

The most popular explanation for the disappointing performance of regulatory agencies is that regulators inevitably become "captives" of the regulated industries. The Interstate Commerce Commission, it is said, serves "mainly to protect the railroads against effective regulation by the public."[1] The Federal Power Commission, likewise, has been charged with consistently making decisions that "enacted by administrative fiat what the pressure groups [natural gas producers and utility companies] had failed to achieve by legislation."[2] If this explanation had some credence in the 1950s (when the above critique was written), it rang false a decade later. Not only did gas producers in the 1960s see the FPC as inimicable to their interests, but gas producers and utility companies often held diametrically opposed positions in rate proceedings before the commission.

What is clearly needed is a theory of regulatory behavior that can account for historical variations in the output of agencies, as well as shifting alliances and conflicts among the major political actors in a regulatory arena. This analysis represents an attempt, through a case study on natural gas regulation, to suggest the outlines of such a theory.

Prominent Theories of Regulatory Behavior

"Regulation," as Marver Bernstein reminded his readers two decades ago, "is intensely and unavoidably political."[3] Nevertheless, key dimensions of the political process have been collapsed in studies of regulation by both economists and political scientists. While single-cause theories have obvious advantages, they often sacrifice explanatory power to simplicity. The first simplification usually encountered in studies of economic regulation is the assumption of a holistic national or consumer interest which regulation is intended to serve (or which, whatever the intention, is the only legitimate end of regulation). Analysis then generally goes on to show how regulation fails to achieve the public interest, and to postulate reasons and remedies for this failure. Blame is usually attributed to the personal characteristics of congressmen and bureaucrats, to the public itself, to the content of the law, or to the internal dynamics of the bureaucratic regulatory process. Despite the attractiveness of unicausal explanations, one culprit seems inevitably to implicate another.

Contemporary consumer advocates often personalize the causes of regulatory failure, suggesting that the public interest may be salvaged if only better men and women can be found to staff the agencies.[4] Similarly, political scientist Samuel Huntington has attributed the "marasmus" (withering) of the once progressive and energetic Interstate Commerce Commission to the commissioners' loss of objectivity. By shortsightedly tying itself to a strategy of promoting railroad interests, the ICC, in Huntington's view, neglected its legislative mandate to promote the public interest in cheap and efficient transportation.[5]

Rather than attributing failure to bureaucratic bias or incompetence, Marver Bernstein argues that regulatory agencies have a natural "life-cycle." From vigorous youth, they seem to move inexorably through maturity to a senescence coincident with complete "capture" by the regulated industry. In this explanation, the blame seems to lie primarily with the public and its elected representatives. Politically isolated because of public apathy, understaffed and overwhelmed by procedural requirements, regulators can hardly be blamed for following the path of least resistance and succumbing to the demands of their active and interested business clientele. The public fails to sustain its support because its attention span is short. That support, according to Bernstein, peaks at the time of enactment of the regulatory statute. The public then breathes a sigh of relief, and retires from the arena as if administrative implementation of legislative goals were automatic. Congressmen, who naturally shrink from the "acrid animosities" of regulatory battles, take their cue from the public and put away their swords.[6] Even more critical of the public's sporadic attention, Murray Edleman argues that reformists are easily lulled into "quiescence" by symbols—in this case, the creation of an agency—and show little or no interest in the substance of the regulatory process.[7]

To Gabriel Kolko, the capitulation of the regulatory bureaucracy is inevitable, not because of public apathy, but because capture was, in fact, the intention of the authors and supporters of the original legislation. In this interpretation, the genesis of the ICC lay not in the demands of farmers and shippers, but in the desire of larger railroads to reduce competition. Thus the establishment of regulatory agencies represents, not the realization of the public interest, but the "triumph of conservatism."[8] Economist George Stigler shares Kolko's cynicism about the motivations and inevitable results of regulation. Stigler maintains that, "as a rule, regulation is acquired by the industry and is designed and operated primarily for its benefit." Thus criticism of the regulatory bureaucracy for pursuing industry over public benefit is completely misplaced. One might as well, in Stigler's words, "criticize the A and P for selling groceries."[9] It is indicative of the appeal of the "original intent" argument that it has appeared in critiques of regulation from both left (Kolko) and right (Stigler).

Both "original intent" and "subsequent capture" theories are at least superficially compatible with the group theory of politics elaborated by Mancur Olson.[10] Law and administration are interpreted by Olson as the outcome of group pressure. In a given legislative arena, producer groups are inevitably stronger than consumer groups because smaller numbers and the salience of publicly provided benefits to producers give them an organizational advantage over consumers. Because regulation has a highly visible impact on their incomes, milk producers, truckers, and broadcasters are more likely to organize to promote minimum price and entry regulation than consumers of milk, transportation services, and television programming are to organize for lower prices and competitive supply. Since the individual members of "the public" are more likely to communicate demands growing out of their producer interests, rather than the diffuse interests they share with the rest of the "public," government policy tends to promote "special" as opposed to "common" interests. Elected officials, likewise, will find it easier to put together supportive coalitions from intense minorities rather than apathetic majorities.[11] In its most extreme form, the "group interest" model describes the policy-making apparatus as an "iron triangle" in which the ostensibly regulated group, the administrative unit, and the congressional committee join in a mutual exchange of benefits outside the public eye.[12] Governmental power in this instance has been almost completely privatized.

Statutes and Politics

In spite of serious reservations concerning past and current regulatory behavior, many political scientists remain convinced that legislators can, and sometimes actually do, write legislation with the national or public interest in mind. Evidence for public interest motives can be found in both legislative sponsorship and the behavior of regulatory agencies at particular times. Alan Stone and James Q. Wilson, for example, point out that regulatory decisions antagonistic to the professed interests of regulated industries are too numerous to be ignored.[13] Writing about the Federal Trade Commission, Stone observes that outspoken industry critics whose motives could hardly be suspect supported the original legislation. FTC statutes were not designed exclusively for either public or private benefit, but reflect "a host of divergent interests and contradictions." Thus, in Stone's words, "any statement beginning, 'the FTC was created for the purpose of . . .' must be arrant nonsense."[14]

Precisely because people with very different motives supported the creation of the regulatory agencies, their statutes are riddled with ambiguities and contradictions. Again it is inappropriate to castigate the regulatory agencies for failing to clearly define and promote the public interest. As Louis Jaffe argues, "When the Congress has not been able to formulate a consensus, we cannot expect the politically weaker agency to do much better."[15]

Theodore Lowi has suggested that if Congress cannot write explicit statutes detailing what it wants done, and how its goals should be achieved, then it has no business making law at all. It is better to have no law than bad law. Most of contemporary economic regulation is based on "bad" law—statutes that merely inscribe a lament calling for some vague problem (or set of problems) to be remedied and leaving it to bureaucrats, judges, and the affected groups to decide what the law is in a given instance. Lowi advocates reinstatement of the Schechter rule (in which the Supreme Court invalidated the National Industrial Recovery Act of

1933 on the grounds that it unconstitutionally delegated legislative power to the executive branch).[16]

In Lowi's view it is unlikely, but not impossible, that Congress will make unambiguous law in the public (majority) interest. However, he apparently expects that presidential and judicial activism on behalf of a non-delegation standard, as well as an explicit limitation on the lifetime of an enabling statute and a rotating senior civil service will be necessary to encourage the legislature to make explicit law on a regular basis.[17] Lowi's work on law and policy has both normative and analytical components. The latter, in particular, are richly suggestive for a historical study of economic regulation. In addition to urging the passage of well-articulated statutes and the codification of administrative decisions, Lowi has developed a framework for classifying public policies and predicting the characteristics of the politics to which a given statute will give rise. Although Lowi does not offer an explanation of how the statute came to be written, given a certain type of fundamental statute, his scheme attempts to predict from characteristics of the statute itself both the nature of the political conflicts that will emerge during legislative consideration and the structure of the implementing bureaucracy.[18] The fundamental characteristic of government, he argues, is its ability to exercise coercion. The intersection of two characteristics of governmental coercion—the nature of its targets (whether coercion is directed at individuals or at classes of actors through system-level constraints) and its immediacy (whether coercion is remote or immediate)—produces a four-fold table into which public policies are classified as distributive, regulatory, redistributive, or constituent.

The degree of specificity present in statutory language varies among the four cells—particularly between regulatory and redistributive policy.

FIGURE 2
Statutory Characteristics and Policy Types
Applicability of Coercion

Likelihood of Coercion	Individual Conduct	Environment of Conduct
Remote	Distributive Policy	Constituent Policy
Immediate	Regulatory Policy	Redistributive Policy

SOURCE: Theodore J. Lowi, "Public Policy and Bureaucracy in the United States and France," paper delivered at the Edinburgh IPSA Congress, Aug. 1976.

Regulatory policies are often worded vaguely, leaving working definitions of terms like "fair competition" to be developed by administrators (with considerable input from regulated firms) and the judges to whom their decisions may be appealed. Redistributive policies are highly explicit because their targets are classes of people or firms whose identity is revealed automatically by the intersection of named properties (for example, people over sixty-five who have incomes of less than four thousand dollars).[19]

Lowi suggests that there is a developmental component in his scheme. In the early years of the American republic, most federal policies were distributive, encompassing the building of roads, bridges, canals, and so forth. Regulatory and redistributive policies (at the federal level) came later, with the emergence of a truly national economy. As one moves counter-clockwise through the typology, from distributive to regulatory to redistributive policy, the focus of the coercive power of the law expands from individuals to classes of people. Enactment is therefore more controversial and the locus of policy leadership moves up accordingly: from committees to the floor in Congress, and from lower-level administrators to the president and his top aides. For Lowi, redistributive laws more nearly approach a legislative ideal. Whereas distributive and regulatory policies are made in a pluralistic setting with groups, committees, and bureaucrats as the major participants, redistributive policy is made by a "parliamentary" Congress, its final outlines determined on the floor rather than behind subcommittee doors. Redistributive policies enjoy the high visibility of genuine national debates, and positions on them tend to aggregate opposing interests into broad and relatively stable coalitions of "haves" and "have nots." The president, party leaders, and high-level administrative personnel play active roles and controversy is high. In making redistributive law the elected representatives of the majority exercise full sovereignty. Coercive potential is high; because it is public, explicit, and majoritarian, however, it is, in Lowi's view, fully legitimate coercion.

Since American liberals fear power, the twentieth-century expansion of government has produced more distributive and regulatory legislation than redistributive statutes. Lowi has labeled as "interest group liberalism" the tendency of liberals to parcel out the power of the expanded state to the de facto control of interested groups. According to the pluralist ethic of American liberals, regulated firms must be allowed to participate actively, not only in the enactment of regulatory statutes but also in their subsequent implementation by the administrative agency.[20] An example of this tendency can be found in the National Industrial Recovery Act of 1933. Under its extremely vague mandate, the federal government allowed industrial trade associations to set their own codes of "fair competition." These codes fixed prices and controlled production, subject to final presidential approval. They created, in effect, publicly sanctioned cartels.[21] Although the broad system of industrial self-government envisioned by the NIRA was aborted by the Supreme Court's Schechter decision, government policy making that relegates to interest groups the power to set the terms of their "regulation" has continued apace.

The complexity of Lowi's formulation is a source of both strength and weakness. In its capacity for generating hypotheses about the relationships among citizens, groups, elected officials, and administrators, the Lowi typology and argument are probably unequaled. There is a compelling logic in the claim that, after all, the content of a public policy—what gets done, how, and with what effect—is rooted in its statutory foundation.[22] Lowi aptly criticizes theories of regulatory "capture," like those of Huntington, Bernstein, and Edelman, that ignore the impact of the organic statute on the "marasmus" or "capture" of agencies and imply that the outcome of the regulatory process will be the same for various agencies regardless of differences in their statutory mandates.[23] The more ambiguous the wording of a statute, the more authority it delegates to bureaucracies and courts to define and proscribe illegal conduct, the more likely it is that the outcome of policy will be the result of a bargaining process between administrators and affected groups. This bargained outcome will bear little resemblance to the "public interest" so loftily enshrined in the statute's preamble.

There are two fundamental problems with the Lowi typology as it stands. The first is the difficulty of classifying policies into the four cells. Not only may different sections of a statute prescribe different degrees and targets of control, but also there are clearly great variations within the cells. Although Lowi does recognize qualitative differences among regulatory policies, he nevertheless maintains that there is a "quantum leap" from regulation to redistribution.[24] The implication is that most of the significant variations in the political process will be found between, rather than within, the cells. When, as in the case of natural gas policy, an ostensibly regulatory policy begins to generate a politics akin to that attributed to redistributive policy without a change in the formal content of the statute, the typology does not readily suggest an explanation.

Second, the Lowi framework focuses on an intermediate slice of the policy process—the politics and administrative structure generated by statutory content. While this represents a provocative turn in policy theory, it leaves unanswered a host of questions that political scientists have always felt compelled to ask. On the one hand, it offers few suggestions as to why a statute came to be written in a given form. What characteristics of the political or economic environment allow (or encourage) congressmen to write laws that promote the well-being of an industry at the expense of the public (or other firms)? Conversely, what forces converge to aggregate group interests into broad coalitions supporting and opposing redistributive statutes?

At the other end of the policy process, the behavior of the officials implementing the statutes also receives little attention in Lowi's scheme. There is now an extensive body of literature that views the administrative process as a logical outcome of rational, goal-seeking behavior on the part of individual bureaucrats. The cultivation of support among interest groups and congressional committees, the development of an organizational *modus operandi*, and attempts to incrementally expand both jurisdiction and appropriations are seen as inevitable bureaucratic behaviors designed to secure and enhance the status of the administrator's job.[25] While legislative politics and statutory foundations determine the degree of freedom administrators have to pursue these activities, causation can also operate in the other direction. Much legislative activity is a reaction to agency behavior, and statutes themselves are often written at the instigation of (or with considerable participation by) administrators. In order to understand the evolution of a policy it may well be necessary to analyze the creative role of bureaucrats.

In the same vein, a theory of public policy must posit some set of assumptions about the behavior of congressmen and presidents. Lowi's framework attempts to specify the impact of policy (that is, statutory foundation) on politics, and not the reverse process. Thus, it offers little illumination of congressional motives for enacting various types of policy, except as they pertain to a generalized liberal preference for eschewing conflict and coopting all affected interests in the policy enterprise. Among students of congressional behavior, it is common to assume that congressmen have ideological predispositions that incline them to support or oppose government regulation of business on behalf of consumers. If the pursuit of ideological goals is instrumentally rational (that is, if taking a given ideological position contributes to one's re-election), it still remains to be explained why voters in some districts support "liberal," and in other districts "conservative," representatives. If, on the other hand, an ideological stance is not related to a re-election motive but is a nonrational feature of personality, then regulation theory that relies on ideology has probably reached a dead end. Conventional "capture" theses seem to assume either that congressmen are lazy, responding fitfully to public outcries and passing problems onto administrators, or that they are the pliant tools of well-organized producer groups. None of these approaches offers a satisfactory explanation for cycles of regulatory activity in which different interests are promoted, nor can they account for variations among individual congressmen on a given regulatory issue.

Natural Gas and Regulatory Theory

The case of natural gas regulation illustrates some of the weaknesses of existing regulation theory. Like much of the economic regulation initiated during the New Deal, the original Natural Gas Act of 1938 was ambiguously worded, highly discretionary, and quite acceptable to both the regulated industry and the consuming public. Within a few years of passage, however, the economic situation that had originally generated demand for the statute changed dramatically. In addition, doctrinal innovation by the Federal Power Commission, accepted and expanded by Supreme Court interpretation, ultimately resulted in a tremendous expansion of the act's jurisdiction—from a few hundred transporters to thousands of producers of natural gas. These changes in jurisdiction greatly changed the pattern of politics in natural gas policy making. Political consensus gradually gave way to polarization as consumers and producers struggled to control the content of regulatory policy.

Thus while the circumstances of original passage seem compatible with "capture," "life cycle," "original intent," or "symbolic acquiescense" theories, the later history of gas regulation is not. The public has been far from "quiescent," and the agency's behavior pattern cannot accurately be described as one of cooptation by producers. Rather, dominance of the regulatory process has alternated between regionally based consumer and producer interests. Conventional theories may facilitate understanding of particular aspects of the energy regulatory process, but not the whole. Similarly, Lowi's "arenas of conflict" theory can illuminate the political changes that follow a revision of statutory content (in this case, "revision" by agency and judicial interpretation of the original statute), but it does not explain the motives of the political actors involved in making and contesting that revision. What is needed is a theoretical framework that both specifies the relationships among political actors— congressmen, commissioners, presidents, judges—and, in turn, links each to a political constituency and an economic environment. What we want to know is not only how the statutory foundation for a policy came to be constructed as it was, but what economic changes and alterations in political balance supported particular agency behavior patterns.

The concept of "political economy" provides a framework broad enough to encompass these objectives, and, hopefully, to integrate a number of important insights from conventional theories of regulation. This study puts forward an explanation of the politics of natural gas regulation from the perspective of political economy. "Political economy" is defined as the efforts of political actors to manipulate the marketplace to their constituents' (and hence their own) advantage. This is, of course, a considerably narrower definition of the term than that used in the seventeenth and eighteenth centuries to describe (usually with strong normative overtones) the aggregate of economic policies pursued by the state.[26] The focus here is on national economic policy (with respect to a particular industry), but the state is not viewed as a monolithic entity. Rather, it is a set of institutions within which elected and appointed officials are involved in making policy, each pursuing goals which, however broadly defined, can generally be linked to the political constituencies that control their tenure in office. Both officials and voters are assumed to be instrumentally rational: that is, they further their own interests through political action. On regulation issues, the voter's principal interest is in maximizing his net income. For the politician, the immediate interest is re-election, and the means to that goal is promotion of his or her constituents' interest (that is, maximization of net income).

While it may be possible for the genuinely disinterested observer to posit an economic policy that maximizes the long-term economic health of the nation as a whole, there is no reason to expect that such a policy will always result from the political process in a democracy. Both voters and politicians are usually interested in the immediate effects of a policy on their incomes or electoral security, respectively; they tend to discount "long-term" benefits. Thus, as welfare economists have often demonstrated, the outcome resulting from the pursuit of rational self-interest by a multitude of actors need not be a "rational" public policy. On natural gas issues, conceptions of "good public policy" or "the national interest" tend to vary with proximity to the wellhead or interstate pipeline.

In the political economy of natural gas regulation, efforts to manipulate national regulatory policy can be traced to four sets of regionally based interests:

   1. producer areas whose private economies and public services depend on the quantity and value of gas production;
   2. gas-deficit consumer areas, dependent on a regulated interstate supply;
   3. regions producing a competing fuel (principally the Appalachian coal fields); and
   4. "spectator" areas which neither produce nor consume significant interstate supplies but are available for alliances with the above interests.

Particular areas of the country have shifted between categories as their supply situations changed, and their political stances on regulation have shifted accordingly. The Federal Power Commission (now FERC) was for forty years the central focus for contending interests in the natural gas policy arena. In order to protect as much as possible of its original and acquired jurisdiction, the commission adapted its behavior to accommodate a shifting congressional balance among the four interests. It has been particularly sensitive to the House and Senate Commerce committees that exercise preeminent influence in FPC jurisdiction and appointments. As regional polarization intensified, however, both the floor of Congress and the president have assumed larger roles in the policy process. The Supreme Court (which itself changes, albeit much more slowly, in response to changes in the electoral base of the president) has played a more passive but highly significant role in setting the terms of natural gas regulation. It has sometimes thwarted the FPC in its efforts to respond to changes in its political environment by overturning commission decisions or "freezing" an interpretation of natural gas law that the commission would like to disavow. In general, it can be said that the Supreme Court has acted to uphold and extend the national jurisdictional claims made by the FPC against competing claims from the states.

This study will trace the interactions of these political actors over the forty-year life of the Natural Gas Act. It explains regulation as the outcome of a dynamic relationship among congressmen, presidents, and commissioners who themselves reflect the changing market positions of their constituents (that is, their relationships as buyers, sellers, and competitors of natural gas). It is assumed that a given regulatory statute creates a set of interests in regulation and that these interests will dominate subsequent political debate on the policy. The focus on the statute and the attempts to amend it over four decades follows the admonition of Lowi and others that policy studies must inquire into the content and purpose of regulatory law. In this case, however, it is difficult to argue that original statutory content has been determining, except in the sense that a vaguely worded statute has permitted the interplay of economic interests to produce, over time, very different policy outcomes. The critical factors, given statutory ambiguity, are the state of the economy and the balance of political interests in regulation at a particular time.

This line of reasoning suggests that "capture" of the regulatory process by producers does not take place unless certain conditions are met. Those conditions probably include the following: (1) the costs of the regulated product or service are diffuse and hidden, as with higher shipping costs or restrictions on competition; (2) consumers are cross-pressured, as, for example, when the regulated industry provides them with valuable services, employment, stock dividends, and tax revenues; (3) the beneficiaries of regulation are numerous enough to have a significant impact on congressional and presidential elections; or (4), in the presence of the first two conditions, the beneficiaries of regulation have the support of a majority of members on the congressional committees that oversee the work of the regulatory agency, and the legislative process encourages reciprocal ratification on the floor of decisions made by "interested" committee members.

On the other hand, if the charges of the regulated industry are highly visible, consumers both numerous and distant from the site of production of the regulated product, and oversight committees dominated by representatives of the consumer region, the regulatory process may well be "captured" by consumers. To reconcile this claim with Olson's argument that large groups (for example, gas consumers) will seldom be able to create organized interests that match the political clout of producers, it is necessary only to fall back on the basis of representation in American politics and the role played by congressmen. The individual congressman is a political entrepreneur who owes his occupational longevity only to his ability to please a majority of voters in his district. If a majority of non–cross-pressured consumers exists in the district, he, in effect, bears the cost of seeking out ("organizing") and channeling that interest into the political process. If the consumer interest in the district is supported by other smaller, but politically active, producer interests (for example, gas-distributing utilities and gas-consuming industries), his task is even easier: he will always vote to control the price and allocation of the regulated product in the interest of his district's consumers.

In the United States, both congressional and presidential elections are determined by candidate-oriented, plurality victories in geographically demarcated constituencies. Because of the territorial basis of American politics and the weakness of integrating mechanisms like political parties, regionalism is a familiar feature of political debate (although it varies in intensity from time to time). Studies of regulation, however, have seldom given much attention to regional interests. When debates over economic policy give rise to acrimonious contests over the distribution of wealth, the usual assumption is that an ideological or class-based struggle is taking place.

Even among economists, explanations of political behavior that rely on regional economic interests have been given short shrift. For example, economist Edward Mitchell contends that "energy policy in recent years has been determined largely by ideology instead of economic interests."[27] There is, of course, considerable overlap among ideological, economic, and partisan interests. For example, most Republicans represent spectator or producer rather than consumer districts. Conversely, most representatives from areas of high natural gas consumption are Democrats, so that there is both a partisan and an economic interest in maintaining fuel price controls. Democrats from Texas and Louisiana oppose their party, however, even when, as in several cases, they are otherwise quite "liberal."[28] Where the interest is clear, principle tends to follow, or at least not contradict, economic (and electoral) interests. Support for federal regulation of natural gas may be described as both a "liberal" and a Democratic position because, since the New Deal, American liberalism has been defined in large measure by support for federal powers to intervene in the marketplace.[29] In this case, however, the ideological and partisan cast are incidental to local economic interests. Because the expense of constructing pipelines in the 1930s and 1940s could only be amortized by laying those transmission lines to the great, densely populated metropolitan areas of the country, the interest in maintaining low interstate prices is felt most keenly in the older urban-industrial cities—places that tend, for a variety of social and economic reasons, to send "liberal" Democrats to Congress.[30]

An argument for the primacy of economic over partisan or ideological interests must rest on fine distinctions. No "region" (such as the South or Midwest) has a homogeneous economic interest on any national regulation issue. Nor do most states have homogeneous interests. In the case of gas regulation, consumers are concentrated in cities and their levels of consumption (hence the impact of gas prices on their incomes) vary according to climate and the uses to which gas is put by residences. Thus, the most relevant factor in determining the "economic" interest of a congressman's constituency (in gas-deficit states) is the percentage of household consumers, weighted perhaps by the per-household consumption level. It is always difficult to find all the information necessary to specify the precise economic situation of a constituency, particularly since not all the voters in a geographically described constituency are actually members of the representative's electoral coalition. As will be shown in Chapters 6 and 7, however, even unrefined measures of economic interest (such as household gas service ratios and residence in a gas-exporting state) are good predictors of congressional votes on the natural gas issue. Over 70 percent of representatives from gas-importing districts where a majority of households used gas opposed deregulation in the mid-1970s, while well over 90 percent of congressmen from gas-exporting states supported it.

In the states that produce gas, household consumers are cross-pressured by the fact that their state treasuries and educational institutions depend on revenues which rise as the price of gas rises. Thus, a measure of "consumer" interest can only be applied to gas-importing regions. Areas producing a competing product (coal, in this instance) have other economic interests in regulation that may be more important than the simple percentage of households consuming gas produced elsewhere. There also exists a large number of political constituencies that have been labeled "spectators" in this study because they do not produce gas or competing fuels for export, nor do a majority of households in these areas consume gas. Through thirty years of legislative controversy over deregulation, there has been a consistent polarization of producer and urban consumer areas, but fluid alliance patterns have prevailed among spectators and, to a lesser extent, coal areas.[31]

The history of natural gas regulation indicates that when producers and consumers are concentrated in different regions, particularly in a situation of growing scarcity, "regulation" takes on the characteristics of "redistribution." In this case, a shift in the focus of regulation, from interstate pipeline companies to regionally concentrated producers gave rise to significant changes in regulatory politics and ultimately to a drastic revision of statutory content. The terms of political debate were altered in ways suggested by Lowi's description of the differences in politics surrounding "regulatory" and "redistributive" policies:

> 1. the original "regulatory" statute was vaguely worded and discretionary as to price setting; the new Natural Gas Policy Act of 1978 is highly specific;
> 2. the president had little involvement in the original act but played a major role in formulating natural gas policy in 1977–1978;
> 3. relatively few congressmen were involved in the construction of the 1938 act, but a large number participated in 1977–1978;
> 4. the original act aroused almost no opposition and passed by voice vote; the new statute (and attempts at policy change in the two preceding decades) elicited broad and relatively stable opposing coalitions of "haves" and "have nots" and was ratified by a narrow margin.

The saga of natural gas regulation illustrates both the strengths and the seemingly inevitable frustrations of the American political process. In this case, it is not naïve to argue that regulation has reflected the will of the majority. The problem is that different majority wills have been brought to bear at different points in time and at different points in the political system. The result can hardly be described as a rational or well-conceived national policy. Cynics will be reminded of the words of H. L. Mencken and Pogo: in a democracy people probably get the kind of government they deserve. Alas, we have seen the enemy and he is us.

2 | The Origins of Natural Gas Regulation

Promotion and Protection: The Evolution of Economic Regulation

Public regulation of business has historically had two purposes that are not at all easy to disentangle: to promote industry and to protect the public. Although studies of regulation by political scientists often seem to imply that only the latter purpose is legitimate, economists seldom make such normative distinctions.[1] Most textbooks on government-business relations treat the two in a matter-of-fact and even-handed way.

Promotional regulation has a long history. Colonial and early state and municipal governments encouraged the development of important services (particularly canals, bridges, ferries, and mills) by granting franchises and direct subsidies for capitalization and operating costs. In return for exclusive or semi-exclusive charters (limiting the entry of competitors into the same business) and secure revenues (either through direct subsidy or guaranteed rates), the holder of the franchise was obligated to provide certain services or products at prices that were not exorbitant. By virtue of this promotional regulation, early transportation and communications networks were built and essential community services established.[2]

Early product regulation provided quality controls that both insured the value of exports and protected local consumers. Regulation also established the legal and monetary framework for business transactions—laws of contract and bankruptcy, patent protection, sound currencies, and so forth. Although "private" interests were the direct beneficiaries, it is easy to argue that these promotional regulatory activities served the public interest as well.

Ultimately it became necessary to institute overtly protective activities that regulated private property and transactions in ways not always desired by affected businesses. A regulatory apparatus was created, under the police powers of the state, to protect the consuming public from fraud, discrimination, price gouging, and physical harm. Just as promotion served the public interest, protection often served certain private interests as well. Kolko argues, for example, that pure food laws aided (and were supported by) large meat packers and food processors who hoped that the new standards would limit competition from foreign and smaller domestic corporations.[3]

An alternative means of protecting the public from exorbitant prices and shoddy goods is to encourage competition. But it has long been apparent that competition is not always a workable (or tolerable) mechanism for combating the evils of the marketplace. Essentially, there are two reasons for skepticism about the virtues of competition. One is that competition itself often causes public harm. Price wars and the scramble to maintain market shares lead companies to cut labor costs and to engage in rebates, bribes, or other sub rosa practices that discriminate among consumers, exploit workers, and can ultimately lead to a wave of bankruptcies. The unemployment, unfair treatment, and interruption in vital services that result can hardly be said to benefit the consuming public. Random, temporary price reduction may not be worth the uncertainty and economic risk of this competitive "jungle." Small wonder then that, in the late nineteenth century, farmers and railway laborers often joined railroads in bemoaning the evils of "cutthroat" competition.[4]

The second justification for substituting regulation for competition is that, in some cases, monopolies or oligopolies can render superior products or services at a lower unit cost. "Natural monopolies" are more efficient than multiple producers; cost advantage is, in fact, their identifying feature. In an area of production where there are heavy fixed costs (for example, telephone service or electricity generation) and economies of scale (that is, the unit cost of production declines when the quantity produced increases), monopoly is "naturally" more efficient than competition.[5] However, the large, capital-intensive enterprise may not arise without the help of government. Entrepreneurs may be unwilling or unable to undertake these large-scale projects without the guarantee of an exclusive franchise, direct subsidy, or guaranteed rate of return. Government, in turn, is reluctant to concede monopoly power without regulation of rates and guaranteed performance of services. This is the traditional basis of public utility regulation.[6] In the case of the public utility, more than any other type of regulation, promotional and protective motivations are inextricably intermingled. As Koontz and Gable put it, "the purpose of public utility regulation is to promote and protect the interests of consumers, investors, and the general public."[7]

Businesses that required utility-type regulation, both to enable them to reap the "natural" advantages of monopoly and to insure that products and services considered essential were not overpriced or undersupplied, were described in British and early American commercial law as "affected with a public interest." The growth of economic regulation from the latter years of the nineteenth century onward was accompanied by the gradual extension of this "affectation" to more and more enterprises.[8]

In the beginning, public utility regulation was an activity reserved to the states, since the operations of the monopolistic enterprises were generally confined to a fairly circumscribed area within a single state. Although several New England states had developed watchful or "advisory" commissions in the early decades of the nineteenth century, the real impetus to the formation of public utility regulatory bodies came in the midwestern, southern, and western states later in the century. Agrarian protest against the monopoly power and practices of railroads, mills, and crop storage facilities led to the enactment of the Granger laws and the formation of public commissions with power over rates and services. When the affected businesses challenged state regulation on the grounds that it, in effect, confiscated their property (a violation of the "equal protection" and "due process" clauses of the Fourteenth Amendment), it remained to the federal courts to determine whether this extension of the concept of utility regulation to private businesses that were not actually monopolies was justified.

The landmark decision of the Supreme Court came in 1877 in the case of *Munn* v. *Illinois*.[9] The plaintiffs, Munn and Scott, operated one of several grain warehouses in the city of Chicago. They were obligated by Illinois law to secure a license for their facilities, post bond (as insurance that they would perform a satisfactory service), and keep their charges below a legislated maximum. The Court upheld the state, ruling that the necessity of the service, its impact on the community at large, and the "virtually" monopolistic position of the elevators justified government regulation. This was, the Court found, an example of a business "affected with a public interest."

The affectation could logically be extended to transportation, water supply, telephone, telegraph, electric and gas manufacturing and transporting companies. These were businesses supplying essential products and services where there were obvious economies of scale and high capital requirements. As more and more of these business operations extended across state lines, it was inevitable that the federal government become involved in their regulation.

The inauguration of federal utility regulation came with the creation of the Interstate Commerce Commission (ICC). The logic behind the nationalization of regulation was clear. State commissions were limited in their ability to control the practices of rail lines that operated across state lines.[10] Although the large railroads probably anticipated advantages from federal control (particularly as opposed to some of the more vigorous state efforts), the Interstate Commerce Act was supported by a broad array of groups including farmers, shippers, and state public service commissions.

The mechanism chosen for federal regulation was the independent commission.[11] The commission form was familiar from state regulatory experience. In the early years of the twentieth century, however, its mode of operation at the federal level was much influenced by progressive thought. The progressives argued for commissions structured and staffed so as to produce a body of impartial experts insulated from political pressure. The ICC exemplified these characteristics, and its form was duplicated in subsequent agencies, including the Federal Power Commission. The terms of members are longer than that of the president, who appoints them, and members cannot be removed for political reasons. The progressives believed that the interests of regulated industries and the consuming public could be balanced in a "nonpolitical" way. Judicialized procedures, in which lawyers representing the industry and various competitor or consumer interests argue their cases before a panel of commissioners, perpetuate the progressive image of the regulatory agency as an impartial court: the agencies are integrated into the federal judicial process by placing their decisions on a par with those of federal district courts. Appeals from those decisions are taken to the applicable circuit court of appeals.

For several decades, the Supreme Court held utility regulation to a fairly restricted category of businesses. Eventually, however, law followed practice, and the restriction collapsed. When, during the Depression, declining purchasing power catapulted prices downward, many businesses began to seek the security of public utility regulation. In 1934, in *Nebbia* v. *New York*, the Court obliged by holding that traditional public utility or "natural monopoly" standards need not be met in order to justify state regulation.[12] The Court noted that "destructive and demoralizing" competition (in this case among milk producers in New York State) had "aggravated existing evils . . . and resulted in retail price-cutting [that] reduced the income of the farmer below the cost of production." In upholding minimum price regulation by the state, the justices declared, "it is clear that there is no closed class or category of business affected with a public interest. . . . The phrase 'affected with a public interest' can, in the nature of things, mean no more than that an industry, for adequate reason, is subject to control for the public good."

The decision in *Nebbia* v. *New York* legitimated a seemingly unlimited application of the techniques of utility regulation—limited entry through the discretionary granting of licenses to do business, imposition of minimum and/or maximum rates and requirements that certain levels and standards of service be maintained—to businesses that might have few, if any, of the characteristics of traditional utilities.

The Depression years inaugurated a phase of economic regulation motivated more by industry demand for price stabilization than by the public's desire to be protected from the ravages of natural monopolies. During the New Deal, economic regulation for the benefit of affected industries took three forms. The first, begun under the National Industrial Recovery Act of 1933, was a broad-based grant of authority to a wide variety of industries to write codes for their own regulation. NRA codes could define and prohibit "unfair" competitive practices, set minimum prices, and limit production. The act exempted the code writers from antitrust laws, which would normally have prohibited such collusion. The price of government approval of the industrial codes was that they recognize the right of labor to organize, and improve wages and working conditions in the industry. Understandably the act drew broad labor as well as business support.

The demise of the NRA in 1935 apparently did not diminish the inclination of Congress to write highly discretionary legislation allowing affected producer interests to bargain out the terms of their own control. Many of the features of the NRA codes turned up in subsequent statutes dealing with discrete industries. Among the statutory descendants of the NRA were laws designed to limit the quantity of production in extractive industries. Fuel producers were especially hard pressed by declining demand and "cutthroat" competition during the 1930s. Threatened, further, with the exhaustion of supplies through overproduction, they appealed for government regulation. NRA codes had brought some relief for the oil and bituminous coal industries. After their demise, Congress responded to industry appeals with the Bituminous Coal Conservation Act and the Connally "Hot Oil" Act (sponsored, respectively, by Pennsylvania and Texas senators).[13]

The Coal Act outlawed unfair competitive practices and divided the coal fields into regions with different price scales. The federal government enforced price and marketing restrictions through a tax and judicially imposed fines. The solution in the oil industry relied on state agencies to control production (on the basis of demand forecasts provided by the Bureau of Mines). The role of the federal government was to prohibit interstate shipments of "hot" oil produced in excess of state quotas. The control of production in the petroleum industry was justified on the grounds that it limited waste and conserved a finite national resource, as well as alleviating economic hardship for the industry itself. In the case of coal, federal price-maintenance regulation ceased when demand and supply came into balance as a result of wartime demand.

The third type of New Deal regulation conferred full-scale utility status on the regulated industries. In two cases, the industries involved could hardly be classified as natural monopolies; in two others, there were more plausible arguments for public utility treatment. The Motor Carrier Act of 1935 and the Civil Aeronautics Act of 1938 provided for restrictions on entry into the trucking and airline businesses through government licensing. The Civil Aeronautics Board and Interstate Commerce Commission, respectively, were empowered to grant "certificates of public convenience and necessity" to prospective entrants. These certificates are licenses to operate over certain routes or in certain territories.

The term "public convenience and necessity" had been used in licensing by state and municiple commissions in the nineteenth century, and was adopted for federal railroad regulation by the ICC. A certificate imposes service obligations on the holder (the "public convenience" facet of regulation). The clear advantage of the certificate from the businesses' point of view is the presumption that when a market is already served by one company, other licenses will not be granted unless the original company is unable or unwilling to expand its service (or cannot do so at a reasonable cost, and the like). In the case of trucking and air transportation, the provision of service by multiple providers clearly entailed no necessary loss of efficiency. Both businesses were very easy to enter. The NRA code for the trucking industry, for example, registered over three hundred thousand trucks for hire. The unavoidable conclusion is that regulation in the transportation industries was instituted primarily to serve the industries by restraining competition.[14]

The anti-competitive impulse can also be seen in the extension of federal public utility regulation to the interstate movement of electricity and natural gas. In these two cases, however, the "natural monopoly" argument had considerable justification, in view of capitalization requirements and economies of scale. Both industries were treated as public utilities and their operations regulated by public service commissions within states. In addition, the pattern of lobbying for the Federal Power Act of 1935 and the Natural Gas Act of 1938 revealed a broader array of interests in support of regulation than was the case with transportation.

Both transportation and gas/electricity transmission filled obvious "gaps" in the regulatory process and illustrate the irresistible momentum of government economic regulation. Once a commission is charged, as the ICC was, with planning and maintaining the health of a transportation industry, there is a strong argument for bringing all segments of the industry under control. Railroad rate and service capacities were obviously affected by competition from trucking, air, and water carriers. As intermodal competition increased, it was inevitable that the railroads and their regulators would argue for the extension of controls to other carriers.[15]

Electricity and gas pipeline regulation filled another type of gap in public control. State regulatory commissions lacked effective control over rates and services of local utility operations when those operations were a part of, or were dependent on, companies headquartered in other states. The regulation of interstate wholesale deliveries of gas and electricity filled the regulatory "void" (such terms as "gap" and "void" were used frequently in legislative debate on these measures). Regulatory saturation in this instance could more convincingly be touted as "in the public interest," since it implied lower rates than would result from an unregulated market (at least in the short term). In the case of transportation, however, the effect was mainly to put a floor under rates. The most convincing "public interest" arguments the transportation industry could marshal involved claims that regulation would protect jobs, improve safety, and promote national defense by preserving a diversified transportation network.

In the 1930s, economic theory evolved to keep step with political demands for regulation. Competition fell into disrepute among leading economists and treatises appeared arguing that unrestrained competition among producers of the same product was both wasteful and unlikely to be maintained.[16] How, then, could the inevitable monopolies or oligopolies be restrained from exploiting their position? Some economists found self-regulatory mechanisms within monopoly itself or between producers and their suppliers or customers.[17] Others argued for a role for government in "reinforcing" self-regulation by monopolistic businesses.[18] The acceptance of bigness had an obvious appeal for those who had, or anticipated, careers in government. The regulation necessary to police firms in the public interest would prove to be a prolific source of employment for lawyers and civil servants. Furthermore, the acceptance of bigness and the explicit or implicit mandate to promote the economic health of the regulated firms (a seemingly inevitable feature of utility regulation) softened the adversarial relationship that can make a regulator's job so unpleasant.

Seen in this context, the regulation of natural gas pipelines was part and parcel of the new, pragmatic philosophy of the 1930s. An unremarkable accomplishment of the New Deal, the Natural Gas Act passed without controversy. As long as the jurisdiction of the act applied only to pipelines, the relationships between consumers, regulators, and businesses were generally harmonious. Each could see advantage in the predictability of utility regulation. When the jurisdiction of the act expanded to encompass producers, that harmony disappeared. Unlike the trucking and aviation companies of the Depression years, natural gas producers in the 1950s faced a situation of rapidly increasing demand and had no desire for federal price regulation. Their loud complaints that gas production had none of the characteristics of a public utility fell on deaf ears, however. That distinction had long since been breached in theory and in practice.

The Natural Gas Industry in the 1930s: Problems and Alternative Federal Solutions

In the first years of the Great Depression, the natural gas industry was in chaos.[19] In the East, it was marked by monopoly, shortage, and increasing prices. In the Southwest, there was an enormous oversupply; thousands of producers with no pipeline outlets scrambled to extract some marketable product from their leaseholds—in the process letting millions of cubic feet of gas escape into the atmosphere. The chaotic state of the industry obscured what would have, in more normal times, been hailed as a milestone on the order of Promontory Point: the completion of the first long-distance, large-diameter gas pipeline from the Texas panhandle to Chicago. This technological feat marked the emergence of a truly national industry out of what had long been a self-contained regional enterprise.

Gas was first used for lighting homes in large northeastern cities around 1820. The product burned, however, was not "natural" gas, but a fuel manufactured from coal or oil. Manufactured gas was in widespread use by 1900, but shortly began to face stiff competition for home lighting from the development of the electric power industry. Since this gas was too expensive to compete for space heating and industrial markets, cooking was its most popular use. Faced with strong competition from electricity and other fuels, urban gas companies turned, where possible, to mixtures of natural and manufactured gas.

However, natural gas was only available to communities that had the good fortune to be located near a gas field. Until the mid-1920s, metals were not available that could withstand the high pressure needed to transmit commercial quantities of gas over long distances. Steels in use in the period were brittle and difficult to weld. As a result, most cities with appreciable natural gas consumption were situated within a hundred miles or so of a gas field.[20] Most were located in or near the Appalachian area (West Virginia, Pennsylvania, Kentucky, New York, Ohio) and in Indiana. On the West Coast, Los Angeles received gas from nearby southern California fields. Most natural gas was discovered in the search for oil, which, because it could be easily transported and stored (and had a wider range of uses), was far more valuable. Because of the primitive state of pipeline metal and welding technology, however, much more gas was produced than could be delivered to cities.

In the late 1800s, huge gas fields were discovered in the Southwest. The Monroe field in northern Louisiana, the Amarillo field in the Texas panhandle, and the Hugoton field in Kansas and Oklahoma were at that time the world's largest known gas fields. Since Kansas and southwestern communities could absorb only a fraction of the current production, however, much of the gas was blown off or flared in order to reach oil reserves. Thus, in the early 1920s, most of the interstate movement of natural gas took place in the northeastern United States, where densely populated urban areas were situated within range of the Appalachian gas fields. Of the one hundred fifty billion cubic feet of gas moved interstate in 1921, about 65 percent was produced in West Virginia. Most of the gas flowed into Pennsylvania and Ohio. Less than 2 percent of the total interstate movement of gas originated in Texas.

Fortunately for both producers and consumers, great strides were made in steel technology in the mid-1920s. From 1926 to 1931, metallurgical advances, along with improvements in welding and compression methods, made possible a rapid development of both the Appalachian and the southwestern gas industry. As easily recoverable reserves began to run out in the Appalachian region, gas companies began to plan connections with the huge southwestern fields.[21] By 1931, pipelines had been completed from the Amarillo field to Denver, Omaha, Minneapolis, Kansas City, and Chicago. By the end of the next year, a pipeline through central Illinois and Indiana connected the Appalachian pipeline system with the Amarillo and Hugoton fields. Another pipeline system sent highly pressurized gas from northern Louisiana (the Monroe field) to the Saint Louis area, and east through Birmingham and Atlanta, terminating in central Georgia. The Depression brought most pipeline construction to a halt after 1932. Although industrial consumption slowed during the Depression, there were seven million residences and commercial establishments using natural gas in thirty-five states by the mid-1930s.[22] The emerging differentiation of producing and consuming regions made possible by the new technology can be seen in Tables 1–3 and Figures 3–4.

The construction of long-distance pipelines was a very expensive undertaking. Often several gas distribution or pipeline companies, which might compete in other activities, cooperated in pipeline ventures. To assure their sources of supply and satisfy investors of the feasibility of the project, the pipeline companies bought up huge tracts of prospective or producing land. In the early 1930s, then, most gas fields had only one pipeline outlet, leaving independent producers in each area at the mercy of a single buyer. As of 1930, almost all companies involved in the local distribution of natural gas were components of integrated utility systems

TABLE 1   THE SHIFTING LOCUS OF NATURAL GAS PRODUCTION

Major Producers	Thousands of Cubic Feet (mcf)		
	1910	1925	1935
West Virginia	190,706	180,345	115,772
Pennsylvania	176,867	101,632	94,464
Ohio	48,232	43,235	49,592
Kansas	59,380	26,917	57,125
Oklahoma	50,430	249,285	274,313
Louisiana	NA	152,620	249,450
Texas	8,110*	134,872	642,366
California	2,764	187,789	284,109
Total United States	509,155	1,188,571	1,916,595

Source: Bureau of Mines, Mineral Resources and Minerals Yearbook.
*Texas and Louisiana are combined here; separate figures not available for 1910.

encompassing production, pipeline transportation, and ultimate delivery to households and businesses.

Vertical integration, however, was only one aspect of the pattern of ownership. As the supplying of electricity and natural gas to urban markets became lucrative enterprises in the first decades of the twentieth century, they attracted speculative investors. By purchasing small but controlling amounts of stock in company after company, speculators like Samuel Insull created utility empires of great size and complexity. A typical holding company of the period controlled vertically integrated gas and electric systems operating in several states.[23] Although the Depression brought financial ruin to a number of these companies, the concentration of ownership was scarcely diminished. In 1934, *Public Utilities Fortnightly* listed only twenty-five separately owned gas utility systems in the entire United States.[24]

Monopoly power led to widespread abuses. Holding companies controlling the Appalachian gas production and distribution systems (principally Standard Oil of New Jersey and Columbia Gas and Electric) divided up markets and ruthlessly drove out competitors. At first the burgeoning supply of southwestern gas was seen as a threat to price maintenance by the integrated utilities of the Appalachian area. To protect their investments in local natural gas production, as well as synthetic gas plants, the dominant companies sometimes prevented the pipeline connections that would have brought inexpensive southwestern gas into their territories. Once they had gained control of the new pipeline systems, they themselves took over the supplying of southwestern gas to midwestern and eastern markets. Columbia Gas and Electric, for example, prohibited the entry into the Detroit area of the Panhandle Eastern Pipeline (which was built by a group of independents) until it gained a controlling interest in the Panhandle company.[25]

TABLE 2   GREATEST RESIDENTIAL NATURAL GAS CONSUMPTION, AT TWENTY-YEAR INTERVALS (TEN STATES—NUMBER OF CONSUMERS)

1925*		1935*		1955		1975	
State	Number	State	Number	State	Number	State	Number
Ohio	1,094,120	California	1,451,000	New York	4,155,000	California	6,181,000
Pennsylvania	582,520	Ohio	1,216,000	California	3,666,000	New York	3,810,000
California	561,710	Illinois	1,147,000	Illinois	1,943,000	Illinois	2,911,000
New York	222,750	Pennsylvania	674,000	Ohio	1,896,000	Texas	2,693,000
Texas	217,240	Texas	568,000	Pennsylvania	1,894,000	Ohio	2,559,000
Kansas	168,790	New York	396,000	Texas	1,824,000	Pennsylvania	2,160,000
West Virginia	167,070	Missouri	378,000	Michigan	1,308,000	Michigan	2,068,000
Oklahoma	155,780	Kansas	203,000	New Jersey	1,296,000	New Jersey	1,624,000
Kentucky	130,780	West Virginia	181,000	Massachusetts	901,000	Missouri	1,085,000
Missouri	100,120	Kentucky	166,000	Missouri	702,000	Massachusetts	1,033,000

Source: Minerals Yearbook.
*Includes commercial establishments.

TABLE 3   PRODUCTION OF GAS FOR INTERSTATE TRANSMISSION IN 1925 AND 1935

	Amount Shipped (millions of cubic feet)			
	1925		1935	
Producing State	*Destination*	*Amount*	*Destination*	*Amount*
West Virginia	Kentucky, Maryland, Ohio, Pennsylvania	110,664	Virginia	69,806
Oklahoma	Arkansas, Kansas, Texas	39,794	Iowa, Kansas, Minnesota, Missouri, Nebraska	25,280
Louisiana	Arkansas, Texas	14,691	Alabama, Georgia, Illinois, Mississippi, Missouri, Tennessee	101,798
Pennsylvania	Ohio, New York, West Virginia	12,677	Canada	30,558
Texas	Arkansas, Louisiana, Mexico	10,071	Colorado, Illinois, Indiana, Iowa, Kansas, Minnesota, Missouri, Nebraska, New Mexico, Oklahoma, South Dakota, Wyoming	149,723
Total interstate flow		199,337		469,024

Source: Minerals Yearbook.

As complaints by independent producers and urban consumers mounted, the Senate directed the Federal Trade Commission (FTC) to conduct an investigation of public utility holding companies. The FTC produced a massive report, covering ninety-six volumes, in 1934 and 1935. The report revealed that more than half the gas produced in the United States, and over three-fourths of the fifty thousand miles of interstate natural gas pipeline, were controlled by eleven holding companies. The four largest holding companies—Columbia Gas and Electric, Cities Services, Electric Bond and Share, and Standard Oil of New Jersey—controlled 58 percent of the total mileage. The same group of holding companies dominated the manufacture and distribution of synthetic gas and electricity, and often had extensive coal and petroleum properties, as well.[26]

The dependence of consumers on these utility combines was not limited to the Northeast and Midwest. Gas distribution in Dallas–Fort

FIGURE 3
Major Natural Gas Fields

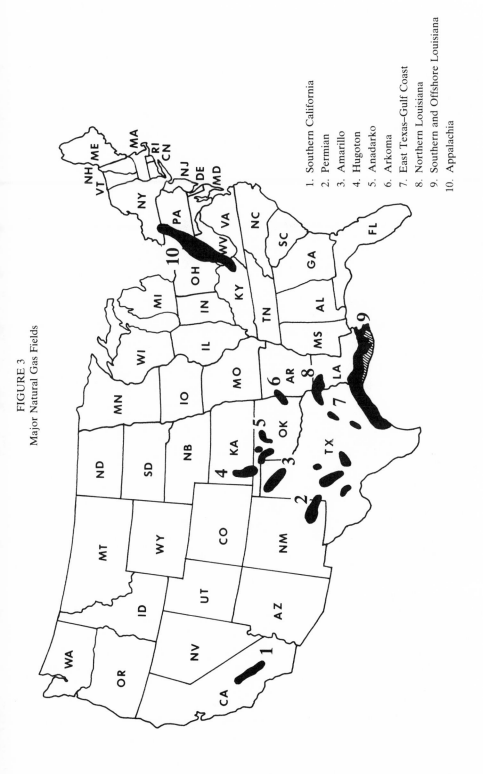

1. Southern California
2. Permian
3. Amarillo
4. Hugoton
5. Anadarko
6. Arkoma
7. East Texas–Gulf Coast
8. Northern Louisiana
9. Southern and Offshore Louisiana
10. Appalachia

FIGURE 4
Major Natural Gas Pipelines, 1932

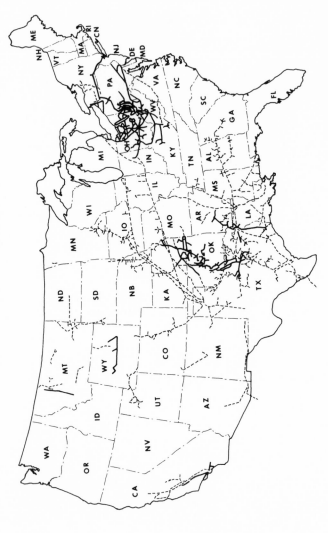

- - - Indicates lines built since December 31, 1925

——— Indicates lines built before December 31, 1925

SOURCE: Federal Trade Commission, Monograph no. 36, Temporary National Economic Committee Report 76-3 (1940).

Worth and 270 other Texas and Oklahoma cities was controlled by the Lone Star Gas Company, the fifth largest of the holding company empires. Lone Star had properties in Texas, Oklahoma, Idaho, Oregon, Washington, and Iowa.[27] It owned 30 percent of the shares in Northern Natural Gas (a pipeline running from the Panhandle to the Twin Cities) and was indirectly affiliated with the Columbia system.[28] The geographical extent of the latter company's holdings can be seen in the following list:[29]

Columbia Gas and Electric Company	Percent of voting stock held
Atlantic Seaboard Co.	100.0
Amere Gas Utilities Co.	100.0
Virginia Gas Distribution Corp.	100.0
Virginia Gas Transmission Corp.	100.0
Binghampton Gas Works	100.0
Bracken County Gas Co.	100.0
Central Kentucky Natural Gas Co.	99.9
Cincinnati Gas and Electric Co.	100.0
Cincinnati Gas Transportation Co.	97.8
Cumberland and Allegheny Gas Co.	100.0
Dayton Power and Light Co.	100.0
Eastern Pipe Line Co.	100.0
Fayette County Gas Co.	99.9
Gettysburg Gas Corp.	100.0
Greensboro Gas Corp.	100.0
Home Gas Co.	100.0
Huntington Gas Co.	100.0
Huntington Development and Gas Co.	99.8
Indiana Gas Distribution Corp.	100.0
Keystone Gas Co.	100.0
Manufacturers Gas Co.	100.0
Manufacturers Light and Heat Co.	99.9
Michigan Gas Transmission Corp.	100.0
Natural Gas Co. of West Virginia	100.0
Northwestern Ohio Natural Gas Co.	100.0
Ohio Fuel Gas Co.	100.0
Pennsylvania Fuel Supply Co.	100.0
Point Pleasant Natural Gas Co.	100.0
Union Light, Heat, and Power Co.	95.8
United Fuel Gas Co.	100.0
Warfield Natural Gas Co.	100.0

In order to compete with other fuels, gas sold to industries had to be priced at levels considerably below those charged residential customers. Prices of gas sold by the same companies to domestic consumers were usually two to five times higher than industrial prices, and in some states

(New York, for example), approached 1970 prices.[30] Consumers who had invested in gas cooking and space heating equipment and had developed a preference for the cleanliness and convenience of natural gas could not easily shift to other fuels when their monthly gas bills were increased.

As public utilities, local gas and electric companies were subject to regulation by state or municipal commissions. However, the control of local distributing operations by companies with multi-state properties made regulation extremely difficult. The essence of utility regulation is the setting of rates designed to produce a fixed return (in this period, 6 to 8 percent) on the company's investment. If the local company was a component in a vertically integrated system, state regulators could inquire into the reasonableness of charges paid by the distributor to its pipeline affiliate. If those charges were excessive, in view of the pipeline's costs, the regulatory body might refuse to count the entire charge when determining the rate to be allowed the distributor (in effect, reducing the distributor's "legitimate" costs—costs on which the rate of return would be figured). However, the process of determining the pipeline's costs could be difficult, if not impossible. The state regulatory body might have to send engineers and accountants to distant states to try to determine the parts of the pipeline company's holdings that were applied to its gas producing and transporting business. This was a costly and time-consuming process, and there was no guarantee that the company would be cooperative or straightforward in making its books available to those agents.[31] The cost figure finally arrived at by the state regulators might be challenged in state and federal courts, causing further delay and drain on the budgets of state agencies.

If the local gas distributor bought gas wholesale from an unaffiliated interstate pipeline, state regulatory bodies had no control over the transportation charge at all. The Supreme Court ruled in the 1920s that "arm's length" transactions (that is, sales between unaffiliated parties) of companies operating in different states constituted interstate commerce and could not be regulated by individual states.[32] Thus, in the absence of federal regulation, such interstate utility transactions were beyond public control.

Like consumers and state utility regulators, independent gas producers had numerous grievances against the large pipeline companies. The FTC heard lengthy testimony from independent operators unable to market their production to monopolistic pipelines owning their own gas leases.[33] The rule of "capture" applied in gas and oil production allowed any leaseholder to pump any amount of gas, even if by doing so he depleted the reserves of a field on which many other producers might hold leases. The "capture" doctrine, in combination with control of transportation by large, monopolistic pipeline companies, frustrated the efficient marketing and production of natural gas in several ways. First of all, a large pipeline constituting the only marketing outlet for an area could force independents to sell their gas at whatever price the pipeline demanded, or see their reserves drained away. If a group of independents attempted to build their own pipeline, however, they might be blocked by the holding company's control of (or influence with) financial institutions and distributing companies. The independently organized Panhandle Eastern Pipeline was, for example, forced into bankruptcy by Columbia Gas and Electric.

Without access to a pipeline or offered prices for their gas that barely met costs, independent producers sometimes resorted to other lamentable practices. In Texas, independents unable to market their gas appealed to state authorities for assistance. The Texas Railroad Commission, which oversees oil and gas production, first attempted to compel the pipelines to buy gas ratably (that is, proportionately) from all producers on a field. The pipeline companies challenged the commission's actions in federal court. Afraid that the pipelines were rapidly draining the gas from their own leases, the independents then persuaded the legislature to pass a law allowing them to set up gasoline plants at the Panhandle field. These plants then proceeded to withdraw gas at rates sufficient to lower the pressure in the interstate pipelines. As they stripped off relatively small amounts of gasoline, the remaining natural gas was blown into the air. A Kansas State University geologist interviewed by the FTC estimated that, from 1933 to 1934, such gasoline plants blew off in one day enough gas to supply a city of fifteen thousand people for five years.[34] To residents of cities unable to get natural gas, or forced to pay premium prices for it, this was an appalling waste.

At the conclusion of its investigation in 1935, the FTC highlighted the following problems associated with unregulated holding company domination of the natural gas industry, calling them "specific evils existing in the natural gas industry."[35]

1. A great waste of natural gas in production.
2. Unregulated monopolistic control of certain natural gas production areas.
3. Discrimination in some instances in field purchase from independent producers.
4. Costly struggles between rival natural gas interests to conquer or defend territories of distribution.
5. Excessive and inequitable variations in city gate [wholesale] rates for natural gas among different localities.
6. Pyramiding investments in natural gas enterprises through holding companies, with attendant evils.

7. Excessive profits in many natural gas sales between affiliated companies.

8. Inflation of assets and stock watering of certain natural gas companies.

9. Misrepresentation of financial condition, investment, earnings, etc.

Finally, the FTC concluded,

natural gas . . . is blown into the air in huge quantities because it has no market, the desire of communities for natural gas goes unheeded, and many producers are helpless to realize on their investment, while the gas is being drained from under them without compensation by competitors who have the necessary marketing facilities in the form of pipelines, or access thereto, or by those who engage locally in those extensive, wasteful and uneconomical processes which result in very small percentages of recovery.

To combat such abuses, the FTC recommended that the federal government scrutinize all holding company operations, forcing divestiture and reorganization where appropriate, and regulating the marketing of their securities. For the natural gas industry, it recommended state production controls supplemented by interstate compacts and federal prohibitions on the shipping of gas produced in excess of state quotas. For the pipelines themselves, the FTC believed that federal utility regulation was a necessity, since the states were unable to effectively regulate the activities of multi-state companies.[36] Parallel difficulties were encountered in the interstate marketing of electricity, and the FTC recommendations for the two industries were similar. The commission cautioned, however, that the problems presented by the natural gas industry differed in fundamental ways from those of the electric industry. Indeed, the commission's opinion was that

they are different from those in any other utility industry. Natural gas must be used practically as soon as produced. Therefore, the public concern is that it be produced only as needed, but that it be produced and delivered when needed, and then that it be used to the highest economic and social advantage. There are no precise parallels in the utility fields for such a situation. . . .

Any proposed Federal legislation should be premised, in part at least, on the fact that natural gas is a valuable, but limited, natural resource in Nation-wide demand, which is produced only in certain States and limited areas, and the conservation, production, transportation, and distribution of which, therefore, under proper control and regulation, are matters charged with high national public interest.[37]

The problems and abuses revealed by the holding company investigation spurred the introduction of legislation regulating holding companies, and instituting federal utility regulation for both the electric and gas pipeline industries. The Public Utility Holding Company Act and the Federal Power Act (actually Title II of the holding company bill) were passed in 1935; the Natural Gas Act, three years later. The Public Utility Act had a significant impact on the structure of public utility systems and was extremely controversial. The other two statutes were, however, considerably more limited in scope.

The Public Utility Act of 1935, as originally conceived, attacked the problems of monopolistic control and waste of fuel resources from several different angles. Title I declared public utility holding companies to be "affected with a national public interest," which required the extension of federal control over their activities. Citing the abuses documented by the FTC, it proposed to reorganize the companies into geographically and economically related units and to abolish all holding companies at the end of five years. Titles II and III closed the "regulatory gap" created by Supreme Court rulings by extending federal utility regulation to interstate sales of electricity and natural gas. Electricity was brought under the jurisdiction of the Federal Power Commission, which had, since 1920, licensed hydroelectric power plants on federal lands and navigable streams.[38]

In the original 1935 bill, certificates of public "convenience and necessity" were required for electricity production for, and sales in interstate commerce, and for the transmission of gas from a natural gas field. The FTC was given authority over the issuance of securities by interstate pipelines and power companies, and over their accounting practices. Both types of utilities were ordered to charge only "reasonable" rates and to extend service where practicable. Pipelines and transmission lines were to be treated as "common carriers." They were obliged to permit the use of their facilities by "other persons" whenever ordered to do so by the commission.

Opposition to the electric and gas titles centered on the common carrier and rate determination provisions. But the greatest furor grew out of the Title I "death sentence" for holding companies. Not only the company directors, but the institutions and individuals holding stock in utility companies protested vigorously against the bill. This was perhaps the only New Deal measure that anticipated a genuine redistribution of wealth and corporate power, and political debate reflected that redistributive content. Trade associations and organizations of utility investors mounted a large-scale campaign to defeat the bill. A Republican representative described the bill as instituting "an extreme length of government dictatorship over private business," permitting the government to "liquidate" lawfully acquired property. Another opponent charged that the bill, even after it was significantly modified, was "the most drastic and extreme measure of regulation ever offered in an American legislative body." Supporters, on the other hand, described the holding companies as "racketeers with their hands on the throats of the American people," and anticipated that the bill would end a loss of over a billion dollars a year in utility overcharges to consumers.[39]

In the final version of the holding company bill, the "death sentence" (mandatory reorganization or dissolution after January 1, 1940) was commuted. The Securities and Exchange Commission was given great discretion in recommending "simplification" of holding company structures, and the companies were invited to demonstrate in hearings before the commission that "substantial economies" could be achieved by retaining the holding company structure. The bill, with Titles I and II, passed the House 222 to 112. Title III (regulation of natural gas companies) was omitted from the version reported by the Interstate and Foreign Commerce Committee. The Federal Power Act (Title II) was modified in its two most controversial sections: electric company transmission lines were not treated as common carriers, and the section on cost determination for rate making was changed to reflect the utilities' objections. These same alterations would be made in the natural gas bill enacted three years later.

The natural gas title of the holding company bill had been drawn up in the office of Commerce Committee Chairman Sam Rayburn of Texas. Although the hearings did not reveal the exact identities of its authors, the three major participants were probably the FTC, the FPC, and Rayburn himself. Title III was described as a response to information in the holding company investigations. Rayburn asked the Trade Commission to draw up a draft of a natural gas bill in 1935. The resulting commission draft would have required the pipelines to buy ratably from all producers in a field.[40] This requirement was not written into Title III, but the provision making the pipelines common carriers had more or less the same effect. Both were designed to insure independent producers a marketing outlet.

Since most of the provisions in Title III were modeled on the Federal Power Act (Title II), the Federal Power Commission must be considered the principle author of the natural gas bill. A committee within the FPC had been working for several years on a draft of a bill that would bring interstate sales of electricity under the agency's jurisdiction. Power commissioner Clyde Seavey and solicitor Dozzier DeVane were its major authors: DeVane provided explanations in committee hearings for both Title II in 1935, and the natural gas legislation considered in 1936 and 1937.[41]

The reason for omission of Title III in 1935 was not specified in floor debate on the holding company legislation, but the gas bill clearly lacked a strong political constituency. Independent producers, particularly on the Panhandle and Hugoton fields, stood to benefit most from the bill's common carrier provision. These beneficiaries, however, were too geographically concentrated to exert political pressure sufficient to overcome the bill's perceived liabilities (even though Rayburn was an influential friend).

The pipeline companies objected vigorously to four of the gas title's provisions. In addition to common carrier status, pipeline representatives protested against the certificate provision. This section required application to the FTC for a certificate to move gas from a developed field, rather than to a given market. Pipeline spokesmen argued that this put them at a disadvantage vis-à-vis intrastate pipelines, which would not have to have an FTC certificate (although they might need approval from state regulators). In the opinion of the national pipeline companies and their financial allies, this was "attacking the problem from the wrong end." The main reason for a certificate requirement, they argued, was to protect a market from invasion by competitors. Thus certificates should be required for anyone proposing to extend a pipeline into a market already served by an existing line.[42]

The pipelines also objected to the bill's standards for determining the costs associated with gas transportation, an objection raised by electric companies as well. A fourth major objection concerned sales of gas for resale to industries. The pipelines wanted these sales exempted from regulation. Pipelines needed industrial markets for sale of gas at "off-peak" hours or during summer months, when household consumption was down. Industrial sales indirectly reduced rates to households by helping to defray general pipeline construction, maintenance, and pumping costs. They were, the companies argued, extremely competitive transactions since industries, unlike households, could easily use other fuels.[43]

In short, while the pipeline companies expressed their willingness to support "constructive" regulation, they saw nothing "constructive" in Title III. They protested that Congress should concern itself with measures to restore public confidence in the utility industry, and make possible an orderly expansion of service, rather than saddling the pipelines with onerous requirements.[44]

Aside from its governmental sponsors, the gas bill drew few endorsements. Even state regulatory commissions found the section on cost determination too ambiguous to be useful. The National Coal Association and coal state congressmen objected to the common carrier provisions. Coal companies often furnished small amounts of gas, tapped in mining operations, to nearby households, and feared that such operations would be brought under federal regulation. In addition, common carrier status might encourage gas sales to industries and utilities, further injuring the severely depressed coal industry. Under this bill, charged Illinois Senator Everett Dirksen, the interests of Illinois coal and utility industries "might be sacrificed upon the altar of the welfare of a State like Texas, which is only too anxious to reap the profits that would accrue from the distribution of billions of cubic feet of natural gas.[45]

Passage of the holding company bill relieved some of the pressure for natural gas legislation.[46] The SEC was now empowered to scrutinize the financial dealings of the utility combines and had the power to order divestiture by one operating company of its stock in other utilities. In the late 1930s, the holding companies began to submit reorganization plans to the SEC. By sales and exchange of stock, the holding companies consolidated their operations regionally, and, in many cases, reorganized themselves into simple operating utilities.[47] Between 1935 and 1947, 306 subsidiary utility companies were spun off by the reorganization process. One hundred and thirteen of these were gas companies.[48] Fifteen years after the act, holding company control of interstate pipeline mileage was reduced from 80 to 18 percent.[49] Interstate pipelines constructed after 1935 often owned substantial gas producing properties, but were seldom integrated with distributing utilities. After the mid-1940s, there was also a sharply declining trend in pipeline ownership of producing properties. The result of this profound change in the structure of the natural gas industry was that producers, transporters (pipelines), and distributors (local utilities) of gas came to have very different interests in regulation. Both pipelines and utilities would prefer a low and stable price level for gas as a commodity—a position diametrically opposed to that of independent producers of natural gas.

The principal immediate advantages of the holding company act for state regulation of the rates charged gas consumers lay in its potential for horizontal divestiture. Many local operating companies (that is, companies distributing gas and electricity to households and businesses) would now be freed from ownership by unrelated interests. One of the abuses perpetrated by the parent holding companies against their subsidiaries was to drive up the "costs" of the operating companies by charging them exorbitant prices for services rendered by the upper layers of the holding company. Such practices inflated the rate base (that is, the costs of providing the service) of the local utilities, driving up rates allowed for their services. By regulating such charges, and by removing many operating utilities from the snares of controllers interested only in short-term gains, the 1935 act halted most of these abuses.[50]

The federal-state jurisdictional problem, however, continued to short-circuit effective utility regulation. When local utilities bought gas from interstate pipelines with whom they were affiliated, there was the problem of assessing costs on a diverse and far-flung enterprise. When the local utility's purchases were at "arm's length" from an unaffiliated pipeline, the state commissions had no alternative but to allow the full purchase price as a cost of operation, even if the pipeline's charges seemed excessive (by comparison, perhaps, with city gate charges in other communities). Nor could state regulators compel the local utility to extend service to a broader population if the pipeline refused to expand its gas sales in a certain area. In other contexts it might be surprising to find state regulatory bodies lobbying for an expansion of federal regulation, but in this case the argument was obvious. The Supreme Court did not allow states to control interstate commerce. Their control of intrastate commerce (the service charges of regulated monopolies) was rendered ineffective when interstate pipelines were subject to no regulation at all. Just as a decision by the Supreme Court had impelled the states to ask for federal railroad regulation in 1887, so the Missouri and Attleboro decisions of 1924 and 1927 created a demand for federal gas and electric regulation. The regulatory "gap" in the electric industry had been closed with the Federal Power Act of 1935. It remained only to bring interstate pipelines into the regulatory net.

The pipelines, however, were in no mood to submit unless the terms of the regulatory contract were changed in their favor. Accordingly, when the natural gas bill came up again the following year, changes had been made which rendered the measure much less objectionable. Hearings were held in 1936 on a revised bill (HR 11662) that exempted industrial sales, omitted the offensive certificate provision of the 1935 title, and included the modified section on cost determination that had gone into the Federal Power Act. Still the pipelines protested that there was simply "no need" for federal regulation. Most local gas distributors were affiliated with pipelines, a Standard Oil representative told the House committee, so that state regulation was adequate to protect the public.[51] It was pointed out by state and federal officials that (1) the pipelines, notwithstanding their professed preference for state regulation, had strenuously resisted state control in federal courts; (2) the states were still unable to regulate nonintegrated utility systems (whose numbers were increasing); (3) the process of investigating finances of integrated interstate pipeline systems was still an onerous task for state commissioners, particularly in view of the unstandardized accounting techniques used by pipeline companies; (4) the absence of federal regulation meant that pipelines could not be compelled to sell gas to municipalities along their routes or expand sales in existing markets; and (5), of the three charges that figured into the household consumer's monthly gas bill, the transportation charge was usually the largest component.[52] The rate charged by the local distributor was a "cost-plus," regulated rate; the price paid to producers, particularly in the glutted southwestern fields, was a miniscule four to six cents per thousand cubic feet. Thus, the major determinant of the price paid by domestic gas consumers was the unregulated pipeline charge.

There were, in short, a number of reasonable arguments for bringing the pipelines under federal regulation. However, as long as the pipelines remained opposed, Congress apparently had little appetite for a regulatory battle. One bruising utility fight was enough for the decade.

In the next Congress, the House Commerce Committee put together a winning formula. The principal change from the previous version was a new section, 7c, which required an FPC certificate for construction of an interstate pipeline to a market already served by an existing pipeline. With this protection from competition, the pipelines acquiesced in federal regulation. Pipeline spokesman W. A. Dougherty, a New York attorney, suggested only a few minor changes in the bill (HR 4008) during 1937 hearings. The pipeline companies had no objection to the measure, he told the Commerce Committee. Although he expressed doubt that any significant consumer benefit would result, Dougherty saw no reason to deny the municipal officials their desire to see Washington control pipeline charges.[53]

The two principal groups lobbying for federal regulation throughout the decade were state public service commissions and representatives of northern cities. The Midwest was disproportionately represented in both groups. A spokesman for the Illinois commission recounted to the House committee the experience of Chicago and other northern Illinois communities in dealing with utility combines. The Natural Gas Pipeline Company of America, organized by Samuel Insull, owned both Panhandle gas leases and the interstate transmission system servicing Chicago and other cities. The company had rebuffed every commission effort to inquire into its finances.[54] In Ohio, Cleveland and other large cities were supplied by the Hope Natural Gas Company of West Virginia, under the control of Standard Oil. A witness representing Ohio cities complained that Hope charged its distributors over forty cents a thousand cubic feet (mcf) for gas moved only two hundred fifty miles, whereas Detroit distributors paid only thirty-three cents mcf for Texas gas moved twelve hundred miles.[55] Another of the big four pipeline systems, Columbia Gas and Electric, had for some time refused to supply natural gas to St. Louis under an informal agreement not to "raid" Standard Oil's territory.[56]

Because of their recent experiences with pipeline monopolies, urban representatives favored a stronger natural gas bill than either the 1936 or 1937 versions on which hearings were conducted (HR 11662 and HR 4008). The Cities Alliance, a group of about a hundred, principally midwestern, urban governments, was organized in the mid-1930s to lobby for federal regulation of pipelines. Bills drawn up by the Alliance were introduced in the seventy-fifth Congress by Representative Robert Crosser of Ohio (HR 5711) and Senator Prentiss Brown of Michigan. The Alliance bill was intended to "remove monopolistic restraints" from the natural gas industry and to secure "a nationwide reduction of gas rates and a savings of many millions of dollars to the American public each year.[57] The bill would have prohibited control of gas pipelines by banking interests. Either the pipelines could elect to be treated as common carriers or, if they purchased gas directly, they were prohibited from showing any undue preference among sellers in a field, when making their purchases. The bill would have required the pipelines to supply gas to any community willing to extend a service line to the main pipeline.

Robert Crosser, the Alliance bill's sponsor in the House, was a member of the Commerce Committee. Representative Crosser deferred to the committee's chairman, Clarence Lea of California, sponsor of the more moderate HR 4008; hearings were held on the latter bill in 1937. Spokesmen for the Cities Alliance, however, objected strongly to the Lea bill's certificate provisions. They protested that the certificate requirement would merely protect powerful entrenched monopolies from competition in supplying natural gas to the nation's cities. Construction of competing lines would be a boon both to southwestern producers (who now lacked sufficient markets) and urban consumers. Without that competition, the Cities Alliance argued, gas would be flared or sold for inferior industrial uses in the producer states, and northern consumers would be at the mercy of a single supplier.[58]

The supporters of HR 4008 responded, in effect, that the price of regulation is the legitimation of monopoly. If the natural gas pipelines were to be controlled like public utilities, argued Republican Representative Charles Halleck of Indiana, then they deserved some assurance that they would not be "crucified" by cutthroat competition.[59] Such guarantees were traditionally incorporated in utility regulation. Chairman Lea, who took responsibility for adding section 7c, voiced the majority's argument for making the regulatory bargain:

> the decided weight of opinion is, for modern regulation, in favor of a certificate of convenience and necessity. The only justification for regulating these utilities is that they do have, in effect, a monopoly. In the absence of that monopoly it might be better to have no regulation so we could depend on competition taking care of the needs of the consumer.[60]

The Cities Alliance wanted regulation to set a ceiling price on gas deliveries, and competition to provide both lower prices and better service. But,

Lea argued, they could not have it both ways, and regulation by the FPC was a better risk than the marketplace. "That is what regulation is," said Lea, "monopoly controlled in the public interest."[61]

The Natural Gas Act of 1938

> Mr. Wheeler. Let me say to the Senator that this bill is unusual in the respect that those who transport the gas favor the bill. All the State public utility bodies favor the bill and the Government has favored the bill.
>
> *Congressional Record*, Senate, August 19, 1937, p. 9313

In April of 1937, the Lea bill was reported unanimously by the House Commerce Committee.[62] It passed the House and Senate with several minor, committee-approved amendments, and was signed into law in June of the following year. Most of the wording of its major provisions paralleled the corresponding sections of the Federal Power Act, the Interstate Commerce Act, and the Federal Communications Act. This was, in Commerce Chairman Clarence Lea's description, "regulation along recognized and more or less standardized lines. There is nothing novel in its provisions."[63]

Regulation was established only for the transportation and sale for resale of natural gas in interstate commerce. Sales at the wellhead by producers not affiliated with pipelines and pipeline sales for distribution solely within the states were exempted (or so it was assumed in the first sixteen years of implementation). Local gas sales would continue to be regulated by state public utility commissions. Wellhead prices would be treated as costs in determining the rates that the interstate pipelines could charge distributors. Hence, the act's jurisdiction was solely over pipelines and not producers or distributors. Section 1b specifically exempted the production and gathering as well as the local distribution of natural gas from federal regulation. The necessity for regulation was explained in the first paragraph of section 1:

> (a) As disclosed in reports of the Federal Trade Commission made pursuant to S. Res. 83 (Seventieth Congress, first session) and other reports made pursuant to the authority of Congress, it is hereby declared that the business of transporting and selling natural gas for ultimate distribution to the public is affected with a public interest, and that Federal regulation in matters relating to the transportation of natural gas and the sale thereof in interstate and foreign commerce is necessary in the public interest.

The Trade Commission's ninety-six–volume report had, of course, explored a variety of ills within the natural gas industry; the Natural Gas Act did not pretend to remedy all of them. For example, the statute contained no provisions directly addressing the problems of monopoly, of waste, or of discrimination in purchases from producers in the field. The stated purpose of the act, according to the Commerce Committee's report, was "to occupy this field in which the Supreme Court has held that the States may not act," by bringing wholesales of gas (by interstate pipelines to local distributors) under federal regulation.[64]

The three major aspects of utility regulation are control over price, control over entry, and control over the extension and abandonment of service. The first is addressed by section 4 of the Natural Gas Act, which requires that natural gas companies (that is, companies transporting and selling natural or mixed natural-manufactured gas in interstate commerce for resale to distributors) charge "just and reasonable" rates and refrain from "undue" discrimination in rates or services among customers. The term "just and reasonable," while extremely ambiguous to the layman, had an accepted interpretation growing out of centuries of utility regulation. The term was widely used in state law, as well as in federal regulation of the transportation, electric power, and communications industries. It was interpreted to imply the setting of rates sufficient to insure that the regulated company could meet its operating costs and receive a fair return on invested capital. To the unpleasant surprise of the pipelines (and ultimately, the producers), however, the Supreme Court's notion of what constituted "just and reasonable" rates began to change significantly in the early 1940s. As the New Deal Court increasingly gave federal regulators more doctrinal latitude than they had had in the past, the FPC itself began to chart new territory in utility rate formulation. In 1938, however, the subsequent abandonment of traditional formulas was probably not anticipated by the pipeline industry.

Under section 4, all rates and charges must be made public and kept on file with the FPC. Any increase in rates to be charged may be postponed for up to five months while the commission investigates the reasonableness of the increase.[65] At the end of the suspension period, if the investigation is not complete (and, in fact, this process may last for several years) the new rates go into effect but the company must post a bond sufficient to refund to its customers that part of the charge (up to the full amount) that the commission may later determine to be excessive. Of course, if there is no objection from customers and the commission itself sees no reason for such an investigation, the increase may go into effect immediately after a thirty-day notice period has elapsed. The FPC can at any time, upon its own initiative or on complaint from state and local commissions or distributing utilities, investigate rates charged by natural gas companies and order that rates be lowered.

Section 7 of the act empowers the FPC to order the companies to extend their services (that is, to establish pipeline connections to adjacent communities) so long as such extension would not diminish service to existing customers. The natural gas companies are forbidden to abandon facilities or services without the commission's approval.

Entry controls were established in section 7c, which prohibited the building of any pipeline into a market already served by an existing natural gas company except on certification by the commission that "the present or future public convenience and necessity require or will require such new construction." The company already in place could, however, expand its own facilities without a certificate.

Other provisions necessary to utility rate regulation were contained in sections 6, 8, 9, 10, and 14. These provisions authorize the FPC to prescribe standardized accounting methods for regulated companies, and to require record keeping and periodic reporting by the companies. The commission is empowered to investigate and ascertain the costs of pipeline properties and to prohibit the companies from charging to their operating expenses unnecessary costs. One of the abuses of pipeline companies catalogued by the FTC investigation was the practice whereby the companies, to forestall competition, would buy up extensive gas producing acreage. These holdings, often far in excess of the company's needs over the next decade or more, would then be charged to its rate base—the result being that gas consumers had to pay inflated charges while being denied the possible benefits of competitive production.

The Natural Gas Act had no provision directly promoting conservation. However, the FPC was authorized in section 3 to control, by issuing permits, both the exportation and importation of natural gas "in the public interest." Section 11 instructed the commission "to aid in the conservation of natural gas resources" and in their "orderly, equitable and economic production, transportation and distribution," by assembling information pertinent to the subject matter of interstate compacts and by making its own recommendations to Congress.

Final sections allowed the FPC to subpoena witnesses and information and to prescribe rules for its administrative proceedings. In the interest of creating a smoothly functioning federal regulatory system, provisions were also established for wide-ranging cooperation between the FPC and the state regulatory commissions.

The 1938 Natural Gas Act was cut from the same cloth as other New Deal economic regulatory statutes. It passed in essentially the form given it in committee, and it had been constructed in committee with an eye to the interests of all affected groups. Typical of the pluralist regulatory model described by Theodore Lowi, the highly discretionary wording of the statute allowed a quasi-judicial body of "expert" administrators to determine the content of the law on the basis of arguments put forward by the affected interests. Although the major groups concerned with natural gas regulation had all approved the new law, they each had a distinct set of preferences for the outcome of the administrative process. In deciding these competing claims, the Federal Power Commission would strive for an image of neutral, professional competence—but always keep a keen eye on the balance of power in its political environment.

3 | The Interests in Regulation

The gas bill's managers on the House and Senate floor described it as conventional public utility regulation "along more or less standardized lines." The targets of regulation ostensibly possessed the characteristics of natural monopolies. They required large amounts of capital to construct, and had obvious economies of scale (since an existing pipeline could extend its service to new customers, within a given area, at a decreasing cost). The fact that the Natural Gas Act contained recognized features of utility regulation and applied them to an industry with the characteristics of a utility is no doubt one reason that it seemed so unobjectionable to all affected interests. The application of federal utility regulation to trucking and air carriers, for which utility status had much weaker theoretical justification, has occasioned some debate and a handful of opposing votes. The gas bill, however, evoked no significant opposition. It was enthusiastically promoted by state and federal regulators, and endorsed, during floor consideration, by representatives of both producer and consumer states.[1] It was apparent that the legislation was perceived by all concerned as an improvement on the status quo.

Beneficiaries of Regulation: The Regulators

The state commissions were the principal advocates of pipeline regulation; the Natural Gas Act was tailored to their needs. Under the new statute, interstate transactions beyond their reach would be kept within the bounds of reasonableness, and a federal agency would assume the burden of ascertaining costs for integrated companies. The NGA treated the state commissioners as colleagues in the regulatory endeavor and granted them open access in the proceedings of the federal agency. In another sense, the Natural Gas Act enhanced the career prospects of the state regulator by adding a higher rung to the utility commissioner's occupational ladder. The state commissions have served as the most important recruiting ground for Federal Power commissioners (see Table 8).

With passage of the 1938 act, the Federal Power Commission greatly expanded its jurisdiction and gained both an important regulatory mission and a stable base of political support. The FPC had been created by the Federal Water Power Act of 1920, and assigned the function of licensing hydroelectric projects on public lands and navigable waterways. Born in the midst of early twentieth-century controversy over public control of hydroelectric power, the Power Commission, in its first decade, was an ineffectual, cross-pressured body. In 1930, the FPC was reorganized as a five-member independent agency; but its members, appointed by a Republican president unsympathetic to public power development, continued to draw heavy criticism from Senate progressives.[2]

With the commencement of the New Deal, however, the agency was rejuvenated. Members appointed by Roosevelt approached their existing regulatory mandate with enthusiasm, and began to lobby for an expansion of the FPC's jurisdiction. In 1935, Congress reinforced the commission's control over water power for interstate electricity transmission. The commission itself had designed the Federal Power Act of 1935 and, of course, the Natural Gas Act as well. The two statutes assured the FPC an influential clientele among the state regulatory commissions, consumer groups, and local utilities.[3] In addition, there was little reason to expect a hostile relationship between the commission and the interstate pipelines. The latter had not opposed the 1938 law. Unlike the railroads, they had no natural competitors (there being no practical way to transmit natural gas except by pipeline) and seemed to possess the characteristics of an industry that could thrive under the grant of a public monopoly (indeed, the pipeline industry has prospered under federal regulation).

In short, the Federal Power Commission in 1938 was in an enviable position for a regulatory agency. It had a vigorous and progressive image—so much so that Congress was willing to enact without question a statute largely of commission design and replete with extremely ambiguous language. Perhaps it is not surprising, in view of this send-off, that the agency within a few years began to overreach itself and set the stage for a tremendous upheaval in its jurisdiction.

Consumers

Household consumers of natural gas from interstate pipelines were, in 1938, concentrated in the metropolitan areas of Ohio, Illinois, Pennsylvania, New York, and Missouri (see Table 4). Most of the interstate gas consumed in Ohio, Pennsylvania, and New York was produced in West Virginia and Pennsylvania; the bulk of interstate gas used in Illinois and Missouri originated in the central-southwestern states of Texas, Louisiana, Oklahoma, and Kansas.[4]

TABLE 4   Consumption of Gas From Interstate Pipelines:
               Ten Largest Importing States in 1935 and 1955

	1935		1955
State	Gas Delivered (Millions of cubic feet)	State	Gas Delivered (Millions of cubic feet)
Ohio	57,147	California	507,157
Illinois	55,874	Ohio	499,439
Kansas	45,019	Illinois	413,885
Texas	33,054	Pennsylvania	404,793
Missouri	32,682	New York	260,829
New York	28,611	Kansas	239,889
Pennsylvania	27,695	Missouri	208,344
Arkansas	20,309	Michigan	199,399
Iowa	19,077	Iowa	141,960
Colorado	16,908	Indiana	138,050

Source: Minerals Yearbook (1938), pp. 1042, 1047–1049.

The advantage to consumers in federal regulation was twofold. First of all, the FPC could prevent price-gouging by pipelines, holding rates to a level guaranteeing a reasonable return on costs but preventing the companies from inflating their costs of transmission (and production, where the companies owned their own reserves). Such price control was particularly important for customers of pipelines owning gas reserves in the Appalachian-midwestern fields. The second advantage lay in the power of the FPC to compel extensions of gas service to communities near pipeline routes. The acquisition of natural gas was a major concern of the Cities Alliance, and became almost an obsession for communities without it in the 1940s. Gas was cleaner and much more convenient to use than coal, and natural gas was significantly less expensive than manufactured gas (which had only half the heating value per volume) or electricity. Gas was also indispensable for certain industrial processes, particularly steel, ceramics, and chemical production.[5] Access to an assured supply of inexpensive natural gas depended on the construction of pipelines from southwestern fields. By facilitating an orderly expansion of the pipeline industry, federal regulation played an indirect, but essential, part in providing urban residential and industrial consumers with a superior and relatively inexpensive fuel.

The Regulated Industry

Between 1935 and 1937, the pipeline industry shifted from opposition to cautious support for regulation. Undoubtedly, the major reason for the shift was the evolution in the content of regulatory proposals. There were four major changes in the gas regulation proposal between 1935 and

1937: (1) the elimination of the common carrier requirement; (2) the modification of the section on cost determination; (3) the change in certification from gas field to distributing market; and (4) the addition of an exemption for industrial sales from the rate-suspension provision of section 4. These modifications stilled the pipelines' objections, and introduced positive advantages in regulation.

Finally, a benign federal regulation was clearly preferable to the sniping of a multitude of state regulatory bodies. Not only did some of the states have laws less favorable to the industry than the Natural Gas Act, but contesting state actions in court produced onerous costs for the companies. In addition, nationalization of the regulatory process held out the hope of surmounting other obstacles put up by the states. Pipeline representatives testified in 1937, and again in amendment hearings in 1941, that public officials and railroads in coal-producing states like Illinois and Pennsylvania sometimes refused to grant the pipelines rights of way through their states for fear of injuring the coal industry and the railroads that depended on coal hauling.[6] Although unable to convince Congress to include a provision granting them eminent domain power, the pipelines apparently hoped that possession of a federally granted certificate to build might be interpreted by the federal courts to convey a right of way.

The growth of demand for natural gas and the changing financial position of the pipelines after 1935 combined to make federal certification a decided advantage. As gas reserves were depleted in the eastern fields, established companies planned pipeline connections with the prolific southwestern fields. However, plans for new lines were not limited to the large, established companies. A spokesman for the Natural Gas Pipeline Company complained to the House Commerce Committee that, after years of planning a pipeline system from Texas to Wisconsin, his company learned that two other companies had similar plans. In the absence of federal jurisdiction, the state of Wisconsin seemed inclined to grant access to one or more of the companies. Alarmed at the prospect of competition for their own project, the Natural Gas representative appealed for federal certification.[7] The larger, established pipeline companies, because they could demonstrate greater reserves and better prospects for financial backing, probably expected to prevail over smaller rivals in the bidding for federal certificates.

Those certificates were becoming increasingly important for pipeline investors. The Public Utility Holding Company Act had effectively removed the holding company as a source of new financing for pipeline companies. Thus, to raise new capital the pipelines turned to banks and insurance companies. These institutions still considered the gas industry a high-risk venture, and placed a number of restrictions on loans, if they granted them at all. To obtain financing, pipeline organizers had to demonstrate not only a secure supply of gas (through long-term contracts or their own reserves), but also a secure market. The FPC-granted certificate provided a market secure from detrimental poaching by competitors. Possession of a certificate became a *sine qua non* for the sale of bonds financing new pipeline ventures.[8]

The 1938 statute required certificates only for "markets already served." In 1942, at the request of the pipelines, coal interests, and the Federal Power Commission, the act was amended to require certification for all new interstate pipeline construction (including lines to unserved markets). The FPC defended this expansion of its jurisdiction as a way to avoid some of the cumbersome investigations needed to define existing markets.[9] The advantage of the amendment to the pipelines—particularly the larger ones—was clear. The House and Senate Commerce committees agreed that the original statute was inadequate to prevent "wasteful" competition and "uneconomic" expansions, the prospects for which seemed "multiple and tremendous" by the early 1940s.[10]

Finally, the pipelines in 1938 had little to fear from rate regulation by the FPC. In 1936 hearings, FPC solicitor DeVane assured questioners that the "prevailing" rates would, in most cases, be those set by the pipelines in their original filings, and that the commission's valuation methods would not be objectionable to the companies.[11] Perhaps the most convincing evidence that the pipeline industry anticipated, and received, considerable benefit from federal regulation is that the industry has never mounted a deregulation effort.

The Competitors

No enterprise was more depressed in the 1930s than the coal industry, and no other economic interest has as much at stake in the price and supply of natural gas. Before the First World War, coal had supplied over 80 percent of the nation's energy consumption; by 1933, as a result of competition from oil, natural gas, and hydroelectric power, only 52 percent of energy consumed was derived from coal. All fuel consumption declined sharply during the Depression, but the coal industry was by far the most severely affected.[12]

The industry's competitive position was of vital importance to the half million men who worked the mines, and to the economics of the eastern coal states—foremost among them being West Virginia, Pennsylvania, Illinois, Kentucky, and Ohio (see Table 5). In the decade before 1933, both the number of coal mines and the number of coal miners fell by over 40 percent.[13] Outside the industry itself, railroads were particularly hard hit by declining coal production. Coal accounted for a large percentage of the tonnage hauled by railroads, and over a fifth of their revenues. Thus,

TABLE 5   THE COAL INDUSTRY IN 1937

Major Producers	Production (tons)	Number of Employees
West Virginia	118,646,343	113,643
Pennsylvania	111,002,289	133,897
Illinois	51,601,638	42,449
Kentucky	47,086,444	55,596
Ohio	25,177,867	30,294
Total United States	445,531,449	491,864

Source: Minerals Yearbook.

when coal production declined by over fifty million tons between 1929 and 1937, the already financially troubled railroad industry was dealt a severe blow. In legislative action on the regulation of competing fuels, these interests—the coal unions and trade associations, the railroads, and elected officials from the major coal-producing areas—would demand to be heard. Together they enjoyed considerable political influence among eastern and midwestern congressmen and in the House and Senate Commerce committees, which have jurisdiction over both natural gas and rail transportation.

By the 1940s, it was clear that coal was losing the battle for cooking and house-heating markets to electricity, oil, and natural gas. Nor could gas manufactured from coal long hope to compete with cheaper, higher-Btu. natural gas from the glutted southwestern fields. For these reasons, the coal interests concentrated on maintaining industrial and utility power plant markets. Any measure that might restrain the expansion of natural gas usage here won endorsement from coal and railway groups. The 1936 natural gas bill, however, exempted industrial sales from the FPC's jurisdiction, and did not restrict pipeline construction because it had no certificate provision. It was of no benefit whatsoever, and the coal industry opposed the bill.[14] In the 1937 hearings, a spokesman for the National Coal Association (NCA) again protested the industrial exemption. The history of all regulation showed, according to the NCA representative, that regulation tends to raise the price of the regulated product. Regulation of natural gas might, he publicly speculated, prove advantageous for the coal industry if the price of gas were kept high enough to restrict its ability to compete with coal for industrial markets. The NCA spokesman pointed out that the coal industry employed ten times as many men as the natural gas business (five hundred thousand, as opposed to fifty thousand). If Congress intended to regulate natural gas, he asked, "why exempt the one class of business that destroys labor?"[15]

The natural gas bill ultimately reported to the floor was rewritten to bring under regulation pipeline sales for resale to industries. In section 4 of the act, pipeline sales for resale (by local utilities) to industries were exempted from the provision that allowed the commission to suspend rate increases while it investigated their fairness. However, this exemption, since it allowed pipelines to charge *higher* industrial prices during the period of the commission's investigation, might work to the advantage both of coal and pipeline companies. What the coal industry wanted from the FPC was a requirement that industrial sales not be priced "unreasonably" low. If industrial sales had been exempt from the FPC's general jurisdiction over rates, the pipelines might have priced industrial gas at, or below, the real cost of transmission, and made up the difference by higher charges for domestic use, a category in which there was much less competition.

With respect to pricing, coal and gas producers in the 1930s had directly opposing interests. Coal wanted high industrial prices; the southwestern gas industry, in its expansion phase, wanted to keep prices attractively low to both residential and industrial customers in order to build markets. The major reservation of gas state representatives on the question of natural gas regulation was that the FPC would, at the behest of coal interests, raise the price of gas to a noncompetitive level, particularly in populous, coal-producing states like Ohio, Pennsylvania, and Illinois.[16] During Senate consideration, amendments were offered on the floor that prohibited the commission from raising the rates submitted by the pipelines, and declared it to be the intention of Congress that gas be sold "at the lowest possible lawful rate consistent with the maintenance of adequate service in the public interest." Both amendments apparently originated with a senator from the Gulf Coast gas-producing region.[17] They were accepted by the House, with minor modification.

Aside from restraining unfair price competition, the major advantage of gas regulation to the coal industry was the certification requirement. Companies proposing to build pipelines into markets already served would have to convince the commission that the "public convenience and necessity" required such construction. The coal industry hoped that the commission would interpret this phrase conservatively and deny certification to pipeline expansion proposals that anticipated increased sales to industries presently using coal. Section 7 of the Natural Gas Act instructed the FPC to give notice to all interested parties when hearings were held on certificate applications. It was at such hearings that the coal industry expected to plead its case against displacement by natural gas. However, during its early years, the FPC interpreted this section narrowly, and restricted coal and railroad participation in certificate hearings. The commission apparently felt that coal interests were not vitally affected by certification, because certificates were only required for entrance into markets already served (where, in effect, coal had already been displaced). When the industry complained about this restricted access, the FPC proposed a remedy: Congress should expand its jurisdiction to include all new interstate pipeline construction. Thus, when pipeline companies requested certificates to build in areas not yet supplied with gas, coal interests would be "vitally" affected, and allowed to participate in the hearings. Section 7 was duly amended in 1942, with the enthusiastic approval of both coal interests and the large pipeline companies. Following this change, the coal industry and its railroad allies became the major intervenors in certificate hearings.

After 1942, to the dismay of the pipelines, the coal and rail interests were allowed to contest all pipeline expansion into states that had been heavy coal users. For example, in 1943, the New York State Natural Gas Company applied to the FPC for permission to build a twelve-inch, high-pressure line across Pennsylvania, in order to deliver Texas gas to New York State. During the subsequent hearings, the construction was protested by representatives of the Anthracite Institute, the National Coal Association (representing most eastern bituminous coal companies), the United Mine Workers Union, and twenty-five railroads. In this case, the certificate was eventually granted, but the pipeline company's deliveries for industrial uses were tightly restricted.[18]

Since no provision of the Natural Gas Act explicitly instructed the commission to consider the effects of its actions on a competing fuel industry, it was necessary to argue that end-use control served the interest of the gas-consuming public by extending the life of natural gas reserves. By prohibiting the use of gas for "inferior" uses (principally, as a boiler fuel for industrial and utility power plants), the FPC could, the coal interests argued, conserve supplies for household service and essential industrial processes.[19] The acceptance of this argument would necessarily imply a very broad construction of the agency's statutory mandate. While the FPC in the early 1940s was steadily pushing at the edges of that mandate, it much preferred that Congress amend the act to explicitly grant conservation authority.[20]

When Congress showed no inclination to authorize end-use control, the commission cautiously began to exercise its own perceived discretion to include conservation considerations in certification decisions. The commission's 1944 ruling on the application of the New York State Natural Gas Company was based on its new authority in the amended section 7 to attach to the issuance of certificates "such reasonable terms and conditions as the public convenience and necessity may require." In a landmark 1944 decision that significantly broadened the commission's rate-determination powers, Supreme Court Justice Robert Jackson invited the FPC to "boldly" interpret its statutory authority: "The commission is free to face up realistically to the nature and peculiarity of the resources under its control, to foster their duration in fixing price and to consider future interests in addition to those of investors and present consumers."[21] This decision, issued just before the FPC ruling on the New York application, further encouraged the FPC to regulate the uses for which gas could be sold. A few months later, the FPC denied the application of the Memphis Natural Gas Company to build a new pipeline from Monroe, Louisiana, to Memphis, Tennessee. The commission declared:

> In view of the limited natural gas reserves shown by the record to be available to Applicant (in the Monroe, Louisiana, gas field), their present rapid rate of depletion, and the effect of excessive rates of withdrawal on the ultimate recovery of gas therefrom, it is necessary and appropriate in the public interest that such natural gas resources be conserved in so far as possible for domestic, commercial and superior industrial uses.[22]

In numerous subsequent decisions, the FPC denied or attached restrictions to certificates in the interests of conserving gas for domestic, commercial, and "higher" industrial uses. The commission's actions, while highly objectionable to the pipelines, did not go far enough in the view of the coal industry. Not only did interstate pipeline sales for industrial uses continue to increase, but there was no federal agency with authority to prevent boiler fuel use within the gas-producing states (since intrastate sales were not federally regulated).[23] From the year of enactment of the Natural Gas Act, coal organizations steadily petitioned Congress to write conservation authority into the commission's statutory mandate, to bring direct industrial sales under its jurisdiction, and to restrict imports of natural gas.[24] However, apart from the commissioners' willingness to consider conservation in pricing and certificate cases, the coal interests realized few victories in their rear-guard actions to prevent displacement by natural gas. Not until the 1970s would a political coalition emerge with sufficient strength to make coal use in industrial and utility power plants a matter of national policy.

The Producers

In passing the 1938 law, Congress paid little attention to the producers of natural gas, and the men who drilled the wells and manned the gathering lines scarcely noticed the arrival of the Natural Gas Act. There were two reasons for their apathy. First of all, gas production was neither a prosperous nor a labor-intensive enterprise; its political influence, as a result, was extremely limited at the national level. Second, while independent producers might have expected some indirect benefit from the law, it was widely understood that the act did not apply to these producers; only interstate pipelines were to be brought under federal regulation. The political actors with whom the producers were most concerned were the state legislatures and state executive agencies which made regulations on the spacing of wells, production rates and levels, taxation of the value of production, and other related matters.

The natural gas producing industry had only nine thousand employees nationwide in 1937. Even in the largest producer states, the role of natural gas in economic life was not highly significant. The wellhead value of natural gas produced in Texas, for example, was less than twenty million dollars. Although the Federal Trade Commission's report had considered the independent producers to be victims of abuse by pipeline holding companies, producer representatives were not called to testify during 1936–1937 hearings on gas regulation; the final bill bore no trace of input on their behalf.[25] Nevertheless, to the extent that the act fostered expansion of the pipeline industry (for example, by enabling pipeline projects to secure financing), it could be of benefit to the producers. The producers' greatest need was for production controls and access to markets. If the federal government could back up interstate oil and gas production agreements, and improve his chances for access to long-distance pipelines by breaking up holding company monopolies, stabilizing the pipeline industry, and perhaps even providing scarce capital for pipeline construction, the producer would be grateful. Otherwise, he probably hoped that the federal government would take no interest in his business.

Some congressmen from gas-producing states were a bit wary of natural gas regulation in 1937 because a few members of the Roosevelt administration had been highly critical of state conservation efforts and proposed ambitious national fuel conservation plans. The gas bill's supporters, however, assured these congressmen that the bill had nothing to do with the production of natural gas.[26] In view of the Supreme Court's later interpretation of these provisions, a few examples of those assurances should be noted:

Congressional Record, Senate, August 14–19, 1937

MR. AUSTIN. Mr. President, I should like to inquire whether the bill undertakes to gain control over the natural resource of gas—that is, the natural gas of any State—to enable the Federal Government to control it? If it does, of course I should object. I inquire whether anyone knows about that?

MR. LA FOLLETTE. Mr. President, it is my understanding, and I think the senator will find from a study of the bill, that all it attempts to do is to give the Federal Power Commission the right to regulate interstate transportation and sale and resale of natural gas which moves in interstate commerce.

MR. AUSTIN. Mr. President, may I ask the senator from Montana (Mr. Wheeler) a question concerning the bill? Does the bill undertake to regulate the production of natural gas, or does it undertake to regulate the producers of natural gas?

MR. WHEELER. It does not attempt to regulate the producers of natural gas or the distributors of natural gas; only those who sell it wholesale in interstate commerce. The National Association of Railroad and Utilities Commissioners have recommended the passage of the bill and have gone on record in its favor by passing resolutions. They are very much interested in it; the city of Detroit and the city of Cleveland and a large number of senators have asked me to take it up.

MR. AUSTIN. Mr. President, will the senator yield for another inquiry?

MR. WHEELER. Yes.

MR. AUSTIN. Is the bill limited in its scope to the regulation of transportation?

MR. WHEELER. Yes; it is limited to transportation in interstate commerce, and it affects only those who sell gas wholesale. . . . There is no attempt and can be no attempt under the provisions of the bill to regulate anything in the field except where it is not regulated at the present time. It applies only as to interstate commerce and only to the wholesale price of gas. . . .

The purpose of the bill is to help the state commissions and the people of the country find out what is the cost of transporting natural gas to the larger cities, such as Detroit, Chicago, Cleveland, and New York City. It does not do any good to give the Illinois commission the power to regulate the price of gas in the city of Chicago if they can be held up—and that is all it is—by pipeline companies which ship the gas to Chicago and be told, "It is going to cost the city of Chicago so much at wholesale for this gas." What good does it do the people of Chicago if they cannot reach the wholesale price and do something to regulate the pipeline companies which transport the gas into the city of Chicago?

The only purpose of the bill is to make effective such provisions of law as will help the State regulatory bodies function in the interest of the people of Chicago, St. Louis, Detroit, and the other large cities, to enable them to get something for their money and not be robbed when they are buying gas brought to them in interstate commerce.

MR. CONNALLY (Texas). Mr. President, I have not had a letter for this bill, nor, so far as I recall, a letter against it. I have no particular interest in the matter, except that the bill does affect a large industry in my state. We want to sell our gas, of course, but we do not want to sell it at a price that is not just and fair.

MR. WHEELER. Let me say to the senator that Representative Rayburn called me up only yesterday and stated to me that he was very anxious that this bill be taken up, and asked me to make a special effort to get the bill passed; and I told him I would do so. Representative

Rayburn was formerly chairman of the Interstate Commerce Committee of the House of Representatives. He has passed upon this bill, and has gone into facts. I do not think he would have called me up and asked me to have the bill passed, if possible, if it was going to hurt the State of Texas, or anybody down there.

When hearings were held by Rayburn's committee in 1936, FPC spokesman Dozzier De Vane explained that the bill conferred no jurisdiction over "gathering rates." Asked to define those rates, he replied,

> the rates that are paid in the gathering field . . . to the man who produces it; that is binding if the transaction is at arm's length. If the transaction is not at arm's length, of course, its reasonableness may be inquired into, under the decision of the Supreme Court.[27]

In other words, prices paid to producers not affiliated with pipelines would not be regulated by the commission. Borrowing De Vane's wording, the committee rewrote section 1 exempting from the bill's jurisdiction "the production or gathering of natural gas." In defending its own interpretation, the Supreme Court would later describe the 1936 and 1937 bills as "completely different." It is clear, however, that they were considered as one by both committee sponsors and participants in the floor debate.[28] The 1937 House report describes the bill as "substantially identical" to that reported by the committee in 1936; the bill's managers on the floor emphasized repeatedly that the only significant change was the addition of section 7c (the certification provision). A careful analysis of the act's legislative history makes it clear that the "natural gas companies" brought under the act's jurisdiction were interstate pipelines, and that "wholesales" or "sales for resale" referred only to sales made by interstate pipelines to other interstate lines or at the "city gate" to local distributing utilities.[29] Furthermore, it is difficult to believe that a bill purporting to control the prices that independent producers could receive for their gas would have been reported unanimously from committee and passed by voice vote in both houses.

Control of natural resources was widely regarded in 1937 (and for some time thereafter) as a matter within the constitutional prerogative of the states. Where federal powers were exerted in these areas, as in the case of coal production, the federal agency was, in fact, an arm of the producers, and achieved its aims—the maintenance of adequate coal prices—by prescribing minimum prices and imposing penalties for overproduction.[30] Thus, what commodity controls existed by federal sanction were instituted at the request of, and operated as directed by, the producers themselves. A law designed to impose maximum price and marketing controls by an independent federal agency on an extractive product could not have been described as "conventional utility regulation" containing no "novel" provisions. Finally, the utility bargain described by Chairman

Lea in the 1937 hearings clearly applied only to pipelines. There were thousands of producers in Kansas and the Southwest; a proposal that some few be granted a "monopoly regulated in the public interest" would have been inconceivable. But without price maintenance and restrictions on competition, Lea implied, regulation would be unfair. With the possible exception of the holding company act, it was not an American custom (and certainly not New Deal policy) to impose federal controls on a reluctant industry.[31]

In summary, then, the Natural Gas Act was probably perceived by both producers and pipelines as a means of legitimating and stabilizing the industry. It would enable pipelines to secure financing for their projects in a period of scarce capital; it would, together with the holding company act, help to reassure potential investors of the general soundness of all utility companies; and it would reassure potential buyers of gas appliances that these purchases were not risky. The FPC would insure that pipeline enterprises were financially sound, possessed of adequate commitments from gas suppliers, and unable to discontinue service except in extreme circumstances. The institution of federal regulation thus became a major factor in the great expansion of natural gas usage that began in the next decade.

The Expansion of the Natural Gas Industry, 1938–1958

Over the twenty years following passage of the Natural Gas Act, the gas industry expanded rapidly. The glutted buyers' market in natural gas gave way to high and sustained demand, as pipelines reached further and further from southwestern fields, and urban dwellers in the Northeast, Midwest, and California clamored for service. Areas of production and household consumption were further differentiated: by 1958, four southwestern states—Texas, Louisiana, Oklahoma, and New Mexico—provided over 80 percent of all marketed production, and about the same percentage of interstate movements; at the other end of the pipelines, California and seven midwestern–mid-Atlantic states contained almost 60 percent of residential gas users.[32]

The bulk of the expansion took place in the decade following World War II. During this ten-year period, the number of households using natural gas increased from 10,959,000 to 21,085,000, and total residential consumption rose from 607 to 2,123 billion cubic feet annually.[33] There are several reasons for the postwar surge. The *sine qua non*, of course, was pipeline construction. After the war, the availability of investment capital was significantly increased and a residential housing boom provided the gas industry with lucrative markets. In 1949, the number of

TABLE 6   Residential Consumption of Natural Gas, 1937–1975
(Number of Households, in Thousands)

	Year					
Region/State	*1937*	*1945*	*1950*	*1955*	*1965*	*1975*
New England						
Connecticut				139	354	373
Massachusetts				643	965	1,033
New Hampshire				25	35	66*
Rhode Island				152	150	154
Vermont				0	0	NA†
Maine				0	0	NA†
Total				959	1,504	1,626
Middle Atlantic						
New Jersey			749‡	324	1,496	1,624
New York	395	437	704	2,506	3,790	3,810
Pennsylvania	651	705	1,633	928	2,095	2,160
Total	1,046	1,142	3,086	3,758	7,381	7,594
East North Central						
Illinois	1,170	1,364	1,607	928	2,500	2,911
Indiana	116	237	424	304	872	1,087
Michigan	516	905	1,017	1,208	1,687	2,068
Ohio	1,157	1,340	1,532	1,761	2,310	2,559
Wisconsin			347	403	642	868
Total	2,960	3,846	4,927	4,604	8,011	9,493
West North Central						
Iowa	110	158	221	323	534	623
Kansas	197	264	350	430	573	651
Minnesota	136	183	283	336	588	724
Missouri	362	457	550	655	864	1,085
Nebraska	111	138	173	217	337	356
North Dakota	NA†	NA†	116§	13	42	65
South Dakota	14	NA†	NA†	35	67	83
Total	930	1,200	1,693	2,009	3,005	3,587
South Atlantic						
Delaware		NA†	NA†	49	70	78
Florida	3	7	13	20	320	373
Georgia	77	106	172	324	663	846
Maryland	191‖	242‖	358‡	436	753#	854
North Carolina				49	177	306
South Carolina				38	205	259
Virginia	NA	NA	294*	266	404	481
West Virginia	174	214	262	299	334	400
District of Columbia		NA	NA	165	NA	
Total	445	569	1,099	1,650	2,926	3,597
East South Central						
Alabama	26	51	173	298	556	603
Kentucky	157	198	252	310	456	585

TABLE 6 (continued)

	Year					
Region/State	*1937*	*1945*	*1950*	*1955*	*1965*	*1975*
Mississippi	35	70	138	194	292	347
Tennessee	40	62	148	213	380	432
Total	258	391	711	1,015	1,684	1,967
West South Central						
Arkansas	64	96	151	206	351	411
Louisiana	157	255	394	506	771	914
Oklahoma	225	308	410	480	595	680
Texas	561	844	1,284	1,678	2,300	2,693
Total	1,007	1,503	2,239	2,869	4,017	4,698
Mountain						
Arizona	26	53	109	189	347	526
Colorado	92	115	170	262	437	679
Idaho					48	119
Montana	34	51	69	82	125	159
Nevada				8	49	109
New Mexico	18	40	84	120	222	240
Utah	28**	65**	NA	105	229	294
Wyoming	20	26	38	49	66	101
Total	218	350	470	815	1,523	2,227
Pacific						
Alaska					7	25
California	1,484	1,967	2,682	3,406	4,938	6,181
Oregon					136	232
Washington					170	289
Total	1,484	1,967	2,682	3,406	5,251	6,727
Total United States	8,348	10,959	16,906	21,084	35,302	41,516

Source: Minerals Yearbook (for 1937–1950, 1965–1975); *Gas Facts* (for 1955).
*Includes Maine and Vermont.
†NA means not available.
‡Includes Delaware.
§Includes South Dakota and Utah.
‖Includes District of Columbia and Virginia.
#Includes District of Columbia.
**Includes North and South Dakota.

certificates issued by the FPC almost tripled that of the previous year. In 1948, the number was smaller, but the total pipeline mileage added was almost eighty-five hundred—an increase of over 70 percent, compared to 1947. The two most important authorizations were issued to Texas Eastern Transmission Company, a Houston concern, and Transcontinental Gas Pipe Line Company, headquartered in Longview, Texas.[34]

Texas Eastern was authorized to purchase two long-distance pipelines built by the government during the war to transport petroleum. Quaintly named the "Big Inch" and the "Little Big Inch," these would be the first gas pipelines connecting East Texas through the Midwest to Appalachia and the Atlantic seaboard (see line no. 48 in Figure 5). The Transcontinental Company was certified to transport gas from the Gulf Coast through the southeastern states to the east bank of the Hudson River (see Figure 6). In 1949, the arrival of southwestern gas in metropolitan New York was greeted by a ribbon-cutting ceremony presided over by city officials.[35] From here the pipelines steadily snaked their way into Connecticut, Rhode Island, and Massachusetts so that by 1958 only Maine and Vermont remained outside natural gas distribution systems. Their small and scattered populations did not justify expensive additions to the pipeline network.

The decline in Appalachian gas reserves further stimulated pipeline construction to southwestern fields. During the extremely cold winter of 1947–48, local gas shortages caused factory closings and residential evacuations in the Appalachian area. By 1949, southwestern gas was supplying 60 percent of the Columbia Gas Company's two million customers in Pennsylvania, Ohio, and West Virginia. California also entered a period of shortage until the El Paso Natural Gas Pipeline linked the state with New Mexico and southwestern Texas fields in 1947.[36] By 1958, California was the largest consumer of gas from interstate pipelines.[37]

Also essential to the expansion of gas consumption was the manufacture of gas appliances. This industry, too, began to boom in the late 1940s. New central space heating and water heating equipment was developed, and gas utilities provided financing for their purchase.[38] New industrial applications were developed, as well. Aside from its convenience and clean-burning qualities, gas was being sold at bargain prices compared to other fuels. From 1938 to 1948, the price of gas to consumers actually declined, while coal prices increased 70 percent and oil prices, almost 80 percent (see Figure 7).[39]

Although urban consumers were delighted to see gas service initiated, the new consumers and their state regulatory agencies were uneasy about this dependence on distant supplies in a situation of high demand and fixed investment in gas-burning appliances. Appreciation for the service in no way diminished the demand for continued federal regulation. The expansion of consumption had, in fact, the contrary effect.

Although gas maintained its price advantage in comparison with other fuels, wellhead prices began to rise sharply in the late 1940s. From 1945 to 1956, prices paid to southwestern producers, which had previously been stable or declining, rose from about three cents per thousand cubic feet (mcf) to about nine cents. The wellhead price of gas was only a small fraction of the final price paid by consumers, but it was the only segment of that price that remained beyond governmental control. As prices in the

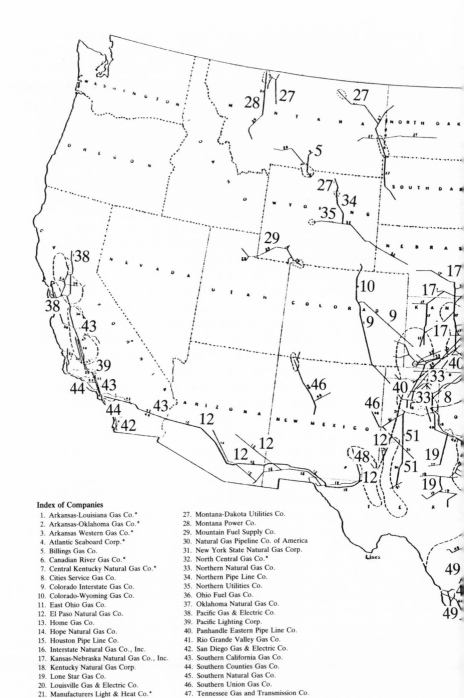

Index of Companies

1. Arkansas-Louisiana Gas Co.*	27. Montana-Dakota Utilities Co.
2. Arkansas-Oklahoma Gas Co.*	28. Montana Power Co.
3. Arkansas Western Gas Co.*	29. Mountain Fuel Supply Co.
4. Atlantic Seaboard Corp.*	30. Natural Gas Pipeline Co. of America
5. Billings Gas Co.	31. New York State Natural Gas Corp.
6. Canadian River Gas Co.*	32. North Central Gas Co.*
7. Central Kentucky Natural Gas Co.*	33. Northern Natural Gas Co.
8. Cities Service Gas Co.	34. Northern Pipe Line Co.
9. Colorado Interstate Gas Co.	35. Northern Utilities Co.
10. Colorado-Wyoming Gas Co.	36. Ohio Fuel Gas Co.
11. East Ohio Gas Co.	37. Oklahoma Natural Gas Co.
12. El Paso Natural Gas Co.	38. Pacific Gas & Electric Co.
13. Home Gas Co.	39. Pacific Lighting Corp.
14. Hope Natural Gas Co.	40. Panhandle Eastern Pipe Line Co.
15. Houston Pipe Line Co.	41. Rio Grande Valley Gas Co.
16. Interstate Natural Gas Co., Inc.	42. San Diego Gas & Electric Co.
17. Kansas-Nebraska Natural Gas Co., Inc.	43. Southern California Gas Co.
18. Kentucky Natural Gas Corp.	44. Southern Counties Gas Co.
19. Lone Star Gas Co.	45. Southern Natural Gas Co.
20. Louisville Gas & Electric Co.	46. Southern Union Gas Co.
21. Manufacturers Light & Heat Co.*	47. Tennessee Gas and Transmission Co.
22. Memphis Natural Gas Co.	48. Texas Eastern Transmission Corp.
23. Michigan Consolidated Gas Co.*	49. United Gas Pipe Line Co.
24. Michigan Gas Storage Co.	50. Virginia Gas Transmission Corp.
25. Michigan-Wisconsin Pipe Line Co.	51. West Texas Gas Co.
26. Mississippi River Fuel Corp.*	*Pipelines not labelled on map

FIGURE 5
Major Natural Gas Pipelines, 1947

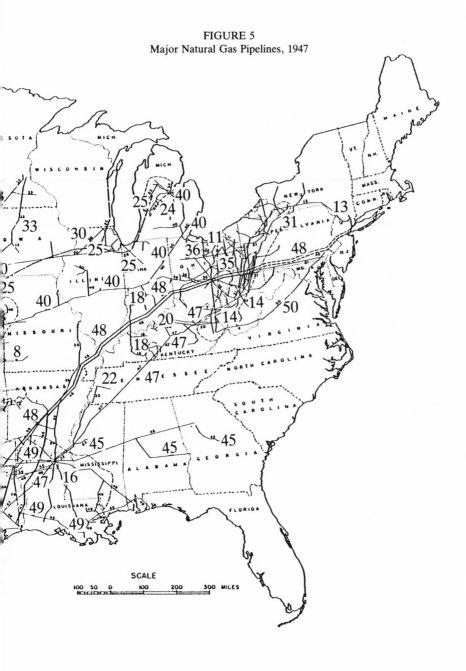

SCALE
100 50 0 100 200 300 MILES

Operating natural gas lines ——————
Other certificated lines
Gas producing areas
SOURCE: Adapted from Federal Power Commission, Docket no. G-580.

FIGURE 6

Major Natural Gas Pipelines, 1954

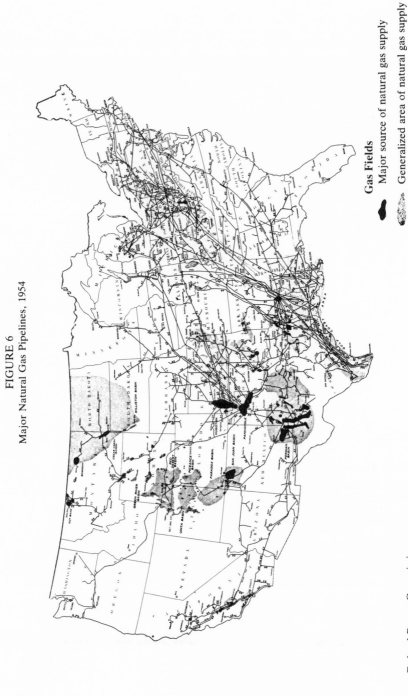

Gas Fields

Major source of natural gas supply

Generalized area of natural gas supply

SOURCE: Federal Power Commission.

FIGURE 7
Gas Price Compared with Other Fuels (Percent of 1940 Price)

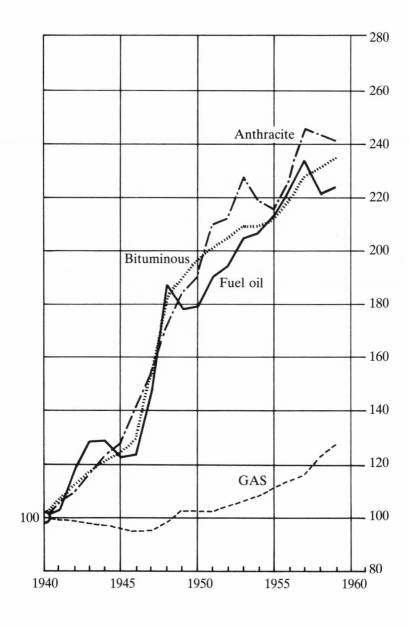

SOURCE: American Gas Association, *Gas Facts* (1960), p. 229.

field began to rise, it was inevitable that state regulatory commissions, particularly those in states with large concentrations of consumers, would begin to urge an extension of regulation to gas production itself.

By the 1950s, the market and corporate structure of the natural gas industry had changed significantly. Not only were producers and household consumers geographically concentrated and distinct, but the industry itself was comprised of three distinct segments: producers, transporters, and local distributors, with little cross-ownership among them. The political demands of consumers, producers, transporters, and distributors overlapped in some instances and diverged in others. The following table suggests some of the ways in which the interests of these groups, and of competing coal producers, could be combined.

The table is meant to be suggestive of general coalition possibilities, and, in several cases, requires considerable elaboration. For example, pricing considerations can be separated into household and industrial components, with somewhat different results. In addition, the actors themselves need not be seen as monolithic. Coal company owners and managers have, since 1970, favored deregulation for all gas prices, with the assumption that prices would rise as a result. Many coal miners, on the other hand, are themselves consumers of gas, and would thus prefer only to see industrial prices rise.[40] Hence, if there is to be a united coal industry position, it will probably have to be on issues subsumed under "entry" and "allocation." Nor does the industrial gas-consuming sector always have a single interest. If gas were scarce in interstate pipelines, those industries for which gas is a fuel that is necessary or difficult to substitute for product manufacture (the steel and glass industries, for example) might well support restrictions on boiler fuel uses of gas.

Table 7 indicates how, by combining price and entry restrictions, the designers of the Natural Gas Act were able to put together a broad-based supportive coalition.[41] After 1950, however, when high demand began to push prices upward and controls were applied for the first time on producers, the coalition dissolved. Allocation, of course, was not a part of the 1938 act. For the FPC to exercise this power required either a loose interpretation of existing powers, or new legislation. In fact, when interstate pipelines began to experience shortages of gas in the late 1960s, allocation became a major issue that ultimately resulted in new legislation. Missing from the table are political groups that, while taking part in decision making on regulation, have no direct interest in its outcome. These "spectators" are, for example, congressmen from areas that consume very little interstate gas. Their willingness to enter into coalitions with one or the other of the interested groups probably depends on other issue positions that they share with those groups at the time gas regulation questions are raised.

TABLE 7   COMMON AND COMPETING INTERESTS IN NATURAL GAS REGULATION

		Area of Regulation and Position		
Interest	Pricing: Low Gas Price in Interstate Market	Entry: Restrict Competition in Interstate Pipeline Construction	Entry: Restrict Imports	Allocation: Restrict Gas to "Higher" Uses
Commercial and residential consumers	Favor	Oppose	Oppose	Favor
Industrial users	Favor	Oppose	Oppose	Oppose
Local distribution utilities*	Favor	Oppose	Oppose	?
Interstate pipelines†	?	Favor	Oppose	Oppose
Independent gas producers	Favor (before 1950) Oppose (after 1950)	Oppose	Favor	Oppose
Coal industry and railroads	Oppose	Favor	Favor	Favor

*Utilities probably oppose restrictions on industrial uses, except in times of shortage, since off-peak industrial sales lower pipeline costs, and thus delivery charges per mcf.
†Pipelines, of course, want to be able to raise prices at their own initiative.

The Impetus to Nationalization

The legislation conceived by Congress as a solution to the problems of the natural gas industry was a noncontroversial, "pareto-optimal" package of benefits. Some of its supporters, however, would have preferred a very different and more fundamental approach to the regulation of a valuable fuel resource. This alternative approach, which contemplated extensive federal control over the production and distribution of both gas and oil, was particularly attractive to residents of northeastern and midwestern states, which lacked petroleum resources but contained populations sizeable enough to control the political apparatus. The nationalization of control was, of course, highly objectionable to the less numerous residents of the states with abundant natural resources. The latter tended to perceive, then as now, national control as a mechanism for the exploitation of southern and western "colonies" by the metropolitan centers of the North and East. The resource-laden minority, therefore, have traditionally sought refuge in the dual sovereignty doctrines of federalism. Because conflict over federal-state jurisdictional boundaries and the national control of local extraction-based economies is deep-rooted and recurrent in American politics, it may be worthwhile to pause briefly and consider some of the arguments made for nationalized controls at the time of the passage of the Natural Gas Act.

The FTC's 1935 admonition that regulation of the gas industry would present problems not encountered in other utility regulation turned out to be correct. Unlike electricity or transportation services, the commission declared, natural gas was a "valuable but limited" commodity, used nationally but produced in quantity only in certain regions. The principal problems documented by the 1935 FTC investigation centered on the supply, price, and conservation of natural gas. Conservation implied both (1) the utilization of methods of extraction which maximize the energy supply of both the oil and gas extracted from a single field and (2) the application of fossil fuels to their most efficient uses. The use of natural gas as a boiler fuel has long been considered an "inferior" use, since it replaces a product (coal) that exists in greater supply and is adequate to the task. The "higher" uses of natural gas include residential cooking and heating, and some industrial processes for which the heat content of coal is inadequate or the products of combustion have undesirable effects.

Both aspects of the conservation issue intruded on sensitive regional and federal relationships. Control of mineral production had traditionally rested with the states, and was a function that they guarded jealously. However, some officials in the Roosevelt administration and in Congress believed that extensive federal control of oil and gas production was needed, not only to counter monopolistic dominance by large national corporations, but also because the states could not be trusted with regulation of production. Oil and gas states would act to protect their own producers and industries even if that meant waste or "inferior" uses of scarce fuel resources. As the Depression lowered tax revenues and increased demands for relief programs, producer states had yet another reason not to limit the fuel production from which a significant portion of their revenues was derived.[42] Unrestricted production would, of course, drive the price down, to the disadvantage of all. But without a production-control agreement encompassing all the major producing states, no one state could be expected to diminish its own production. This line of reasoning underlay most arguments for federal control.

The producer states recognized the need for better production methods, both for conservation and in order to avoid national control of their economies. By 1936, all the major southwestern producer states had enacted laws designed to improve recovery techniques, prevent waste, and allocate production quotas among fields and leaseholders.[43] The Connally "Hot Oil" Act, passed by Congress in 1935 and renewed in 1937 and 1939, instituted federal penalties (fines and imprisonment) to discourage petroleum shipments produced in violation of state law. In 1935, the states of Texas, Oklahoma, New Mexico, Kansas, Illinois, and Colorado ratified an interstate compact pledging each state to enact and effectively enforce laws against wasteful production methods. An Interstate Oil Compact Commission was created, with representatives from each of the states, to coordinate production policy. Monthly estimates of demand were provided by the Bureau of Mines for each state, and most of the major producer states adhered fairly closely to these estimates in allocating production quotas within their states.

The state-controlled system, however, had serious flaws in the view of its critics in the Roosevelt administration and consumer states. California, one of the largest oil and gas producers at that time, had no effective conservation laws as late as 1939. Illinois, although a party to the compact, violated the terms of the agreement and allowed production far in excess of its quota in 1938 and 1939.[44] When overproduction caused a sharp drop in the price of oil in 1939, the Texas Railroad Commission (the regulatory body that oversees oil and gas production in that state) ordered a two-week shutdown of all production. The head of the Railroad Commission defended this action as in the interest of "conservation," but to representatives of consumer states, the Texas action exemplified the price-fixing efforts of a producer cartel.[45] Clearly, the term "conservation" carried different connotations in different regions. Underproduction for price maintenance had little to do with the FTC's conception of sound extraction methods and priority allocation to household consumers.

Far from encouraging reliance on state efforts, the FTC seemed to argue that nationalization of the oil and gas industries might be necessary. Particularly where, as in the Appalachian fields, producing properties were controlled by a few giant corporations, the FTC report cautiously suggested that the situation "insistently raises questions of regulatory policy involving the very basis of the validity and expediency of present theories of private ownership, control and exploitation of natural gas resources."[46]

There was, then, a strain of opinion in the Depression years that the production and pricing of essential fuels should not be left to loosely structured market forces. The market was not an unfettered arena for buyer-seller transactions, but was, at least in one region, marked by monopoly control. In the other, more important producing region, the constraints of the federal system allowed producer state governments to put the interests of their own constituents above the more numerous fuel consumers in other states. A coherent national policy for fuel allocation and conservation could hardly be derived by reliance on traditional federal solutions.

In 1938 President Roosevelt instructed his high-level research and planning agency, the National Resources Committee, to develop recommendations for "policies, investigations and legislation necessary to carry forward a broad national program for the prudent utilization and conservation of the Nation's energy resources."[47] The committee issued a controversial report in 1939 that advocated federal controls over oil, gas, and coal production.[48] For the petroleum industry such controls would prescribe methods and quantity of production, and the number and spacing of wells on each field. Interior Secretary Harold Ickes, chairman of the National Resources Committee, was a major advocate of federal production controls in the interest both of conservation and of protecting consumers from unreasonable prices. A national petroleum conservation policy could not, he told the House Commerce Committee in 1934, "be simply an aggregation of the separate policies of individual oil producing states."[49] Since the major interest of these states would be to restrict production in order to keep prices high, only federal regulation could provide both conservation and consumer protection.[50]

In 1939, the House Commerce Committee again held hearings on the need for federal production controls, this time on a bill written by Secretary Ickes and introduced by Commerce subcommittee chairman William Cole of Maryland. Although more limited in its provisions than the National Resources Committee recommendations, the Cole bill drew adamant opposition from producer state officials.[51]

In the face of such opposition, advocates of stronger, national controls relented in favor of interstate oil and gas compacts and legislation like the

Natural Gas Act. The latent interest in nationalization of control remained, however, and would rise again when scarcity and price increases
combined to pit consumers against producers. The operation of the
American political system normally makes it very difficult to enact legislation controlling the price of a resource produced in one region on
behalf of consumers in another region. Since natural resource–producing
states are over-represented in the Senate, and since the committee system, dual chambers, and separately elected president provide a multitude
of veto points, the enactment of such legislation would normally require
an extraordinary majority intensely committed to its position. In the case
of natural gas, the "intense majority" position was achieved through a
Supreme Court decision. Consequently, with producer regulation instituted by judicial interpretation, it now requires an extraordinary majority
in the legislature to undo regulation.

The Natural Gas Act of 1938 was the result of a political consensus
achieved on the basis of the extraordinary economic conditions of the
1930s. Demand for national regulation of the gas industry had developed
in the Northeast and Midwest, where a few large holding companies
monopolized the production, transmission, and local distribution of
rapidly declining Appalachian gas supplies. A thousand miles to the
southwest, gas production was plagued by hypercompetition, overproduction, and falling prices. Southwestern producers, also victims of pipeline monopolies that blocked their outlets to market, hoped that federal
regulation of interstate pipelines would facilitate the disposal of their
surplus gas. A few years after passage of the NGA, these market conditions began to change drastically. By the early 1950s the Northeast and
Midwest were receiving most of their gas from Kansas and the Southwest,
and supply could barely keep up with expanding demand for natural gas
in urban households. As a result, gas prices were rising rapidly. In
addition, the early dominance of the industry by a few vertically integrated holding companies was a thing of the past. By the 1950s, there
were three distinct segments to the natural gas industry: producers,
pipelines, and local distributors. The last two segments were publicly
regulated utilities; production, however, was (at least in the aggregate) a
highly competitive enterprise.

In the face of these profound alterations in the relationships among
sellers, transporters, distributors, and final consumers of natural gas,
pressure inevitably arose for a reinterpretation of the meaning of the
Natural Gas Act. Since the legislature was not sympathetic to a redefini-
tion that would expand federal control over energy resources, the Federal
Power Commission and the courts became the focal points of the struggle
for national control of gas prices.

4 | The Changing Meaning of the Natural Gas Act

The Regulatory Bureaucracy

> I have no hesitancy in making the assertion that the work of the FPC constitutes one of the truly outstanding regulatory performances of the decade since 1935, and one of the most auspicious signs for the future of regulation in this country.
>
> Ben W. Lewis, 1945[1]

> The Federal Power Commission represents the outstanding example in the federal government of the breakdown of the administrative process.
>
> James M. Landis, 1960[2]

The opinion of political analysts concerning the performance of the Federal Power Commission changed significantly between 1945 and 1960. Superficially, this change might be attributed to personnel changes on the commission. In 1940, for example, the appointment of New Deal theorist Leland Olds as chairman of the FPC was an indication that the agency would aggressively exercise its new powers under the Natural Gas Act. However, as later experience demonstrated, the commissioners sometimes changed their minds on the proper conduct of the agency within a relatively short time. In addition, changes in the commission's membership reflected broader changes within its political environment. Olds himself became a casualty of such a political shift in the late 1940s.

In any case, a theory of agency behavior cannot be built on an analysis of personnel turnover alone. A more generalized explanation of bureaucratic behavior can be constructed with the help of a few simple assumptions. The first such assumption is that agency appointees are ambitious professionals who wish to retain their positions. The second assumption is that agency personnel will attempt, whenever possible, to expand their jurisdictions.

In order to retain their positions, political appointees must maintain favor with those who appoint them (the president) and those who confirm appointments and provide the agencies with statutory authority and appropriations (the Congress). If reappointment becomes unlikely for any reason, an incumbent commissioner will probably shift his or her position toward the interests of those who are in a position to offer subsequent employment (for example, the regulated industry, state government, or other federal administrative posts). It is probably safe to assume that careerists predominate among regulatory commissioners, and give the agencies their adaptive qualities. On the other hand, short-term appointments (which are common in highly politicized agencies) provide an even more sensitive reflection of shifting political currents because their approaches to regulation are generally well known at the time of appointment. Federal Power Commissioners of the 1920s were often criticized for favoring private power companies over public applicants for hydroelectric licenses. However, the commission in the twenties was composed ex officio of cabinet members from the Departments of War, Interior, and Agriculture; there is no particular reason to expect the short-term political appointees of a Republican president in this era to do otherwise than lean toward private industry.

Commissioners appointed to the reconstituted agency in the thirties could look forward to considerably longer careers, so long as their regulatory philosophies were in step with the prevailing political majority.[3] It was not impossible for Republican commissioners to be reappointed by Democratic presidents, and vice versa, since the agency was bipartisan by law. Roosevelt reappointed two members of the Hoover commission. One of these appointees, Wyoming Republican Claude Draper, showed remarkable adaptability. First appointed by Hoover in 1930, he was considered antagonistic to public power. As the 1932 election approached, however, Draper broke with President Hoover and sided with commissioner Frank McNinch in advocating federal jurisdiction over hydroelectric development in the controversial New River case.[4] Both Draper and McNinch were reappointed by President Roosevelt. Draper went on to serve for twenty-six years on the commission, lasting through four different administrations and several notable shifts in the political climate surrounding natural gas regulation.

Compared to the various state commissions and private legal practices from which appointees so often came, a position on the Federal Power Commission must have been quite attractive in the 1930s and early 1940s. Voluntary turnover was low. Even with the change in administrations, the average commissioner appointed during the period from 1932 to 1945 served almost ten years. During the next fifteen years, however, as natural gas regulation became a divisive political issue, the average length of term dropped to a little over four years.

Those who pursue careers in an agency presumably will attempt to expand the agency's jurisdiction and budget, so long as that growth does

TABLE 8   MEMBERS OF THE FEDERAL POWER COMMISSION, 1930–1978
(FEDERAL ENERGY REGULATORY COMMISSION, AFTER 1977)

Name	Party	State of Residence	Principal Occupation(s) Prior to Appointment	Appointed by	Years Served
Draper, Claude L.	R	Wyo.	ICC Bar and staff of National Association of Railroad and Utility Commissioners	Hoover, Roosevelt, Truman, Eisenhower	1930–1956
Garsaud, Marcell	D	La.	New Orleans Port Commissioner	Hoover	1930–1932
Williamson, Ralph B.	R	Wash.	D.C. attorney for irrigation project	Hoover	1930–1933
McNinch, Frank R.	D	N.C.	Mayor; practicing attorney	Hoover, Roosevelt	1930–1937
Smith, George O.	R	Maine	U.S. Coal Association; U.S. Geological Survey	Hoover	1930–1933
Drane, Herbert J.	D	Fla.	Congressman	Roosevelt	1933–1937
Manly, Basil	D	D.C.	U.S. Senate staff; attorney for N.Y. Power Authority	Roosevelt	1933–1945
Seavey, Clyde L.	R	Calif.	California Railroad Commission	Roosevelt	1934–1943
Scott, John W.	D	Ind.	U.S. Assistant Attorney General	Roosevelt	1937–1945
Olds, Leland	D	N.Y.	N.Y. Power Authority; presidential study commissions	Roosevelt	1939–1949
Smith, Nelson L.	I	N.H.	Economist, N.H. Public Service Commission	Roosevelt, Truman	1943–1955
Sachse, Richard	D	Calif.	California Railroad Commission	Truman	1945–1947
Wimberly, Harrington	D	Okla.	Publisher; State Democratic Committee	Truman	1945–1953
Buchanan, Thomas	D	Pa.	Public Utility Commissioner	Truman	1948–1953
Wallgren, Mon C.	D	Wash.	Governor of Washington	Truman	1949–1951
Doty, Dale E.	D	Calif.	U.S. Department of Interior	Truman	1952–1954
Kuykendall, Jerome K.	R	Wash.	Chairman Wash. Public Service Commission	Eisenhower	1953–1961
Digby, Seaborn L.	D	La.	Unknown	Eisenhower	1953–1958
Stueck, Frederick	R	Mo.	Public Service Commissioner; Insurance company vice president	Eisenhower	1954–1961

Name	Party	State	Position	President	Years
Connole, William R.	I	Conn.	Attorney for Public Utility Commission	Eisenhower	1955–1960
Kline, Arthur	R	Wyo.	Federal judge	Eisenhower	1956–1961
Hussey, John B.	D	La.	Unknown	Eisenhower	1958–1960
Sweeney, Paul	D	Md.	Attorney, Justice Department	Eisenhower	1960–1961
Swidler, Joseph	D	Tenn.	TVA attorney	Kennedy	1961–1965
Morgan, Howard	D	Oreg.	Construction company executive	Kennedy	1961–1963
O'Connor, L. J., Jr.	D	Okla.	Oil company; Department of Interior	Kennedy	1961–1972
Ross, Charles R.	R	Vt.	Chairman Public Service Commission	Kennedy	1961–1969
Woodward, Harold C.	R	Ill.	Ill. Commerce Commission	Kennedy	1962–1964
Black, David S.	D	Wash.	Wash. Public Service Commission; attorney; Department of Commerce	Kennedy	1963–1966
Bagge, Carl E.	R	Ill.	Railroad attorney	Johnson	1965–1971
Carver, John A., Jr.	D	Idaho	Senate staff; Interior Department	Johnson	1966–1973
White, Lee C.	D	Nebr.	TVA; Senate staff (Kennedy); presidential counsel	Johnson	1966–1969
Brook, Albert B.	R	Ky.	Senate staff (Morton)	Johnson, Nixon	1969–1975
Nassikas, John	R	N.H.	Attorney; Senate Minority counsel	Nixon	1969–1976
Walker, Pinckney	R	Mo.	Professor of economics	Nixon	1971–1973
Moody, Rush	D	Tex.	Attorney	Nixon	1971–1975
Springer, William L.	R	Ill.	Congressman (IFC Committee)	Nixon	1973–1976
Smith, Don S.	D	Ark.	Public Service Commission	Nixon, Carter	1974–
Dunham, Richard L.	R	N.Y.	N.Y. Budget Director; White House staff	Ford	1976–1977
Holloman, John	D	Miss.	Attorney	Ford	1976–1977
Watt, James G.	R	Wyo.	Interior Department	Ford	1976–1977
Sheldon, Georgiana	R	Pa.	AID; Civil Service Commission	Carter	1977–
Curtis, Charles	I	Pa.	SEC; House staff (IFC)	Carter	1977–
Hall, George R.	D	Calif.	Defense Department (Resource Planning)	Carter	1977–
Holden, Matthew	D	Wis.	Professor; Public Service Commission	Carter	1977–

not destabilize the agency's political support. Expansion is pursued through aggressive rule making, broad interpretation of existing authority, and pursuit of formal additions to the agency's statutory mandate. Regulators will generally prefer to accomplish their goals by administrative action rather than by the passage of an explicit statute that limits administrative flexibility. However, expansion of jurisdiction through vaguely worded, highly discretionary legislation will usually be supported by the agency. Rule making and broad interpretation require judicial legitimation; statutory expansion must be accomplished by Congress, and generally requires prior approval by the committees that oversee the agency.[5] For the FPC, these have been the House and Senate Committees on Interstate and Foreign Commerce.[6]

Particularly in the House, where members generally serve on only one major committee, Commerce has traditionally been particularly attractive to urban congressmen interested in its jurisdiction over domestic and foreign trade and transportation.[7] Through the first half of the 1940s, the Democratic majority reflected the interests of urban gas consumers and supported an activist Power Commission. After 1946, however, when the Republican party returned to national power, a new majority coalition began to form on the House committee. Made up of suburban Republicans and southeastern Democrats—both from districts with lower gas consumption than central cities—and a few southwestern producer state congressmen, this coalition took a dim view of the FPC's expansive behavior.[8] In the Senate the Commerce Committee had always contained a large core of southern and western members who were interested in railroad regulation but were not supportive of most other forms of federal economic intervention. Less sympathetic from the beginning to arguments for federal control of natural resources, the Senate committee became openly hostile after the 1946 Republican landslide and the addition of new members from gas-producing states.

The distinct periods in the life of the Federal Power Commission after passage of the Natural Gas Act are outlined in Table 9. In the beginning, with a supportive congressional, executive, and judicial environment, the commission broadly exercised its loosely worded statutory mandate. Ultimately it went too far, however: the widespread consensus under which it began started to evaporate. The commission got into trouble, not only because it misread the mandate of 1938, but because the political balance itself was shifting. There was a Republican resurgence in the postwar period, and southern Democrats, once the Depression was over, became far less supportive of the northern-based national Democratic administration. The FPC began to backtrack and during the Eisenhower years argued a different side of the principal gas regulation issue. In the 1960s, the New Deal commission appeared to have been reborn, only to

TABLE 9   SEVEN PERIODS IN FEDERAL POWER COMMISSION REGULATION

Period	Party in Control of Executive	Position of Oversight Committees*	Agency Attitude	Gas Supply to Interstate Pipelines
1938–1945	Democratic	Pro-regulation	Activist, pro-consumer	Surplus
1946–1952	Democratic	Anti-regulation	Divided	Regional shortages, high demand
1953–1960	Republican	Moderately anti-regulation	Reluctant regulation, pro-producer	Abundant
1961–1968	Democratic	Pro-regulation	Activist, pro-consumer	Stable†
1969–1973	Republican	Pro-regulation	Cautious, leaning to producer	Shortage
1974–1976	Republican	Moderately pro-regulation	Moderately pro-producer	Shortage
1977–1980	Democratic	Divided	Pro-consumer	Expanding supply, creation of national market

*The reference is to the position (on control of wellhead gas prices) of the majority coalition on the committee, which may be bipartisan. In terms of party control, the Republican party held a majority in the House and Senate only during 1947–1948 and 1953–1954.
†The implication of the word "stable" is that additions to reserves and production levels were adequate to supply current pipeline demands.

give way in the 1970s to an agency attitude closer to that of the Eisenhower commission. Each shift represented an adaptation to changes in the agency's political environment.

The Evolution of Regulatory Doctrine

Following the passage of the Natural Gas Act in 1938, the FPC quickly began to break new ground in utility regulation. In its first decade, the FPC formulated a standardized system of utility accounting (as the act directed it to do), and cast its regulatory net wide enough to encompass a number of producers and intrastate gas distributors—both of whom had considered themselves explicitly exempted from the act. The commission also succeeded in establishing, to the dismay of the regulated pipelines, a new standard for determining the costs (or rate base) of providing utility service. In academic circles and among other state and federal regulatory bodies, the new standard was hailed as a brilliant innovation. In the case of jurisdictional claims affecting producers and distributors, however, the commission's innovations were not well received. In both of the latter cases, vociferous complaints from the affected groups resulted in congressional efforts to rein in the commission through statutory amendments.

Until the early 1940s, the Supreme Court judged the fairness of regulatory commission rate decisions according to a formula laid down in the landmark 1898 case of *Smyth* v. *Ames*. Smyth was a member of the Nebraska commission that controlled railroad charges. The commission had set a maximum rate based on the current value of railroad property, rather than its original cost. Since this was a period of declining prices, the cost of reproducing railroad investments was generally less than it had been earlier. The result of using reproduction, rather than original cost, was a reduction in rates. Railroad investors (Ames et al.) challenged the decision as a violation of the Fourteenth Amendment, charging that this rate-making procedure confiscated their property (that is, lowered the value of their investment) without due process of law. There is considerable irony here. Later, in inflationary times, regulated industries would argue for rates based on reproduction costs and regulatory agencies would prefer original costs, for obvious reasons.

The Supreme Court in 1898 upheld the state of Nebraska against the railroads, finding that the commission's method could, indeed, yield a fair return (that is, a return that would not violate the Fourteenth Amendment). However, the doctrine set down in *Smyth* v. *Ames* proved extremely ambiguous.[9] The Court admonished regulatory bodies to grant public utilities a "fair return" on the "fair value" of their investments. "Fair return" has generally been interpreted as close to the current interest rate—at the turn of the century, about 6 percent. But what was "fair value"? It seemed to be some sort of compromise between the original and reproduction costs of the property used in providing the service. According to Justice Harlan,

> In order to ascertain that value, the original cost of construction, the amount expended in permanent improvements, the amount and market value of its bonds and stock, the present as compared with the original cost of construction, the probable earning capacity of the property and under particular rates prescribed by statute, and the sum required to meet operating expenses, are all matters for consideration and are to be given such weight as may be just and right in each case.[10]

The state commissions, of course, had no idea what weight to assign these factors in each case. The ambiguous Smyth standard, therefore, made their task extremely difficult, and invited extensive litigation. By the 1930s there was great dissatisfaction with the method, and several of the more adventurous state commissions began to formulate simpler standards. The most appealing was the use of original costs. It was easy enough, from the company's records, to determine what it had cost to put together the utility. By discounting or ignoring "unwise" or excessive expenditures, regulators could then establish a "prudent investment" figure and, using a formula of the type below, fix a rate to be charged for the service:

$$\text{Allowable rate} = \frac{\text{Rate of return [a fraction]} \times (\text{Original cost} \times \text{Depreciation}) + \text{Taxes} + \text{Current operating expenses}}{\text{Units sold}}$$

A number of complications remain. For example, in the case of pipelines, the assessed property must be allocated between jurisdictional (interstate) and nonjurisdictional (intrastate) investments.[11] Nevertheless, the process is considerably easier and less open to judicial challenge than attempting to discern what each part of the company's property would cost to put together at today's prices.

When it seemed that the Court was amenable to replacing the Smyth doctrine, the FPC joined the argument for a prudent investment standard. In 1935, the commission tried to convince Congress to write a prudent investment standard into the natural gas and electricity titles of the holding company bill.[12] In both titles, the sections on rate setting (which the FPC itself had written) directed the commission to investigate and determine "the actual legitimate prudent cost" of the property used in providing the service. Pipelines and electric companies were alarmed by this wording. Congress, for its part, was not inclined to revolutionize utility rate making in 1935, even though the FPC insisted that a "fair value" determination would be costly and time consuming. The final versions of both the Federal Power Act and the Natural Gas Act omitted the word "prudent," and settled on "the actual legitimate cost" and "other facts which bear on . . . the fair value of such property." This was ambiguous enough, however, to enable the FPC to pursue a judicially legitimated prudent investment standard. In the late 1930s, the commission filed amicus curiae briefs in cases involving state regulatory decisions based on the new standard. Finally, it applied the new doctrine in its own rate-making decisions.[13]

Immediately upon passage of the Natural Gas Act, a number of municipalities and state commissions petitioned the FPC to investigate pipeline charges in their areas. The city governments of Toledo, Cleveland, and Akron, Ohio, along with Pennsylvania officials, challenged the rate charged by Hope Natural Gas Company for West Virginia gas sold to distributors in the two neighboring states. The FPC undertook an investigation of Hope's charges, and proceeded to order rate reductions based on prudent investment calculations. The company argued for an 8 percent return on the "present fair value" of its property. The commission granted a 6.5 percent return on Hope's depreciated original costs, and ordered rate reductions totalling over three and a half million dollars. Hope appealed the decision, handed down in 1942, and was upheld by a circuit court which agreed with the company that a "just and reasonable" rate must reflect replacement costs. The FPC appealed this decision, which reached the Supreme Court in 1944.

In the 1940s, the Supreme Court contained a Roosevelt-appointed majority clearly sympathetic to the argument of state and federal regulators that they be given more flexibility in rate doctrine. Recognizing that the Smyth "fair value" standard was a barrier to effective regulation, the Court upheld the commission's use of "prudent investment" costs. No particular formula need be followed, Justice Douglas wrote for the majority, so long as the end result was one that balanced the interests of investors and consumers. From the investor's point of view, wrote Douglas,

> it is important that there be enough revenue not only for operating expenses but also for the capital costs of the business. . . . The return to the equity owner should be commensurate with returns on investments in other enterprises having corresponding risks . . . [and should] be sufficient to assure confidence in the financial integrity of the enterprise, so as to maintain its credit and to attract capital.[14]

The commission had argued that Hope was, and would remain under the allowed rates, a strong company with "protected, established markets," and secure gas supplies. Thus the company was in "a strong position to attract capital on favorable terms when it is required," and that strength was enough evidence that the FPC's rates were not unfair. The Court agreed.

The Hope case represented a landmark in regulatory doctrine. The decision was a victory for a young and active FPC, and one that found consumers, regulators, and the New Deal Court in perfect harmony on the scope of regulation. However, the decision created considerable consternation among both pipeline companies and gas producers. Hope, a subsidiary of Standard Oil, was a large pipeline that owned a substantial quantity of gas reserves in West Virginia. In its decision, the FPC had applied cost-based regulation not only to the company's transmission facilities, but to its producing properties as well. The prudent investment method had been designed for pricing the services of publicly sanctioned monopolies. To apply this method to an exhaustible commodity produced at considerable risk by multiple producers seemed highly inappropriate even to some members of the Supreme Court. Justices Jackson, Reed, and Frankfurter dissented on this and other grounds.

Jackson was particularly emphatic in his objections, both here and in later decisions involving the Power Commission and pipeline-owned production. He argued that the value of gas had nothing to do with the capital invested in drilling a particular well. Why, he asked, should one gas producer receive five times as much for his gas as another, simply because he has been unlucky and had to spend more to find it? And was it not "capricious," he argued in a similar case the following year, to put five of a company's major leaseholds into its rate base at less than ten cents an acre (at depreciated original cost), when the gas reserves contained therein had a market value of over three million dollars?[15] Applied to a commodity like natural gas, this was, to Jackson, a "fantastic" rate method. The result, Jackson felt, was particularly unfortunate from the standpoint of conservation, since low prices would encourage wasteful industrial use.

The state of West Virginia contested the method in an amicus curiae brief. Cost-based evaluation of gas production, it argued, "brings consequences which are unjust to West Virginia and its Citizens," which "unfairly depress the value of gas . . . and gas leaseholds, unduly restrict development of their natural resources, and arbitrarily transfer their properties to the residents of other states without just compensation therefore." Since West Virginia had a production tax based on the value of gas sold, the rate fixed by the FPC would cost the state thousands of dollars in lost revenues, discourage new exploration, and squander its diminishing resources, all "for the benefit of Ohio and Pennsylvania consumers."[16] A decade later this argument would be repeated by the southwestern producer states.

Justice Frankfurter, dissenting from the majority's decision, argued that the "public interest" the commission was directed to consider was "a texture of multiple strands" that included "more than contemporary investors and contemporary consumers."[17] The majority, however, claimed that it had searched the legislative history of the Natural Gas Act for any indications that Congress had intended for the interests of the producing states to be considered in the commission's rate making, and found nothing that would compel the commission "to let the stockholders of natural gas companies have a feast so that the producing states may receive crumbs from that table."[18]

Although in the Hope case the FPC had allowed the company to count as an expense the full amount it paid for gas purchased from independent producers, the commission's activism and the tendency of the Supreme Court's reasoning aroused considerable opposition in the producer states. Even before the Hope decision, FPC actions had begun to alarm the producers. In the first few years of regulation under the Natural Gas Act, the commission took the position—about which there was little controversy—that it had no jurisdiction over sales of independent producers. Four of five commissioners took this position in a 1940 ruling involving the Columbia Fuel Corporation. The four-man majority included three who had been on the commission when the act was passed, and newly appointed New York Democrat Leland Olds. Another newly appointed commissioner dissented, however, arguing that the sale of gas to an interstate pipeline was not a part of the "production and gathering" process exempted in section 1b. In addition, the majority left open the possibility that "further experience" with the act might change its opinion on the exemption.[19] Later, in its Billings Gas Company ruling, the FPC held that when gas was transported beyond the end of the producer's gathering lines, the sale was in interstate commerce, and, therefore, subject to the commission's jurisdiction even though it was the first sale by the producer to a pipeline.[20] Still, "arm's length" sales by independent producers at the end of their gathering lines remained unregulated.

Two years later, in 1942, the commission faced directly the question of how to treat sales by companies that both produced gas for sale to interstate lines and transported gas for resale. Since interstate pipes were clearly subject to its jurisdiction, the commission decided to apply cost-based regulation to the entire system, including production facilities used for interstate sales. The companies involved (the Colorado Interstate and Canadian River Gas Companies) challenged the ruling. They argued that since section 1b of the Natural Gas Act exempted "production and gathering," a fair market price should be allowed for the gas they produced, and the production and gathering facilities should be excluded from the rate base in determining their pipeline charges. The Supreme Court in 1945 upheld the ruling of the commission, thus denying the "production and gathering" exemption to leases owned by producers whose transmission business brought them under regulation.[21] In 1943, in the Interstate Natural Gas Company case, the commission again claimed jurisdiction to set cost-based rates for producer sales of gas to affiliated companies, and again it was upheld in court. Moreover, in deciding the Interstate challenge in 1947, the Supreme Court went so far as to argue that sales to interstate pipelines, even first sales at the completion of gathering, were a part of the area Congress had intended to occupy in passing the 1938 act. The Court held that the exemption in section 1b merely prohibited federal regulation of the "physical" process of production, not the sale by producers of gas destined for consumption in other states.[22]

This very broad interpretation of FPC jurisdiction went beyond any previous claim of authority made by the commission, and clearly indicated that wellhead sales by independent producers would eventually be included in federal regulation. Even before the final Supreme Court decision in the Interstate case, a storm of protest arose from pipelines and producers, and resounded in Congress. The commission now recognized that it had set in motion a process that would generate great controversy, and quickly sought to retrace its steps to firmer ground. After the Interstate ruling was upheld in circuit court in 1946, a number of bills were introduced to clarify the Natural Gas Act by explicitly denying FPC jurisdiction over sales by independents, and allowing market-determined prices for gas produced by pipeline companies. The FPC, in congressional testimony, opposed the most extreme of these bills—the Moore-Rizley bill, named for its two Oklahoma sponsors—but declared itself unanimously in support of legislation that would exempt independent producer sales while continuing FPC regulation of gas produced by pipelines. The commission itself drew up such a bill and it was introduced in the House by Commerce Committee Democrat Percy Priest of Tennessee. However, the House passed the stronger Moore-Rizley bill by a large margin in July of 1947.[23] The drive for amendment had been strengthened by increasingly severe gas shortages in the Appalachian area and the widespread belief that confusion about the FPC's regulatory intentions would cause many southwestern producers to withhold their gas from the interstate market.[24]

In 1938, when supplies were ample, price control was a prominent motive for establishing federal regulation over pipelines. In 1947, when shortages of gas threatened industrial closings and residential evacuations, price regulation seemed far less important than facilitating adequate supplies. State public utility commissions, which had championed federal regulation in 1938, now supported limitations on FPC authority. Those limitations were seen as necessary conditions both for securing additional gas supplies and for persuading the commission not to intrude upon the jurisdiction of state regulatory boards.

During its expansionist phase in the 1940s, the FPC had begun to assert jurisdiction over the strictly intrastate operations of local gas-distributing companies. Many of these companies owned high-pressure stub lines that ran between the interstate pipelines and the point of pressure reduction— usually at the "city gate." When they transported purchased gas through these short lines to their own distribution facilities, or allowed their connector lines to be used for sales by the interstate pipeline to other users or distributors, the FPC asserted jurisdiction, requiring that certificates be obtained for the construction of such lines and that extensive cost inventories be made by the companies owning them. The local utilities complained of the burden and expense of this paperwork, which, in most cases, duplicated reports they were required to file with state regulatory bodies.[25] For their part, the state commissions were highly offended by the federal intrusion into a situation that they contended was adequately supervised by the states. The FPC had thus alienated an important part of its clientele. Gas producers were able to make common cause with distributors, state regulators, and urban consumers by including in the Moore-Rizley bill a "clarification" of the distributor exemption in section 1b. The Moore-Rizley bill as a package, then, was promoted by its sponsors as a way to improve gas supplies to urban areas in the Midwest, South, Northeast, and Pacific Coast by overcoming the reluctance of both producers and distributors to take actions (that is, selling gas to interstate pipelines or building stub lines to interstate pipelines) that threatened to bring them under federal control.

Anxious to reassure Congress and retain as much as possible of its statutory authority, the commission in two cases before it in 1947 held that it had no jurisdiction over arm's length sales at the end of gathering lines.[26] Furthermore, the commission pointed out that these decisions were consistent with its 1940 ruling in the Columbia Fuel case and indicated that it had never really abandoned the earlier position on exemption of independent sales. Following the August 1947 Supreme Court ruling in the Interstate case, the FPC immediately issued Opinion no. 139, disclaiming the authority given it by the Court. Veteran commissioner Claude Draper dissented from the statement in Opinion 139, but Leland Olds, perhaps sensing his growing unpopularity in the Senate, voted with the majority.

Not only had producer state representatives awakened to the dangers inherent in discretionary regulation under the Natural Gas Act, but the partisan balance in Congress had also shifted dramatically. In the 1946 elections, the Democratic Party in the House of Representatives declined from a 242-seat majority to a 188-seat minority. In the Senate, the Republican Party captured a majority for the first time since 1930. The 1947 change in partisan control, in combination with a reorganization of the committee system, dramatically changed the composition of one of the committees overseeing the work of the Federal Power Commission. The House Commerce Committee shifted from a fifteen-to-eleven Democratic majority, chaired by former California Public Service Commissioner Clarence Lea, to a sixteen-to-eleven Republican majority, with New Jersey Representative Charles Wolverton in the chair. Lea opposed the Moore-Rizley deregulation bill; Wolverton supported it, as did all other Republican members of the committee.

Sentiment against the commission's perceived expansionism ran high in the Republican-controlled House, as exemplified by the following excerpts from the debate on the Moore-Rizley bill:

> MR. WORLEY (Democrat, Texas). If this legislation is not passed, there is absolutely no limit whatsoever to how far the Federal Power Commission will go in reaching out to get more and more powers which the Congress never intended them to have.

MR. SABATH (Democrat, Illinois). The Federal Power Commission is acting for the Government, for the protection of the American people. . . .

MR. SCOTT (Republican, Pennsylvania). I cannot quite share the complete confidence expressed by the gentleman from Illinois in any federal agency just because it is a Federal agency. . . . I do not like law handed down by interpretation or by administration. I think when there is a substantial doubt as to what is coming next, as there is in this case, we better say by statute precisely what we mean.

MR. GAVIN (Republican, Pennsylvania). I come from a district in Western Pennsylvania that has been producing gas for many years. Last winter it was necessary for us to ration gas, the first time it has been rationed to my knowledge. I am greatly interested as are my people and the industrial life of my district in serving an additional supply of gas to supplement the rapidly depleting gas supply in Western Pennsylvania.[27]

The Supreme Court, secure in its tenure, might continue to expand the frontiers of regulation, but the FPC, a creature of Congress, could not ignore the new political climate. The commission was eager to reassure the new Republican majority that it would take a narrower view of its powers in the future. However, a number of municipalities, state regulatory boards, and consumer area representatives, the core clientele for gas regulation, were supporting the Court decision, and urging the extension of regulation to producers. In addition, there was still a Democratic president who clearly allied himself with the consumer interest, and who might be re-elected in 1948 in spite of the Republican trend.

The commission became schizophrenic. In response to the mounting complaints against its actions, it had undertaken in 1945 an extensive investigation of the natural gas industry and the effects of federal regulation, conducting hearings in the consumer, producer, and coal regions of the country. A report based on this investigation was issued in 1948. There was now one vacancy on the commission and the remaining four members were unable to agree on recommendations for future gas regulation. Commissioners Smith and Wimberly (the latter an Oklahoma Democrat) urged that independent producer sales be exempted from regulation, and that gas produced by pipelines be allowed market-sensitive prices. Draper and Olds defended the need for regulation, without explicitly arguing for the control of all independent producer sales. They did, however, strongly defend cost-based regulation for pipeline-owned production, and argued for an extension of FPC jurisdiction to the end-use regulation of natural gas.[28]

President Truman tipped the balance on the commission in 1948 by appointing Thomas Buchanan, a Pennsylvania Democrat who took the side of expanded regulation. Truman also renominated consumer advocate Leland Olds the following year. By this time, however, the opposition aroused in producer state delegations (and among other opponents of commodity regulation) by the Supreme Court decision in the Interstate case had focused on the commission's activists. A Senate Commerce subcommittee chaired by Lyndon Johnson held hearings on the Olds nomination in 1949. These hearings provided a forum for extended debate on the natural gas issue, and served to define the battle lines.

Couching their arguments in expansive, emotion-laden rhetoric, each side attempted to build a majority coalition. Olds was strongly defended by elected officials, Democratic Party organizations, and labor groups from the consumer regions, as well as a number of public power organizations. Morris Cooke, who had served with Olds on the New York State Power Authority, presented the issue in these terms:

> I have never wavered in my loyalty to our American competitive, freely operating, enterprise system. . . . But, among the influences seeking to break it down, the closely knit private utility system appears to be the strongest single force as it tries either to sabotage existing regulation or to escape entirely from its control as is now the undisguised effort of the natural gas industry located in the southwestern part of our country.
>
> Clearly the battle over the confirmation of Leland Olds as a member of the Federal Power Commission is a battle between the great body of people who are consumers, on the one side, and the monopolistic power and oil-gas interests on the other. It is a part of the battle which has been going on for years to bring these vital interests under some measure of public control. This battle must go on if democracy itself is to survive.[29]

Almost all of the witnesses testifying against the renomination were from the major gas-producing states. Their views of the consequences of a "wrong" decision by the Senate were no less apocalyptic. The chairman of the Oklahoma state commission for oil, gas, and utility regulation warned that

> Mr. Olds is imbued with a philosophy of centralized and nationalized government that would lead to a complete usurpation of the jurisdiction and regulatory power of our commission over the production, gathering, and field sales of natural gas, and would eventually lead to the destruction and usurpation of the constitutional powers of the State to regulate and control local business activities.[30]

Olds had begun his career as a labor organizer and journalist in New York. He had worked for the reform of utility regulation, and later served on the staff of a New York State commission for water resource planning and hydroelectric power development. Before his appointment to the Federal Power Commission, Olds had undertaken two assignments for the Roosevelt administration: first, a report on the European cooperative movement; and second, a contribution to the administration's controversial 1939 *Report on Energy Resources and National Policy.*[31] That report, it will be recalled, advocated a larger role for the federal government in hydroelectric power development and the production of oil, gas, and coal. During House hearings on deregulation in 1947, Representative Rizley described the 1939 report as "an element of a national plan to federalize all of the energy resources of the nation to the end that the entire national economy may be controlled through federal administrative decrees."[32] Olds' career, together with early writings for the labor press in which he appeared to advocate state socialism, connected him with the perceived trend to nationalization. Thus, he became an obvious target for those who opposed federal involvement, not just in natural resource development, but also in business regulation in general. In the emerging cold war period of the late 1940s, a few congressmen from producer states seized the opportunity to link Olds with a growing Communist Menace. Texas Representative John Lyle claimed that his opposition to Olds' appointment ("an utterly unthinkable appointment for the time in which we live") was based on the fact that Olds had—

> through a long and prolific career—attacked the church; he has attacked our schools, he has ridiculed the symbols of patriotism and loyalty such as the Fourth of July; he has advocated public ownership; he has reserved his applause for Lenin and Lenin's system, and he has found few words of praise for our American system; and yes, gentlemen, he has seen fit to attack the men who serve as elected representatives in our government—men such as you. He has characterized you as mere administrative clerks handling administrative details for "an immensely powerful ruling class." Yes, unbelievable as it seems, gentlemen, this man Leland Olds, the man who now asks the consent and approval of the Senate to serve on the Federal Power Commission, has not believed in our constitution, our government, our Congress, our representative form of government, our churches, our flag, our schools, our system of free enterprise.[33]

The subcommittee unanimously recommended defeat of the Olds nomination, and the full Senate rejected the appointment by a vote of thirty-three to fifteen. This action by the Senate, however, cannot be interpreted solely as a vote on the scope of natural gas regulation. The overwhelming rejection was as much indicative of a broader opposition to Olds' regulatory philosophy as to his position on the natural gas issue. In fact, the opposing coalitions on natural gas regulation were very closely matched in 1949. The political balance was held by spectator states, and by presidents who might decide the outcome by using the appointment power or the veto.

The strongly antiregulation Moore-Rizley bill that passed the House in 1947 died in Senate committee in 1948. In 1949, the Democrats regained control of the House, and, by a two-seat margin, the Senate as well. The demand for a limitation on FPC jurisdiction remained strong, however. In the House, Oren Harris, a Commerce Committee Democrat representing a gas-producing district in Arkansas, introduced a bill similar to the more moderate Priest bill of the previous Congress.[34] In the Senate, Robert Kerr of Oklahoma introduced a companion bill "clarifying the status of independent producers and gatherers." With Buchanan now on the FPC, a three-man majority of the commission opposed this limitation of its authority.

The House and Senate Commerce committees were themselves divided. When the Harris-Kerr bill came to the floor in 1949–1950, the House committee split eighteen to ten, and the Senate committee, five to four, in favor of deregulating independent producers. Producer state representatives on the committees built alliances with Democrats from mountain states (in the Senate) and the Southeast (in the House), but relied mainly on their Republican colleagues for support. Midwestern and northeastern Democrats on the committees opposed Harris-Kerr.

The deregulation bill passed the House 183 to 131 in 1949, and the Senate, 44 to 38, in the following year. Supporters based their arguments on original legislative intent, and maintained that the fundamental issue was whether Congress or the bureaucracy should make law. They insisted that gas production was a highly competitive enterprise, and that the independent producers, who made most gas field discoveries, required free market prices as an incentive to explore for gas. Furthermore, as supporters of the bill pointed out, the wellhead price of gas had declined in the past eleven years and composed less than 10 percent of the total price per thousand cubic feet (mcf) paid by household consumers.[35]

Opponents of deregulation perceived a very different natural gas industry. Where a Louisiana congressman saw thousands of farmers and small businessmen drilling for gas on modest leaseholds, a Michigan senator saw giant monopolies sanctioned by the producer states themselves, and determined to charge their distant customers all that the traffic would bear. They insisted that the original intent of Congress had been to protect consumers from exploitation at the hands of large gas companies. Since the price of gas had recently begun to rise, and seemed likely to be pushed higher by ever-increasing demand, the continuation of FPC regulation was essential. A Chicago representative pointed out that a five-cent increase in the wellhead price of gas would cost his constituents over six and a half million dollars. The issue, as consumer representatives saw it, was not "who shall make the law," but rather, "should monopolistic industries be regulated or not?"[36]

The narrower House vote on the Harris bill, compared with the large majority in favor of the more extreme Moore-Rizley bill in 1947, was indicative both of continued growth in natural gas consumption and the effect of a shift in partisan control of Congress. Between the two House votes in 1947 and 1949, the Big Inch and other new pipelines were certified to transport gas to the Northeast and Pacific Coast. Pipelines from the Southwest first reached eastern Pennsylvania, New York, and New Jersey during 1949. Along the new transcontinental routes, North and South Carolina received their first supplies of natural gas; Tennessee, Alabama, and Georgia had their interstate pipeline mileage almost doubled.[37] Between 1946 and 1949, the number of household consumers of natural gas increased by 3.8 million, and the amount of gas consumed by them rose by over three hundred billion cubic feet.[38] Each new interstate consumer acquired a vested interest in regulation.

Two explanations may be offered for the shift in policy position when a seat changes party. First, Republicans generally represent a more affluent segment of the district's voters, one that is less concerned with the immediate effect of a monthly utility bill than with the broad principle of business freedom from government price regulation. In addition, most partisan turnover in this period occurred in mixed urban-suburban or urban-rural districts. The percentage of gas consumers among center city households tends to be significantly larger than in the suburban or small-town areas that form the constituencies of many Republican congressmen.[39] It was, after all, the dense concentration of potential urban consumers that originally justified the expense of constructing long-distance pipelines. Many small towns and suburbs were unable to obtain gas service (which they would have preferred to more costly or less desirable fuels) as late as 1970. In general then, because of their lower gas consumption and/or higher incomes, the impact of gas price increases was less burdensome for Republican voters.

A comparison of the 1947 and 1949 positions of the Ohio delegation illustrates the effects of partisanship and gas consumption levels on natural gas votes (see Table 10). In 1947, nineteen of the twenty-two-member Ohio delegation were Republicans; sixteen of them supported the Moore-Rizley bill.[40] In 1949, the state's delegation contained only eleven Republicans, and produced only eight votes for the Harris bill. Among Democratic districts, the average percent of households supplied with utility natural gas was 65; among Republican districts, the average was only 53 percent.[41]

These figures are roughly indicative of the net interests of the representative's constituents on the gas regulation issue. Other important factors must be considered along with residential gas usage ratios, however. Household statistics, for example, do not indicate the amount of gas

TABLE 10   NATURAL GAS VOTES IN THE OHIO
CONGRESSIONAL DELEGATION IN 1947 AND 1949

	Year							
	1947				1949			
	Delegation		Vote		Delegation		Vote	
	Democrat	Republican	Favor	Oppose	Democrat	Republican	Favor	Oppose
Partisan division	4	19			12	11		
Vote on deregulation*			16	4			8	11
Percentage for deregulation	0	84			8	60†		
Average percentage of households using gas‡		—			65	53		

*The 1947 vote is on recommittal of the Rizley bill in favor of the Priest substitute. The 1949 vote is on passage of the Harris bill.
†Four Republicans did not vote.
‡Local gas consumption data are taken from American Gas Association, *Survey of Residential Gas Service by County*, 1949. County data are not available for 1947.

consumed in the district. Where gas is used only for cooking, or for heating where winters are mild, monthly gas bills are likely to be modest, and generate no great pressure for control (at least, as long as there are no sharp increases). Because the winters are relatively severe, the growth in the use of gas for house heating in the Midwest and Northeast during the late 1940s and 1950s probably had a significant effect on the politics of regulation.[42] Furthermore, as was proposed earlier, affluent households probably pay less attention to the size of their monthly gas bills than do low-income users. Thus Republican districts would generate less pressure for regulation than would Democratic districts with the same number of consumers.

Finally, a congressman represents not an entire district, but some subset of its voters. For example, in the sixth district of southern Ohio, the overall consumption level was low because three of the district's six counties had no natural gas service in the late 1940s. The district's Republican congressman in 1947 received a majority of his total vote from the three counties with no natural gas, and voted for the Moore-Rizley bill. He was replaced in 1949 by a Democrat who received the majority of his support from the three counties with natural gas. The Democratic congressman opposed deregulation.

The emphasis here has been on comparisons of residential gas consumption, since household use seems a better indication of the interests of individual voters than commercial and industrial use. The largest industrial users of natural gas are found in the producer states, where large quantities of gas have been used as a boiler fuel by electric utilities. Outside the producer states, much of the gas used by industries is obtained through direct sales (not resales by local distributors), and those sales are not regulated by the FPC. Therefore, the assumption here is that residential consumption figures offer the best indication of the interest of a political constituency in the regulation of (interstate) natural gas sales. However, congressmen undoubtedly receive communications from industrial, as well as household, gas consumers in their districts concerning natural gas regulation, and in some cases the interests of the two classes of gas consumers may diverge.

By the early 1950s, the greatest concentrations of residential gas consumers were found in the east north central and mid-Atlantic states, and in California (see Table 6). The five states with the greatest numbers of household consumers (aside from the producer state of Texas) were New York, California, Pennsylvania, Illinois, and Ohio.[43] In none of these states did a majority of the congressional delegation support the Harris bill in 1949. Within these delegations, members representing urban areas were overwhelmingly opposed. Only two votes were cast for deregulation among the forty-three representatives from New York City, Cook

County (Chicago), and Philadelphia. In Wayne County (Detroit), Michigan, only one of six representatives supported the deregulation bill.[44]

In the producer state delegations, the vote was unanimous. Every representative from the states of Kansas, Oklahoma, Louisiana, New Mexico, Texas, and Wyoming supported the Harris bill. Spectator state congressmen were of different minds. Some represented areas that hoped to obtain gas service eventually, and believed the possibility to be jeopardized by regulation.[45] Others followed the lead of regional majorities. In general, mountain and Pacific states with relatively small consumption opposed the Harris bill; south Atlantic and east south central states overwhelmingly supported the southwestern position; New England and west north central spectators were about evenly divided.

The tendency of congressional voting to reflect the producer and consumer interests of constituents generally overrode partisan considerations. Democrats in the House split ninety-three to ninety-seven on the Harris bill; Republicans, ninety to thirty-four. Twenty-six of the Republican votes against deregulation represented changes in position from the vote two years earlier. Apparently, a number of Republicans who had voted for the extreme deregulation bill in the gas-shortage year of 1947 reconsidered their positions once the pipelines brought southwestern gas into their districts. For example, Republican Representatives Kenneth Keating and John Taber, from districts in western New York state, switched their votes from no to yes in 1949. Camden, New Jersey, Republican Charles Wolverton had chaired the House Commerce Committee, and backed the Rizley bill in 1947. In 1949, after the arrival of the Transcontinental Pipeline in Camden, Wolverton opposed even the more moderate Harris deregulation bill. Similarly, Republicans Jacob Javits and Henry Latham of New York City shifted into the opposition column when the Big Inch line brought southwestern gas to metropolitan New York. In Ohio, Cincinnati Republican Charles Ellston switched from support to abstention after narrowly winning re-election in a district where over 70 percent of households used natural gas in 1949.

Just as congressmen tended to reflect the interests of their electoral constituencies on the natural gas issue, so, too, did presidents. Beginning with Roosevelt's second term, Democratic presidents were increasingly attentive to the interests of the gas-consuming urban and industrial region that constituted, after 1936, their core electoral support. During Democratic administrations, FPC appointees have come disproportionately from these states. From 1938 until the end of the Truman administration, the five largest consumer states supplied four of seven appointees to the FPC.

The eleven southern states voted 104 to 4 in favor of deregulation in 1949. However, the South had dropped from a position of dominance to a minority faction within the Democratic party, and was becoming increasingly isolated within the party. The region's unhappiness with the civil rights and labor policy of the Truman administration was punctuated by the Dixiecrat revolt of 1948. Truman's victory in 1948, however, demonstrated that a Democratic candidate could win the presidency without "solid" support in the South.[46] Forced to choose between the regions on divisive issues such as civil rights, labor, urban development, and natural gas regulation, President Truman aligned his administration with the northern, metropolitan wing of the party. Like Roosevelt after his first term, Truman appointed pro-regulation activists to the Federal Power Commission. On other energy policy issues he also favored the extension of national jurisdiction over petroleum resources. For example, when Congress, in response to federal court decisions asserting national jurisdiction, passed a bill granting the states drilling rights in submerged lands on the continental shelf, Truman vetoed the bill.[47] The president also antagonized the oil and gas producing states by consistently opposing their efforts to specify the exemption of wellhead prices from the provisions of the Natural Gas Act.

In response to the growing polarization within the party, President Truman vetoed the Harris-Kerr bill in 1950.[48] He was supported in that action, not only by the congressional representatives of the consumer states, but by three of five Federal Power Commissioners: Draper, Buchanan, and new Truman appointee Mon Wallgren (who replaced Leland Olds). The commission itself reflected the regional polarization between producers and consumers. Four of the five took the same stand on the new bill as did the majority of their home state delegations. Only Claude Draper, first appointed in 1930, was out of step with his native state. While Draper took the consumer position on the veto, Wyoming now produced and exported substantial quantities of natural gas and allied itself with producer states on the regulation issue.

In the wake of Truman's veto, the frankly consumer-oriented FPC majority rescinded Order no. 139 (which had stated its intention to continue the exemption of independent producers). But it was clear that the presidential veto did not mark the end of congressional attempts to restrict FPC rate-making authority. Deregulation forces were strengthened by the 1950 elections in which the Republican Party gained five Senate and twenty-eight House seats. By late 1951, dissatisfaction with the Truman administration increased the prospects for additional Republican victories—both congressional and presidential. To head off further attempts to restrict its jurisdiction, the new FPC majority once again reconsidered its position. The Phillips Petroleum Company case in 1951 gave the commission the opportunity to announce its changed opinion to a more conservative Congress. The Phillips decision also set the stage for a final judicial settlement of the vexing question of producer exemption and established clearly demarcated battle lines between consumer and producer regions—lines that have moved little in the last three decades.

5 | Regulating Producers

The Phillips Decision

Section 1b of the Natural Gas Act states that the act's provisions shall apply to "natural gas companies" engaged in the transportation or sale of gas in interstate commerce, "but shall not apply to any other transportation or sale of natural gas or to the local distribution or to the production or gathering of natural gas." The issue in the Phillips case was whether Phillips was a "natural gas company" as defined in the statute and thus subject to FPC price regulation. Phillips was one of the larger American petroleum companies. Its operations included production, refining, and processing of both oil and gas and their products. The company did not, however, own interstate transmission facilities, but sold the gas it produced to nonaffiliated pipelines. Phillips' counsel argued that these sales occurred at the conclusion of the production and gathering process and were, therefore, exempt from regulation. Phillips argued that the company was not in any way similar to a public utility, and claimed that it "should be permitted to conduct its gas business just like it conducts its oil business, in open competition with other people who are engaged in those various businesses, as the rest of the vast majority of business in the United States is conducted."[1]

Basing their argument on original legislative intent and a broad interpretation of the "production and gathering" exemption, the commission agreed with Phillips that it was not a "natural gas company" within the meaning of the statute, but an independent producer whose arm's length sales at the end of its production and gathering lines were not subject to FPC regulation. The commission majority—Draper and Wallgren concurred with Smith and Wimberly on the Phillips exemption—drew on its earlier rulings in the Columbia and Billings cases, ignoring the later inconsistent (and controversial) decisions involving the Colorado Interstate and Interstate Natural Gas Companies. To accommodate the Supreme Court's ruling in the Interstate case, the commission found a loophole in the wording of that decision. The court had remarked that

FPC authority over sales of natural gas should be limited to situations in which such transactions were not "so closely connected" with the production and gathering process "as to render rate regulation by the FPC inconsistent or a substantial interference with the exercise by the state of its regulatory functions." The commission majority found that sales by independent producers such as Phillips were indeed that closely connected, and thus were not within FPC jurisdiction.[2]

Dissenting sharply from this interpretation, Commissioner Buchanan set forth the arguments traditionally made for federal regulation of producer sales, and presented a detailed refutation of the technical arguments made by the majority.[3] The Senate promptly rewarded Draper for his change of heart by confirming his reappointment to a fifth term. Buchanan, however, was denied confirmation by the Senate when President Truman renominated him in 1952. The reversal on the FPC, which was solidified with subsequent appointments by President Eisenhower, quieted congressional demand for statutory amendment. Meanwhile, the issue was moving toward a climax in the federal judicial system. Federal judges, appointed for life, had no reason to reverse their positions in response to transitory political majorities.

The FPC's Phillips decision was immediately challenged by the Public Service Commission of the State of Wisconsin. Ninety percent of Wisconsin's gas consumers were supplied with gas sold by Phillips to the Michigan-Wisconsin Pipeline Company. It was the Wisconsin Commission, along with the Detroit City Council, that had originally petitioned the FPC to assume jurisdiction over Phillips' sales. The Federal Court of Appeals for the District of Columbia reversed the FPC, finding that Phillips' sales took place after the production and gathering process. The case was then appealed to the Supreme Court by Phillips, the FPC, and the states of Texas, New Mexico, and Oklahoma.[4]

The case for extension of regulation to independent producers was argued by the Wisconsin Commission and the cities of Detroit, Kansas City, and Milwaukee. In a five-to-three decision in 1954, the Supreme Court upheld the appeals court reversal.[5] The Court held that

(1) This Company is a "natural gas company" within the meaning of the Natural Gas Act, and its sales in interstate commerce of natural gas for resale are subject to the jurisdiction of, and rate regulation by, the Federal Power Commission.

(2) The sales by this Company are not a part of the "production or gathering of natural gas," which are excluded from the Commission's jurisdiction under section 1(b), since the production and gathering end before the sales occur.

(3) Congress did not intend to regulate only interstate pipeline companies. Rather, the legislative history indicates a congressional

intent to give the commission jurisdiction over the rates of all wholesales of natural gas in interstate commerce, whether by a pipeline company or not and whether occurring before, during, or after transmission by an interstate pipeline company.

(4) Regulation of sales in interstate commerce for resale made by a so-called independent natural-gas producer is not essentially different from regulation of such sales when made by an affiliate of an interstate pipeline company.

The Court found in the original act a legislative intent "to give the commission jurisdiction over all sales in interstate commerce." The term "production and gathering" contained in the section 1b exemption was defined by the Court to be a process ending just prior to the first sale to an interstate transporter. Thus, a sale "in interstate commerce" was, in effect, any sale to an interstate pipeline regardless of where that sale took place. Independent producers selling their gas to interstate pipelines were to be treated as public utilities and their sales regulated by the FPC.

Justice William O. Douglas dissented from the majority opinion. Although granting that there was "much to be said, from the national point of view, for regulating sales at both ends of these interstate pipelines," and it was clearly within the power of Congress to do so, there was nothing in the legislative history and early implementation of the act that evidenced any intent of Congress to regulate producer sales. The effect of such regulation on the production and marketing of natural gas was "certain to be profound," Douglas argued, and added, "If that ground is to be taken, the battle should be won in Congress, not here. Regulation of the business of producing and gathering natural gas involves considerations of which we know little and with which we are not competent to deal."[6]

Precedents for the Court's broad interpretation of FPC jurisdiction had been established in the decade between the Hope and Phillips decisions. Given this record, there seemed to be no possibility that the implications of the Phillips decision would be softened in subsequent rulings. Without statutory revision, the commission had no choice but to begin the enormous new task of regulating sales by thousands of independent producers. In a series of rulings in the summer of 1954, it instituted a moratorium on price increases, and ordered producers to file prescribed forms for certification.[7] From 1954 to 1959, 8,496 independent producers filed for certificates (before 1954, the FPC had only exercised jurisdiction over a few hundred pipelines).[8] The commission did not proceed very rapidly to exercise its new authority, however. The Congress, President Eisenhower, and his new FPC appointees anticipated and were sympathetic toward a legislative reversal of the Phillips decision.

Political Mobilization

The legislative situation in 1955 was not as favorable to producer interests as it had been in the previous Congress: both houses were captured by the Democrats in the 1954 elections, and gas consumption (and the strength of consumer interests) were increasing rapidly. Nevertheless, House Commerce Committee Chairman Percy Priest supported deregulation, along with a razor-thin majority of the committee's membership. In the Senate, Commerce Committee Chairman Warren Magnuson opposed amendment, but the committee membership favored revision by almost two to one. House Speaker Sam Rayburn and Senate Majority Leader Lyndon Johnson, both Texans, strongly endorsed deregulation and could promise favorable floor procedures when and if the legislation was reported. Furthermore, Congress had recently overturned unpopular judicial rulings in two related areas: the local distributor exemption under the Natural Gas Act and the right of states to control and profit from offshore oil and gas discoveries.

After the Supreme Court upheld the FPC's jurisdictional claims over intrastate distributors, the Republican-controlled eighty-third Congress passed, early in 1954, an amendment spelling out the distributors' exemption. In the first session of the eighty-third Congress, a law was passed that upheld the claims of coastal states to tidelands oil and gas deposits. The tidelands bill, an earlier version of which had been vetoed by President Truman, was also a response to a Supreme Court ruling upholding national government powers vis-à-vis the states. President Eisenhower had supported both legislative actions and appeared sympathetic to an amendment exempting independent producers from federal regulation. In February of 1955, his Advisory Committee on Energy Supplies and Resources Policy issued a report that recommended such legislation.

Lengthy hearings were held on the issue in the spring and summer of 1955. Testimony before the House and Senate Commerce Committees revealed the sharp differences that separated the urban consumer regions from the gas producing states. A long list of big-city mayors, consumer state governors and regulatory commissions, labor union leaders, a coalition of gas utilities, and the Americans for Democratic Action constituted the core pro-regulation alliance. Mayors and city officials supporting the Phillips decision included representatives of Louisville, Philadelphia, Baltimore, Cincinnati, Cleveland, Pittsburgh, Syracuse, Milwaukee, Buffalo, St. Louis, Youngstown, Minneapolis–St. Paul, Chicago, Birmingham, Memphis, Nashville, Providence, and Portland, Oregon.[9] These officials complained of city gate deliveries costing over 50 percent more than comparable supplies five years earlier. Unregulated producers would, they feared, soon charge "all the traffic will bear," as competition for supplies intensified.[10]

In support of deregulation, a coalition of producer and mountain state office holders joined with officials from a scattering of smaller cities and suburbs in north central and southern states that wanted gas pipeline service but had so far been unable to obtain it. High-consumption cities with long-term supply contracts could afford to advocate continued regulation, but growing cities with inadequate gas service tended to support deregulation as a means of expanding supplies. Southern cities illustrated the different positions on the regulation issue. Representatives of rapidly growing cities such as Jacksonville and Tampa voiced fears that producer regulation would increase the attractiveness of intrastate southwestern markets, and create shortages in the interstate pipelines on which they depended for the future supplies considered essential for growth and development. Older southern cities with adequate supplies—Birmingham, Nashville, and Memphis, for example—opposed amendment.[11]

Bills to amend the Natural Gas Act were introduced by Arkansas Senator William Fulbright and Representative Oren Harris in 1955. Unlike the 1947–1950 deregulation bills, the 1955 attempt at revision allowed some FPC pricing authority over the first sales by independent producers. The commission could indirectly regulate producer prices by its power to disallow excessive prices paid to producers when determining pipeline costs. The standard by which prices were judged excessive would not be a utility standard, however. Instead, producers were to be allowed a "reasonable market price."[12] Although imprecise, this standard implied considerably less FPC discretion than the old "just and reasonable" guideline. It would presumably set a price close to the average contract price established by arm's length bargaining between producers and pipelines in the unregulated market. In addition, pipelines that produced some of the gas they sold were to be allowed a "reasonable market price" for that gas.[13]

The FPC, with Commissioner Smith joining a new, Eisenhower-appointed majority, endorsed the Harris-Fulbright bill. Although the bill limited its newly acquired pricing authority, it promised to reestablish a degree of harmony between the commission and the producer-centered majority in Congress, and, at the same time, to relieve the agency of a great regulatory burden. Between June 1954 (the month of the Phillips decision) and June 1955, the commission received 6,047 certificate applications and over 10,000 rate filings by producers. Furthermore, the Harris bill compensated the FPC for the jurisdictional limitation by granting an increment to its jurisdiction that the commission had urged for years: authority over the pricing of imported gas.

In a letter to Chairman Percy Priest of the House Interstate and Foreign Commerce Committee, FPC Chairman Jerome Kuykendall reiterated the commission's opinion that natural gas producers did not have the characteristics of utilities. Independent producers were competitive, not monopolistic. Should marketplace competition later be found deficient, the commission suggested antitrust proceedings as a more appropriate remedy than price regulation. Without amendment, the commission warned, the uncertainties of regulation might lead producers to limit gas sales in interstate commerce. In addition, the agency cautioned, the threat of governmentally controlled pricing would result in

> the establishment in the areas where natural gas is produced, in preference to other areas, of petrochemical and other plants using large volumes of natural gas as well as the movement of industries from those points outside of and remote from them into areas in which intrastate gas is available. . . . Remote domestic and other natural gas consumers may find themselves facing, not only a declining supply of such gas, but the fact that some of the industries upon which the economies of their communities depend may have moved from their midst.[14]

In what turned out to be a prescient warning, the FPC pointed out the contrast between the short-term interest in maintaining an inexpensive fuel price through manipulation of the political economy, and the long-term possibility of fuel shortage and economic decline in the consumer regions. Elected officials, however, seemed to be more sensitive to the immediate effects of policy decisions on constituent incomes than to complex, long-term consequences that might not occur in their political lifetimes and, if they did, might be too remote from specific legislative decisions for unambiguous attribution. In any case, the distinction between intrastate and interstate markets was itself a political one. As consumer state politicians discovered in the 1970s, a political boundary can be politically erased.

The deregulation majority in the House, both on the Commerce Committee and on the floor, was slim. The committee voted sixteen to fifteen to report the Harris bill. Opponents objected that the bill did not outlaw "favored nation" clauses in gas contracts.[15] These provisions allowed automatic increases in the price of gas sold under contract when the pipeline later made other purchases in the same area at higher prices. In this way, gas sold under a long-term contract was not frozen at the original price, but floated upward with the prevailing market price. In two minority reports, eight Democrats and two Republicans on the committee (representing the gas-importing states of New York, Pennsylvania, Maryland, Alabama, Massachusetts, Georgia, Michigan, Ohio, and New Jersey) argued that the bill was "not in the public interest," and would allow natural gas companies to reap "windfall profits" from the sixty million consumers who depended on natural gas "for warm homes and warm food."[16] Three dissenters—one Democrat and two Republicans—in a second, more strongly worded minority report, discounted the FPC's warning about diminishing interstate supplies. The pipelines would continue to be well supplied, they argued, since gas would continue to be found in the search for oil, and producer state markets were too limited to absorb interstate sales.[17]

The majority report argued the need to exempt producers from inappropriate utility regulation "and thus restore the law to what it had been generally believed to be for sixteen years prior to the Supreme Court's decision of June 7, 1954." The majority insisted that the "public interest" did not require producer regulation. Instead, competition among producers and between gas and other fuels prevented exorbitant pricing. They pointed out that only about 10 percent of the price paid by the ultimate consumer represented reimbursement to producers. The rest went for transportation and distribution charges, which were controlled by state and local regulatory boards. In New York City, for example, FPC records showed that the average cost of natural gas was $2.42 per thousand cubic feet (mcf). Of that total, only 7.8 cents were paid the producer. Pipeline charges comprised another twenty-four cents. The remaining $2.10 went to the distributor, Consolidated Edison.[18]

The floor vote in the House on Harris-Fulbright was as closely balanced as the committee vote (see Figure 8 and Table 12). The bill passed 209 to 203. The party breakdown found Republicans supporting the bill 123 to 67, and Democrats opposed by 136 to 86.[19] Producer state Democrats (from Texas, Louisiana, Oklahoma, Kansas, and New Mexico) were unanimously in favor; northern urban Democrats solidly opposed it, as did many urban Republicans in the consumer states.[20] Florida representatives, who seemed to feel that their state's future growth would be imperiled without an expansion of interstate gas service, voted unanimously with the producer delegations. North and South Carolina, where gas service was available to very few communities, also gave overwhelming support to the Harris bill. Other southern states along the pipeline routes, however, were abandoning the deregulation movement as their own consumer constituencies grew to political significance. Despite a massive lobbying effort directed at the South by oil and gas companies in 1955, fourteen of the eighteen representatives from Alabama and Tennessee, nine out of ten from Virginia, and four of ten from Georgia opposed deregulation (see Table 11).[21] In 1949, 95 percent of the repre-

FIGURE 8
Support for Deregulation in the House of Representatives, 1955

Key

Vote on Passage:

Yea

Nay

Abstention

Speaker

Metropolitan Districts

	Y	N
San Francisco	3	2
Los Angeles	10	2
Chicago	4	9
Baltimore	0	3
Boston	1	6
Detroit	0	6
St. Louis	1	2
Newark	1	7
New York	0	24
Cleveland	2	2
Philadelphia	1	6
Pittsburgh	0	4

TABLE 11   The Growth of Residential Gas Service and Support for Federal Regulation in the South from 1949 to 1955

State	1949			1955		
	Number of Households	Percentage of All Households	Support for Deregulation*	Number of Households	Percentage of All Households	Support for Deregulation*
Alabama	167,805	21	100	324,000	39	22
Tennessee	109,921	13	90	245,000	21	11
Georgia	152,344	17	90	321,000	33	60
Virginia	690†	0	100	281,000	29	10
North Carolina	0	0	83	47,000	4	83
South Carolina	0	0	83	47,000	8	67
Florida	10,456	1	86	25,000	2	100

Source: *Minerals Yearbook* and *Congressional Quarterly Almanac.*
*Percentage of state delegation supporting Rizley or Harris deregulation bills.
†Includes mixed (natural and manufactured) gas.

sentatives from these four states had supported the amendment. Thus, as the interstate natural gas network expanded, so did the size of the electorate possessing a vested interest in low, government-controlled prices. The economic success of gas marketing in the 1950s carried with it the seeds of political failure.

In 1955, the producer states were more strongly represented in the Senate than in the House, and were able to build an alliance in the upper chamber with a number of western spectator states, whose economies were also dependent on natural resources. The Harris-Fulbright bill passed the Senate fifty-three to thirty-eight. There were twenty states in which both senators supported the deregulation bill. These states included the largest producers (based on the volume of reserves, marketed production, and surplus for interstate sale): Texas, Louisiana, Oklahoma, and Kansas; the state of Wyoming, which had expanding oil and gas as well as coal production; and Arkansas, with small but at that time economically significant gas production. In addition, there was solid support among senators from five mountain states (Arizona, Nevada, Montana, Utah, and Idaho);[22] five southeast–south Atlantic states (Mississippi, Florida, South Carolina, Delaware, and Maryland); and California and New Hampshire. All but New Hampshire were located in the region below the Mason-Dixon line or west of the Mississippi. There was no strong sentiment for deregulation in any of the urban-industrial states of the northeast, north central, Great Lakes, or mid-Atlantic regions. Opposition to the Harris bill was strong in coal-producing areas, for reasons that will be discussed later. In the fourteen major coal-producing districts in the House, there were only four votes in favor of the Harris bill. Given the intense commitment of the gas-producing states and the even split among spectators, coal votes were crucial to consumer representatives in the fight against amendment of the Natural Gas Act.

The Deregulation Drive Stalls

Shortly before the vote was taken on the Fulbright bill in 1956, South Dakota Senator Francis Case announced to the chamber that an attorney for Superior Oil Company had offered him a twenty-five hundred dollar campaign contribution. He suggested that the money was intended to influence his vote on deregulation. Much was made of the incident by deregulation opponents. The company, of course, denied any impropriety, describing the money as part of a general fund-raising effort for Republican candidates. For the deregulation forces, the timing could not have been worse. In view of the strong hint of scandal, President Eisenhower vetoed the bill. Although he supported its objectives, the Superior affair made it imprudent to sign the bill in an election year.[23]

TABLE 12   PRODUCER, CONSUMER, AND SPECTATOR STATES, 1955–1956

	Support for Deregulation			
	House		Senate	
State	Percent	Number	Percent	Number
*Producer states**				
Texas	100		100	
Louisiana	100		100	
Oklahoma	100		100	
New Mexico	100		50†	
Kansas	100		100	
Wyoming	100		100	
Mississippi	83		100	
Total	98	50/51‡	93	13/14
Consumer states§				
Arizona	50		100	
California‖	73		100	
Colorado	75		50†	
Connecticut	17		0	
Delaware	0		100	
Maryland	43		100	
Illinois‖	56		50	
Indiana	82		50	
Massachusetts‖	36		50	
Michigan‖	33		0	
Missouri	36		0	
Nebraska	75		100	
New Jersey‖	14		0†	
New York‖	12		0	
Ohio‖	43		50	
Pennsylvania	43		50	
Rhode Island‖	0		0	
Total	42	102/245	47	16/34
Spectator states				
Maine	100		50	
New Hampshire	0		100	
Vermont	0		50	
Wisconsin	20		50	
Minnesota	11		0	
Iowa	50		100	
North Dakota	100		50	
South Dakota	100		50	
Virginia	10		0	
North Carolina	83		50†	
South Carolina	67		100	
Georgia	60		0†	
Florida	100		100	
Tennessee	11		0	

TABLE 12 (continued)

State	Support for Deregulation			
	House		Senate	
	Percent	*Number*	*Percent*	*Number*
Alabama	22		0	
Arkansas	100		100	
Montana	50		100	
Idaho	50		100	
Utah	100		100	
Nevada	100		100	
Washington	57		0	
Oregon	50		0	
Total	50	63/125	54	24/44
Coal states				
West Virginia	33		0	
Kentucky	0		0	
Pennsylvania	54		50	
Illinois	56		50	
Total	46	29/69	25	2/8

*States producing more gas than they consumed in 1955. West Virginia is classified as a coal-producing state.
†One senator did not vote.
‡Pairs are counted for or against the bill, as specified by *Congressional Quarterly*.
§States in which consumption exceeded production, and more than 50 percent of households used natural gas. Pennsylvania and Illinois are also grouped with coal states.
‖States in which over 60 percent of households used natural gas.

In the next Congress, yet another effort was made to amend the Natural Gas Act. The new bill, again sponsored by Representative Harris and endorsed by the FPC, provided for more limited deregulation. The commission would regulate producer rates directly, rather than indirectly, through approval of pipeline costs. The pricing standard, however, would still be a "reasonable market price" rather than a utility rate based on original costs plus a fixed return. Once again, in 1957, the deregulation movement fell victim to the excesses of oil men. This time, a Texas independent producer arranged a premature victory celebration for deregulation. He planned an "appreciation dinner" for the Republican minority leader, whose assistance, he suggested in the invitation, would assure passage of the Harris bill. The contents of the invitation were picked up by the press, and the resulting adverse publicity made it impossible to muster a majority for the bill in the closely divided House of Representatives.[24]

Limited deregulation bills were introduced in subsequent Congresses, but by then the favorable political environment for amendment had changed.[25] The 1960 elections inaugurated a new era of consumer dominance in natural gas policy. In Congress, the election of more Democrats from heterogeneous northern districts strengthened the pro-regulation forces. In the South and on the West Coast, the continued expansion of gas consumption made congressmen unsympathetic to deregulation throughout the 1960s. Southeastern congressmen enamored of "free enterprise" in the 1940s became defenders of federal price regulation after natural gas pipelines passed through their districts. The state of California became one of the most active consumer intervenors in FPC cases as the ratio of domestic production to interstate imports diminished.[26] Democratic presidents with electoral support centered in gas-importing urban areas also opposed deregulation. When he was a Texas senator, Lyndon Johnson was a champion of deregulation and leader of the opposition to Leland Olds' confirmation; as president, Johnson appointed consumer advocates to the FPC. In each case, positions on the federal control of natural gas prices were tied to the economic interests of constituents.

Post-Phillips Regulation: The FPC and Its Political Environment

As a new majority began to form on the natural gas issue, the agency charged with implementing regulation also underwent a metamorphosis. A comparison of the operation of the Federal Power Commission under Republican and Democratic presidents illuminates two facets of bureaucratic behavior. First, contrasting patterns of regulation reveal the ability of bureaucracies to adapt to changes in their political environments. Second, the similarities in FPC behavior illustrate the constant bureaucratic imperative: protect and expand, where feasible, the agency's jurisdiction.

The FPC in the 1940s had steadily extended the boundaries of its jurisdiction until this expansionism generated significant congressional hostility toward the agency. Critical congressional hearings, passage of deregulation amendments, and rejection of Federal Power Commission appointments were clear signals to the commission that its claims of jurisdiction over producers were politically destabilizing. Thus, in the Republican decade between 1951 and 1961, the FPC first disclaimed and then interpreted its court-granted authority over producer prices in a manner favorable to the producers.

In areas other than wellhead pricing, where jurisdictional expansion was not politically destabilizing, Republican commissions have favored such expansion to about the same degree as Democratic ones. For example, in the 1950s (under Eisenhower-appointed Chairman Jerome Kuykendall), the FPC requested that Congress amend the Natural Gas

Act, giving the commission the power to approve security issues of natural gas pipeline companies; to order emergency pipeline interconnections; to suspend proposed rates for resales for industrial use; to make more comprehensive investigations of the gas industry; to prohibit pipelines from selling off gas reserves; to make safety regulations for pipeline companies; to allocate gas among customers in case of shortage; and to increase its authority over imports, exports, and end uses of natural gas. These same legislative recommendations were made by the Kennedy-appointed FPC in the 1960s.[27] In addition, both Republican and Democratic commissions, from the late 1950s through the 1970s, claimed far-reaching authority to compel producer sales to interstate pipelines. The principal difference between Republican and Democratic commissions, then, and the difference in behavior that is most indicative of bureaucratic adaptation to change in the political environment, has been in pricing policies. The FPC under Eisenhower and Nixon supported high wellhead prices, while the Kennedy and Johnson commissions resolutely depressed producer prices in response to the expressed interests of consumer areas.

The commission had already begun to adapt its behavior to a new political balance in 1951, but its transformation was hastened by President Eisenhower's appointments in 1953. Whereas the majority of Roosevelt-Truman appointees had come from the largest gas consumer states, none of Eisenhower's nominees were residents of those states. Three of his seven appointments to the FPC were made from the gas-producing states of Louisiana and Wyoming. Expecting (and supporting) legislative reversal of the Phillips decision, the Eisenhower commission pursued with little enthusiasm the new producer pricing authority imposed upon it by the Supreme Court. From the time of the Court's ruling through 1956, more than one-half the dollar amount of the rate increases requested by producers were allowed to go into effect with only minimal review.[28] Not until the Eisenhower veto of the Harris-Fulbright bill did the FPC begin in earnest to cope with the task of regulating producer prices, but even after 1956 there is no evidence that FPC regulation in the 1950s held wellhead prices below market levels.

The commission's rulings in the 1950s reflected the interests of gas producers in three major ways: in its willingness to certify initial producer sales at comparatively high contract prices; in allowing market prices for gas produced by pipelines; and in setting area rates for producers that were close to those prevailing in the unregulated intrastate market. In the last case, these prices had no sooner been put into effect than the subsequent Kennedy commission began to roll them back. In the first two areas the commission was reprimanded (and reversed) by the federal courts for its inadequate price regulation efforts.

One such reprimand stemmed from the CATCO case, so named for the four gas companies involved.[29] The companies applied for an FPC certificate to sell gas to the Tennessee Gas Transmission Company at an initial contract rate of 22.4 cents per mcf—a price significantly higher than the pipeline had ever before paid. The FPC offered to grant a conditional certificate with later investigation of the reasonableness of the contract price. When the producers then threatened not to sell the gas to the Tennessee company unless granted a permanent certificate, the commission acquiesced. The producers and pipeline company had presented evidence at the certification hearing that the price was justified by the size of the CATCO reserves—the largest ever committed to one sale—and their convenience to Tennessee Gas transmission lines, as well as by drilling costs (these were offshore leases carrying higher drilling costs than onshore) and the availability of higher intrastate prices. Nevertheless, the New York Public Service Commission objected to the contract price and the Appeals Court for the District of Columbia overturned the FPC's decision to certify the sale. The court held that the commission had no authority to grant certificates to producers who, in effect, limited the scope of the commission's authority by threatening not to sell gas in the interstate market if a lower price were imposed. The Supreme Court upheld the lower court's decision in 1959, establishing what came to be known as the "in line" standard: new sales should not be certified if they were not "in line" with existing prices in the same area.[30]

The Natural Gas Act had conferred on the commission no explicit authority to deny initial certificates on the basis of contract prices. (Rather, such rate determinations were presumably to be decided only after investigation, as provided in section 5.) In 1942, however, an amendment to section 7 allowed the FPC to attach conditions to certificates granted. The major purpose of this new provision was to make possible consideration of the arguments raised by coal and railroad interests against industrial sales. However, the commission in the 1940s began to examine the level of proposed pipeline charges as evidence for granting certificates. The alternative method for controlling pipeline charges was provided in section 5, which allowed the FPC to fix a lower rate after an investigation of reasonableness. Such investigations tended to be long and complex, however, and any decision in favor of a lower rate was not retroactive.

Price control through certification had several advantages. If the FPC issued a certificate for sales at a lower rate than the pipeline had proposed, the pipeline might later file for a rate increase. The request for an increase, however, would come under section 4. Under the terms of this section, the burden of proof was on the company to justify higher rates. Moreover, if the new rates went into effect after the suspension period, refunds could be ordered by the commission when (and if) the new rates were later found to be "unreasonable." No refunds could be ordered under section 5 procedures for existing (that is, certified) rates.

After the Phillips decision, producer contracts became subject to the same certification procedure and what had been a discretionary practice—the examination of initial contract rates—came to be required by virtue of court decisions. The Eisenhower commission was willing to forego certificate requirements that threatened to discourage producer sales to interstate pipelines. In a number of cases prior to CATCO, it issued unconditional certificates to independent producers in spite of strenuous objections by distributors.[31] Ultimately, however, the courts were not impressed by producer arguments that they could sell their gas in the unregulated intrastate market since, until the 1970s, intrastate prices were generally at or below interstate prices, and the ability of the producer state market to absorb much more of the gas produced there seemed doubtful. In addition, the threat not to sell was, in itself, held to be an infringement on the FPC's authority. Since, in the words of one legal commentator, "a threat not to sell is an almost necessary preliminary to any bargain and sale agreement," condemnation of this practice "can only imply that sellers of gas must come to the FPC agreeing to sell at any rate the commission imposes."[32] Indeed, the trend of later commission and court interpretations has been to confirm the "capture" of gas producers, and to compel them to sell gas at the regulated interstate price.

After the Supreme Court established that producers were subject to regulation, Federal Power commissioners appointed by both Democratic and Republican presidents have held that, once a producer has made a sale to an interstate pipeline, the gas from that leasehold belongs to the regulated interstate market until such time as the commission may allow such sales to cease. The Eisenhower commission early began to insist on issuing producer certificates for an indefinite time period, although the producers, for obvious reasons, preferred the certificates (that is, the requirement for sales to interstate pipelines) to last only as long as the original contract.[33] Thus the requirement of continuous service, long essential to utility regulation, came to be applied to gas producers. Producers would not be allowed to terminate their interstate sales without FPC permission as long as gas remained in the leasehold.

Without this requirement, which has been consistently upheld by the federal courts, it is conceivable that some pipelines would have gone bankrupt. Even before the Phillips decision, larger independent producers had insisted on having "escape clauses" in their contracts with pipelines. These provisions allowed the producer to terminate sales if any federal agency attempted to assert jurisdiction over them. After the

Phillips decision, a number of producers did cancel sales, and others filed abandonment proceedings. The FPC, however, ordered reconnection. The pipeline companies were thus able to convert limited-term contracts into "life of the field" commitments.[34] The interest of the FPC in maintaining its original regulated clients is clear. If producers had been able to discontinue sales and pipelines been bankrupted as a result, the agency's jurisdiction would have severely contracted. In the immediate aftermath of the Phillips decision, a number of producers who had not yet contracted with interstate transmission companies refused to do so. Some pipelines that were projected or under construction saw their potential supplies evaporate overnight, and were forced to rely on imports from Mexico or Canada.[35] To prevent such losses of supply where the FPC lacked jurisdiction to compel connection, the commission in the 1950s was willing to allow favorable wellhead prices. Subsequent commissions, however, discounted the risk of shortage, and mandated lower producer prices in the interest of consumer savings.

In addition to allowing market prices to independent producers, the Eisenhower commission also attempted to grant pipelines commodity prices for the gas they produced. Here, too, the commission's free-market philosophy found disfavor in the federal courts. Since the institution of cost-based pricing for pipeline gas in the 1940s, pipelines had begun to sell off the gas reserves that were no longer profitable. By 1955, interstate pipelines owned only 13 percent of the gas they transported.[36] The FPC first attempted to prevent sales of gas leaseholds by pipelines, but the Supreme Court in 1949 reversed the commission, finding nothing in the Natural Gas Act that permitted it to ban such transactions.[37] Later, the Eisenhower commission decided that it was in the public interest to permit transporting pipelines to own gas leaseholds, both from the point of view of assuring their supplies, and because such ownership might improve the bargaining position of the pipelines in their purchases from independent producers. The commission therefore began, in 1954, to allow pipelines a "fair field price"—a weighted average of payments charged by independent producers for similar gas from the same field. The governments of Detroit and Wayne County, Michigan, challenged the FPC ruling, and in 1955 the District of Columbia Appeals Court reversed the commission. The court held that, although the Natural Gas Act and the 1944 Hope ruling did not prohibit market pricing, the primary aim of the statute was to protect consumers against excessive rates. Therefore, the cost of producing the gas must be the standard for rate determination, and any deviation from cost-based pricing requires convincing evidence that a higher price is necessary to encourage exploration and drilling by pipelines.[38]

The Establishment of Area Rates

In its 1954 decision in the Phillips case, the Supreme Court did not specify on what basis the FPC must regulate producer prices. The producers argued that the establishment of a price close to that prevailing in the marketplace between nonaffiliated buyers and sellers would satisfy the "just and reasonable" standard of the Natural Gas Act.[39] The commission's professional staff, on the other hand, argued for cost-based regulation, but the FPC was reluctant to apply the traditional utility standard to independent gas producers.[40] Hearings on the Phillips rate case were finally begun in June 1956—two years after the Supreme Court decision. Eighteen months of hearings were held in an attempt to ascertain the production costs attributable to the gas Phillips sold to the Michigan-Wisconsin pipeline. In 1959, an FPC examiner estimated those costs at just over fifty-seven million dollars. Phillips' revenues from the sales, however, came to only forty-six million dollars. Since costs exceeded revenues, even allowing for interim rate increases, the original contract, which had led to the landmark 1954 Court decision, was allowed to remain in effect.[41]

It was obvious that the estimation of costs for each of the more than five thousand producers who sold gas interstate would be an immense and time-consuming task. In order to simplify the process, the FPC announced in 1960 that it would fix producer charges by an "area rate" method. The commission would find a fair price "based on the reasonable financial requirements of the industry for each of the gas producing regions in the country."[42] The termination of the Phillips proceedings and the intended abandonment of individual cost-of-service regulation were challenged by the states of Wisconsin and New York, and other consumer-area plaintiffs, but the commission was upheld by the Supreme Court.[43] The Court was willing to allow the FPC methodological leeway, as long as independent producers were regulated and the prices that were established through regulation did not offend the tribunal's interpretation of "just and reasonable."[44] Initial consumer state apprehension about the abandonment of the traditional rate method turned out to be unfounded; the area rate procedure proved perfectly compatible with the goal of price restraint.

By the time final hearings began in the first area rate proceeding, the composition of the FPC had changed significantly. By September of 1961, President Kennedy had appointed four of the five commissioners. By the end of the year, former Chairman Kuykendall, who had supported deregulation bills in the 1950s, was also replaced. During the Kennedy and Johnson administrations, commission majorities were clearly pro-consumer, and established generally close relationships with Democratic majorities on the congressional oversight committees. Recruitment to the FPC again reflected political geography. Whereas three out of seven Eisenhower commissioners had come from producer states, only one of nine Kennedy and Johnson appointees did. Appointments of strong consumer advocates such as Joseph Swidler, Lee White, and Charles Ross reflected the mood of the Democratic majority.[45]

The first area rate proceedings for the Texas–New Mexico Permian Basin region began in December 1960, but were conducted and brought to conclusion during the Kennedy and Johnson administrations. During the proceedings, producers presented data on their costs of production; consumer state regulatory commissions (principally those of Wisconsin and California) filed opposing briefs. The hearing transcripts ran to over thirty thousand pages. Clearly, the process of determining an "average" area cost of production was a complicated one. The FPC's rate-setting opinion for Permian area producers was not issued until August 1965.[46]

The Permian decision was anxiously awaited by both producers and consumers, since it not only set prices for a major producing region, but also indicated the form commodity regulation would take in the future. The decision created a two-tier pricing structure (an approach later to be used in oil price control), with a somewhat higher price ceiling for "new" gas than for "old." The price differential was intended to encourage exploration efforts. The commission set a minimum rate of nine cents per mcf for pipeline-quality gas, and a ceiling of 16.5 cents for new gas. The latter price was even lower than that recommended by the hearing examiner, which was itself linked to a cost factor considerably below the average national cost of gas production. The FPC also went beyond the examiner's recommendations on the requirement that the producers make refunds when their current prices exceeded the new area ceilings. Rate increases above the area rates were prohibited for existing contracts (the Kennedy commission had already prohibited escalator and "favored nation" clauses in new contracts), and a moratorium was declared for rate increase filings until 1968.[47]

In federal courts, the producers challenged the Permian decisions as arbitrary and unfair. They maintained that the proposed rates would prove "confiscatory." Since those rates were based on average producer costs in an area, they would in some cases fail to generate revenues that matched expenses. As a result, producers charged, some small producers—particularly those unlucky enough to find gas in commercial quantities only after numerous drilling attempts—would be driven out of business. In opposition to the producers, associations of California and eastern gas distributors and the California public utility commission intervened in support of the commission.

The court of appeals declined to overturn any of the commission's Permian rulings. "A producer," the court argued, "has no constitutional right to be reimbursed for dry-hole expense." The court did, however, require the FPC to hold further hearings on several technical points concerning the rate decisions because the commission had disregarded the old Hope standard that regulated prices should allow companies to remain in business, maintain credit, and attract capital.[48] The constitutionality of the new procedure was finally upheld by the Supreme Court on a seven-to-one vote in 1968. Justice Douglas dissented, as he had in the Phillips case in 1954.[49]

The implementation of the area rate method marked the culmination of the transformation of federal involvement in the natural gas industry from conventional utility regulation to redistributive policy. Where the Eisenhower commission, in proposing the method, had been inclined to let market prices in a producing area set limits for "just and reasonable" producer prices, the FPC of the 1960s insisted on cost-based regulation, but divorced the standard from individual producer costs. The commission replaced the Hope rule protecting individual companies with the new concept of a fair aggregate price-cost relationship for all jurisdictional producers in a given area. The general effect of the new method was to lower wellhead prices below the market-determined levels of the 1950s, and this was clearly their intended effect. The commission was, it announced in 1963, "determined to hold the line against increases in natural gas prices."[50]

The Permian Basin proceedings were followed by those for another major southwestern producing region, southern Louisiana. The Eisenhower commission had set a "guideline price" for southern Louisiana gas at 23.6 cents per mcf. The Kennedy commission first reduced the guideline to 21.2 cents, and then, in 1964, to twenty cents. In its first formal rate decision for southern Louisiana, the FPC rolled the price back even further, to 19.5 cents. In the past, the average initial contract price for all interstate gas from the southwestern states had risen from 13.3 cents in 1953, to 18.6 cents in 1958, and remained at about that level through 1960. In 1961, the price dropped below eighteen cents, and in 1964, to 16.2 cents. In 1967 the average new interstate contract price still had not regained the level of 1958. New gas prices in the unregulated intrastate market reached 20.3 cents in 1970, while the regulated interstate ceiling remained at 16.5.[51]

As the new, lower prices took effect, the commission ordered the gas industry to make refunds from the higher levels permitted earlier. FPC Chairman Swidler later testified in congressional hearings that refunds ordered from 1961 to 1965 alone totalled almost a billion dollars.[52] The benefits of regulation were felt, not only by residential consumers, but also by industrial users, gas-distributing utilities, and pipelines in the gas-importing states. The costs were borne by producers, their state treasuries, and, to some extent, by competing fuel producers deprived of their markets by natural gas. This assessment of costs and benefits is probably valid only in the short term, however. Long-term regional cost-benefit calculations depend on what weight is assigned to losses incurred by those unable to obtain gas (for example, future fuel users deprived of gas by present overconsumption), and the extent to which differential regional growth rates may be ascribed to gas price and supply differences in the Northeast, the Midwest, and the gas-producing states. Some of the unintended consequences of producer price regulation and the subsequent regulatory proposals to which those consequences gave rise will be considered in Chapters 6 and 7. As a preliminary to that discussion, however, a summary of the opposing positions on gas price regulation is in order.

Cost-Based Regulation of Independent Producers: The Contending Arguments

The institution, in the mid-1960s, of full-scale utility regulation of independent producers clarified the essential issue in natural gas regulation: what was at stake was a massive regional transfer of wealth. The issue was seldom debated in explicitly regional terms, however. To do so would have limited the ability of both producer and consumer areas to form the broader alliances necessary to control the federal regulatory apparatus (which control, of course, was necessary to maximize or minimize the regional transfer of income). Instead, the opposing sides emphasized the characteristics of the gas-producing industry that made regulation either necessary or undesirable. It may be useful at this point to pause and summarize those opposing arguments.

The Producers

The arguments of producers against regulation may be grouped under three broad contentions: first, that the gas-producing industry had none of the characteristics of a public utility; second, that price regulation of natural gas was both unnecessary and unfair; and third, that price regulation would ultimately have several undesirable consequences from the point of view of gas consumers and the interests of the nation as a whole.[53]

In support of the first contention, producers pointed out that there were over eight thousand independent producers who competed both with each other and with other fuels for markets. Such competition, they maintained, was sufficient to prevent exorbitant pricing in the absence of regulation. In response to the charge that in fact relatively few large producers controlled the bulk of gas reserves, producers countered that the concentration ratio among natural gas producers was far lower than in other major (and unregulated) industries. An economist from Standard Oil presented evidence in 1955 congressional hearings that the twenty largest companies controlled only 46 percent of gas production; the four largest, only 17 percent.[54] Other economists have noted that the gas-producing business is marked by ease of entry: in the 1950s, for example, less than one hundred thousand dollars was necessary to capitalize a gas drilling operation.[55] In addition, producers argued, it was the gas producer who was dependent on the pipelines, and not vice versa. With their extensive network of interconnections, the pipeline companies could "shop around" from producer to producer in search of better prices. In this situation, the advantage was with the large buyer, not the seller.[56] For the foregoing reasons then, gas producers have denied that their industry can be characterized as a monopoly requiring public regulation. In further support of their contention that utility regulation was inappropriate for the industry, the producers maintained that their product was no more "necessary" to the public than a host of other products that remained unregulated.[57]

The producers have consistently argued that price trends for unregulated wellhead sales did not justify the consumer alarm generated in the 1950s. Producer representatives testified in congressional hearings that, adjusted for inflation, there was no real increase in wellhead prices between 1945 and 1953, and the price increase in response to the high demand conditions of the 1950s was still less than either the increase of other fuel prices or consumer prices in general (see Figure 7).[58] In addition, the price of gas in the 1950s was less, and by the late 1970s significantly less, than the price of an equivalent heating quantity of coal or oil.[59] Producers argued, therefore, that consumer estimates of the costs of deregulation should take into consideration the alternative costs to consumers of a regulation-induced shortage of natural gas.

Of the price paid by the residential gas consumer, only a small fraction—usually less than 10 percent—went to the producer. A field price increase of five cents per mcf—a 30 percent increase at 1955 prices—would have cost the average residential consumer less than eight dollars a year. If consumers were concerned about the size of their monthly bills, producers argued, they were better advised to scrutinize the delivery charges of pipelines and local utilities—which comprised 75–90 percent of their gas bills—and to demand more effective utility regulation from their state commissions.[60]

Residential consumers, pipeline companies, and distributors objected strongly to the price escalation clauses contained in producer contracts in the late 1940s and 1950s. These provisions generally took one of the following forms:[61]

1. *Price redetermination clauses*. The producer and pipeline agree that at specified intervals (for example, every five years), the wellhead price will change to reflect the average new price being paid for gas of similar quality in the area.

2. *Price adjustment provisions*. The contract price is periodically moved up or down according to a standard index (such as the Wholesale Commodities Index).

3. *"Favored nation" clauses* (so named for international treaties embodying a similar principle). The buyer increases the price to the supplier whenever he purchases gas from another producer in the same area at a higher price.

4. *"Spiral" escalation clauses*. The buyer increases the price to the producer whenever he is granted a higher price for his deliveries to distributors.

The producers defended such clauses as essential to secure a fair price for their gas in an inflationary economy. No other commodity, they argued, was sold at a contract price fixed at the original level for twenty years or more. They had been obligated to accept such long-term contracts for the benefit of the pipelines. Pipeline companies had to present to their investors, and to the FPC in certification hearings, evidence of long-term supply commitments at low to moderate prices. To enable them to obtain financing and certification, the producers agreed to long-term contracts, often at low initial rates, with the provision that prices would be raised later. Price increases through escalation clauses thus represented to the producer a way of obtaining "fair" prices under constraints that prevented a direct response to changing demand conditions. For the government to fix the price of gas according to a utility standard was, then, both unnecessary (since price increases were relatively modest and were limited by competition) and unfair, because they subjected gas prices to a degree and type of control not imposed on other commodities.

Utility pricing was also unfair, they argued, in that it unreasonably penalized a business on which the economies of south central and southwestern states depended, in order to subsidize fuel consumption in other regions. An artificially depressed gas price deprived producer state citizens of royalties and tax revenues used to fund education and welfare services.[62] At the same time, these citizens must consume products produced at unregulated and ever-increasing prices in other areas. In the past, the application of utility regulation had represented an exchange of benefits between the regulated industry and its public controllers. In return for a guaranteed profit and market franchise, the industry provided stable prices and service. As applied to natural gas producers, however, regulation was a bad bargain. It granted them no monopoly and did not guarantee a profit. Producers therefore considered themselves unwilling participants in a redistributive transaction.

Finally, producer representatives argued, utility regulation of wellhead prices would ultimately work against the interests of consumers and the national welfare in general. Utility rate methods, they contended, would inevitably force many small producers out of business. In 1953, for example, forty-eight hundred dry holes were drilled by small independent producers. Utility rate setting would not compensate all expenses associated with unsuccessful drilling, and thus would discourage exploration—particularly by the small "wildcatters" who brought in over 75 percent of all gas wells. Small independents would also be especially penalized by the burden of paperwork and legal fees imposed by regulation. It was claimed, for example, that merely to secure copies of FPC testimony related to his contracts could cost the producer over ten thousand dollars in the 1950s.[63] Moreover, the effect of FPC decisions, upheld by the courts, was to bind the producer to the regulated market for the life of his reserves, whether the price granted for his gas was profitable or not. As Justice William Douglas pointed out in his 1968 area rate dissent, even in other regulated industries individual firms may at least withdraw from the business if they are losing money. Gas producers, however, may not cease interstate sales without FPC approval.

Thus, whenever possible, an independent producer would withhold his gas from the interstate market. The price available in the intrastate market might not be significantly higher, but the costs and uncertainties associated with the transaction would be considerably less. Interstate consumers would therefore see their gas supplies threatened and be forced to shift to other more expensive and less desirable fuels. In the meantime, producers warned, much gas would be used wastefully. Not only would holders of long-term contracts at artificially low prices be encouraged to overconsume, but gas would be sold for boiler-fuel use in the producer states rather than residential use in the regulated interstate market. Wasteful gas consumption would deprive competitive fuels of their markets, deprive households of a superior fuel, and increase dependence on imported oil and gas. Regulation would therefore be self-defeating. It would provide short-term benefits to a few favored consumers but only at substantial long-term costs to the nation as a whole.

The Consumers

In 1956, Illinois Senator Paul Douglas, a leading opponent of the Harris-Fulbright bills, authored a ringing rebuttal of the producer arguments for deregulation. In an article entitled "The Case for the Consumer of Natural Gas," Douglas set out to prove that the gas-producing industry was indeed characterized by monopoly, and that the costs to consumers of wellhead deregulation would be staggering.[64]

Of the fifty-five hundred producers who sold to interstate pipelines in 1954, Douglas pointed out, only 197—3.5 percent—sold almost 90 percent of the gas carried interstate. In the individual gas fields, competition was even more restricted than these aggregate national figures suggested. In the two major producing fields (Panhandle and Hugoton), for example, a few large companies controlled most of the reserves dedicated to interstate pipelines.[65] It was these giant oil and gas corporations that stood to reap most of the gains from deregulation, Douglas argued, and those gains would constitute a huge unearned windfall. At 1955 consumption levels, a five-cent increase in wellhead prices would cost the nation's consumers over three hundred million dollars.[66]

The traditional argument for utility regulation was that the large fixed costs necessary to provide a given service to the public both rendered competition uneconomic and necessitated a publicly guaranteed market monopoly. Senator Douglas and other consumer representatives turned this argument on its head. It was the consumers and distributors, not the producers, of natural gas who had a large fixed investment, and must be granted a "monopoly" interest in a gas leasehold. Regulation of producer contracts was necessary to protect the value of the buyer's investment and guarantee his supply. The average household, Douglas estimated in 1956, had invested over five hundred dollars in gas-burning appliances. These appliances made household consumers "captives" of the gas industry. When prices rose they were helpless, since they could hardly scrap this expensive investment to purchase new appliances using electricity or other fuels. Similarly, pipeline companies had expended forty thousand to one hundred thousand dollars per mile on their transmission facilities, and these lines could not "be moved at will like a garden hose," in search of lower prices at other fields. Local utilities were particularly hard hit by price increases in the 1950s. Regulatory bodies often denied them price increases sufficient to compensate for higher gas costs; even if an increase was granted, it usually came only after a considerable lag. The cost to utilities to provide gas hookups was estimated at five hundred dollars per household in the mid-1950s.[67] Thus utilities had incurred substantial debt in converting to natural gas, and, particularly in the Northeast, where coal and oil prices were competitive, a sharp increase in the price of gas could drive many small utilities into bankruptcy.[68]

Much of the hostility directed at gas producers reflected consumer perceptions that the oil and gas industries were one and the same.[69] The large multinational oil corporations, which have never enjoyed great popularity in the public mind, lost even more ground after the steep price increases of the 1970s. Not only were the oil and gas corporations seen as monopolistic and exploitative, but they also had, in the opinion of many, used their tremendous wealth to manipulate both state and national governments to their own advantage. At the national level, they had secured, primarily during Republican administrations, favorable tax

FIGURE 9

Residential Consumption of Natural Gas by County, 1955 (Outside Producer States)*

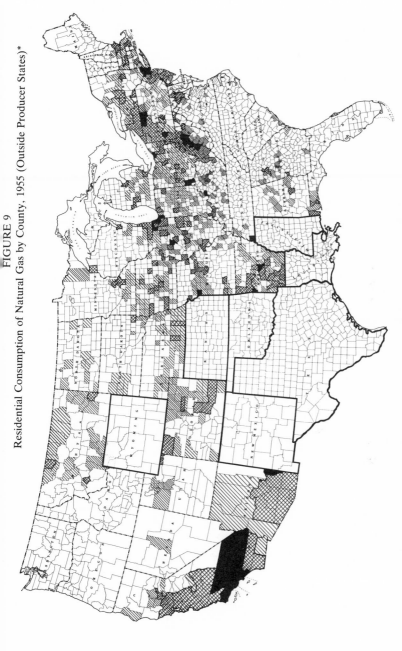

*Producer states in 1955 were Wyoming, New Mexico, Oklahoma, Texas, Louisiana, and Mississippi.

†The ranges listed refer to the percentage of households in each county that have gas service.

treatment through depletion allowances and other provisions.[70] In addition, the oil companies and producer states had persuaded the Eisenhower administration to restrict imports. Since imported oil at that time was priced considerably below domestic production, the effect of the program was to raise prices to consumers—principally in the import-dependent Northeast—to the advantage of the oil companies and producer states. In 1972, a coalition of New England governors filed suit to abolish the oil import program, which was estimated to cost U.S. consumers almost five billion dollars a year. The governors of the four large oil-producing states—Louisiana, Oklahoma, Texas, and Wyoming—intervened in support of the program.[71] The depletion allowance was abolished for major oil and gas producers in 1975, and the effect of import controls was reversed after 1973 when imported oil became more expensive than domestic. Nevertheless, the experience with these programs generated considerable resentment of the political power of the petroleum industry, and hardly encouraged the movement to decontrol gas producer prices.

The producer states attempted to disassociate themselves from the unfavorable public image of "Big Oil" by emphasizing the role in gas production of the shoestring wildcatter and the small farmer-leaseholder, as well as the widespread benefits of oil and gas royalties and severance taxes to public schools, hospitals, and welfare institutions. There is little evidence, however, that such arguments persuaded any congressmen who were not already predisposed to support deregulation. "Reduced to its simplest terms," wrote one economist in 1951, "the issue [in natural gas regulation] is whether Mr. Getty shall buy a yacht . . . or whether thousands of New Jersey citizens shall enjoy an extra 'evening on the town' in Manhattan once a year."[72] Argued in more serious terms by Senator Douglas, there were seven states in 1955 that were net exporters, and thirty-five that were net importers of natural gas (see Figure 9). In all, there were over twenty-one million households consuming gas, and only about fifty-five hundred producers for interstate consumption. If there could be said to exist a "national interest" in gas regulation, then surely the presumption of such interest lay with the more numerous consumers, not with the producers of natural gas.

Finally, consumer advocates (both in Congress and on the FPC) discounted producer warnings that regulation would lead to interstate gas shortages and a general decline in exploration because of inadequate price incentives. Four major arguments have been advanced against this contention of the producers. First of all, according to Senator Douglas, since gas production was dominated by giant oil companies, plenty of capital would be available for exploration even if gas prices were controlled. The oil companies, reaping large profits from (then) uncontrolled oil prices and tax benefits, would not suffer a shortage of investment capital. Furthermore, gas would inevitably be discovered in the search for oil, since it was very difficult to predict whether oil or gas deposits would be reached in the course of a drilling operation, and a large percentage of wells yielded both. Thirdly, consumer representatives scoffed at the producers' claim that they could, and would, sell their gas in the intrastate market if interstate prices were controlled. This argument was fallacious, Douglas contended in 1956, because the producer states lacked the population and industrial base to absorb much more of their own production. And if they hoped to attract industry, he argued, the intrastate price itself would have to be kept low, for "no big user is going to move from New York to Texas to pay a higher price for gas."[73]

A fourth argument made by Douglas and by later opponents of deregulation was that a higher price would not elicit greater supplies of gas because the price-supply relationship was inelastic. They showed that production grew significantly even after the Phillips decision. Later, in the 1970s, consumers pointed out that production continued to decline despite the fact that the Nixon commission implemented significant price increases.[74] Consumer spokesmen on the commerce committees in the 1970s pointed to evidence that United States gas reserves were near depletion, and production could not be increased significantly at any price level. Deregulation in a situation of rapidly diminishing reserves would simply repeat the experience of the Appalachian area in the 1920s: producers would charge more and more exorbitant prices as gas became scarcer. As Federal Power Commissioner John Carver argued in 1971, "in a period of commodity shortage, it would seem to be the worst time to relieve that commodity of regulation."[75]

The Coal Industry

In 1971, the president of the National Coal Association (NCA), Carl Bagge, testified in hearings before a House Interstate and Foreign Commerce subcommittee in favor of a limited deregulation bill. Bagge told the subcommittee:

> The Nation's coal industry has historically opposed wellhead producer price regulation in the natural gas industry. The rationale for the coal industry's opposition to natural gas producer price regulation was based historically upon the wholly artificial and totally discriminatory competitive advantage accorded the distribution and marketing segments of the natural gas industry. Such artificial and discriminatory gas pricing policies which were established by producer price regulation since the *Phillips* decision have resulted in the displacement of coal from a broad range of industrial and commercial markets.
>
> The coal industry believed and continues to maintain the position that it is being discriminated against by a national policy which has

established an artificially low price for natural gas. Recent United States Bureau of Mines figures show that in 1970, based on price per million Btu.'s, natural gas at the wellhead was priced at only 68 percent of the price of an energy equivalent amount of coal at the mine. This, notwithstanding the more limited reserves of natural gas, has affirmatively encouraged the use of gas as a utility boiler fuel and in a broad range of industrial uses. Thus, natural gas has, in the past, effectively displaced coal in many markets solely on economic grounds because the artificial restraints on the price of gas have created an artificially high level of demand.[76]

Bagge's testimony actually represented a change in the position of the NCA. His statement about the industry's "historical opposition" notwithstanding, coal industry spokesmen did not support deregulation bills on which congressional hearings were held in 1947, 1949, and 1955, and most representatives of coal areas voted against the bills on the floor, as Table 13 demonstrates.[77]

There are essentially two reasons for the coal industry's opposition. First, the major coal-producing states—Kentucky, West Virginia, Pennsylvania, Illinois, and Ohio—also have high gas consumption. The coal unions, in particular, have opposed the deregulation of residential gas prices. Second, the principal goal of the coal industry and its railroad allies—the prohibition of "inferior" gas uses—has been perceived by the industry to require more regulation, not less. In 1955, for example, representatives of coal and railroad executives and the railway and mine workers' unions all testified in favor of bills introduced by Representative Harley Staggers and Senator Harley Kilgore of West Virginia.[78] The Staggers-Kilgore bills had four major features: an extension of FPC jurisdiction to direct industrial sales by pipelines; a requirement that rates be set, for sales of gas to industry, that reflected the full cost of transportation of gas; a restriction on gas imports; and amendment of FPC certification powers to make mandatory a consideration of the economic health of competing fuel industries. While passage of the Harris-Fulbright bills would almost certainly have raised gas prices, and in that way eventually discouraged industrial sales, the coal industry much preferred direct

TABLE 13   MAJOR COAL-PRODUCING DISTRICTS:
VOTES ON DEREGULATION BILLS IN THE
HOUSE OF REPRESENTATIVES

Year	In Favor	Opposed	Not Voting
1947	4	8	2
1949	4	7	5
1955	4	10	0

prohibitions. Deregulation, if it stimulated gas production and improved the supply situation for interstate pipelines (as the producers claimed it would), might even worsen coal's position. In absence of end-use regulation, any increase in residential sales in the interstate market would result in increased industrial sales, since pipelines would have to make large-volume, attractively priced gas sales to off-peak users in order to meet their expanded operating costs. Thus, while the coal industry urged gas price increases for industrial uses in administrative hearings before the FPC, its attitude toward statutory deregulation of wellhead prices ranged from ambivalent to hostile. This position was not immutable, however. When circumstances changed in the 1970s, both the coal industry and coal area congressmen began to reconsider their position on deregulation.

The Politics of Producer Regulation

Because it hears final appeals from the decisions of regulatory agencies, the Supreme Court has always played an important role in economic regulation. In the case of natural gas, the Court has not only legitimated significant innovations in regulatory methods but has reached beyond the contemporary political consensus reflected in Congress and the executive branch to radically alter the meaning of the regulatory statute.

The change in the meaning of the Natural Gas Act accomplished by the Supreme Court's decision of 1954 turned national gas regulation upside down. With the jurisdiction of the act expanded to include first sales by independent producers, federal regulation of the natural gas industry acquired the potential for transferring wealth between regions. Since 1954, congressmen and presidents have struggled to make natural gas, like numerous other forms of economic regulation, work to the advantage of their regional constituencies.

Because the two major parties tend to represent constituencies with different stakes in the outcome of regulation, the Federal Power Commission's interpretation of its mandate has varied significantly between Republican and Democratic administrations. However, this variation has occurred principally with regard to gas pricing. In other regulatory decisions (particularly those involving supplies to interstate pipelines) there is less difference between Republican and Democratic commissions. Both have broadly interpreted the agency's powers to compel deliveries to the interstate pipeline companies that were the original and are still the core regulated clientele of the FPC under the Natural Gas Act. Maintenance of a healthy pipeline industry implies no particular gas-pricing strategy on the part of the commission. Thus, in its pricing decisions, the FPC has adapted itself to its political environment, holding the price low in response to consumer-area dominance of Congress and the White House and raising gas prices when the Republican-producer coalition has the upper hand.

The regionally based contenders—gas-producing and importing regions and coal areas—do not, of course, argue the issue in crass, localistic terms. Each can make a compelling case for the hardship, exploitation, and economic pathology that would result from alternative approaches to regulation. Faced with passionate and plausible arguments on both sides, it is no wonder that federal power commissioners and representatives of spectator areas align themselves with either producer or consumer coalitions, depending on their estimation of political reward.

In retrospect, the arguments of consumer-area representatives in the 1950s and 1960s may appear short-sighted. Their assumptions about the inelasticity of the price-supply relationship and the ability of producer state economies to absorb increasing supplies turned out to be mistaken. But it is difficult to blame the political actors of the past for not being omniscient. With the information available to them at the time, and the responsibilities imposed by representative democracy, their positions were understandable.

6 | The Politics of Scarcity

In 1968, two developments combined to signal the beginning of a new period in natural gas regulation. In the industry itself, evidence accumulated that the supply situation for interstate pipelines was changing for the worse. In the political arena, a new Republican president was elected whose FPC appointments and legislative recommendations would support natural gas policies much more favorable to the producers than those of previous Democratic administrations.

For the first time in the country's history, more gas was being sold than discovered. In the first year of the Nixon administration, the quantity of United States proven reserves dropped by over twelve trillion cubic feet; the ratio of total reserves to total production declined to a new low of 13.3 (see Table 14). The accepted standard in pipeline certification had long been a reserves to production ratio of twenty. The number of wells drilled for hydrocarbons had peaked in 1956 at about fifty-seven thousand; in 1969 it stood at thirty-two thousand. Exploration had dropped sharply, even as gas sales reached record highs (see Figure 10). During the decade from 1960 to 1970, consumption of natural gas more than doubled, while the number of gas wells brought in declined by over 25 percent.[1] The predictions of shortages, so often made by producers during the long debate on regulation, had apparently come to pass.

As a result of federal regulation, the interstate pipelines' share of total marketed production began to decline in the 1960s. From 1965 to 1975 the percentage of total marketed production that moved interstate dropped from 61 to 53 percent. In the Permian Basin, which by the end of the decade accounted for 10.5 percent of United States natural gas reserves, almost all additions to reserves after 1965 were committed to intrastate buyers.[2] In 1970, 77 percent of all gas sold under new contracts remained in the producer states.[3]

Between 1966 and 1970, total United States reserves committed to interstate pipelines dropped from 198 to 174 trillion cubic feet.[4] The average new contract price for gas in the producer states exceeded the new price set for interstate sales in 1970. The wellhead price, however,

TABLE 14 UNITED STATES NATURAL GAS SUPPLY, 1956–1973
(ALL VOLUMES IN TRILLIONS OF CUBIC FEET)

Year	Production	Reserve Additions	Reserves/Production Ratio	Total Wells Drilled for Hydrocarbons	Gas Wells	Dry Holes
1956	10.9	24.7	21.8	57,170	4,531	22,111
1957	11.4	20.0	21.4	51,995	4,475	20,156
1958	11.4	18.9	22.1	46,941	5,005	18,162
1959	12.4	20.6	21.1	47,563	4,931	18,589
1960	13.0	13.9	20.1	45,547	5,129	18,185
1961	13.5	17.2	19.9	44,254	5,459	17,382
1962	13.6	19.5	20.0	44,158	5,353	17,078
1963	14.5	18.2	19.0	41,467	4,570	16,762
1964	15.3	20.3	18.3	42,293	4,694	17,694
1965	16.3	21.3	17.6	38,773	4,482	16,226
1966	17.5	20.2	16.5	35,730	4,321	15,193
1967	18.4	21.8	15.9	32,234	3,659	13,246
1968	19.4	13.7	14.8	30,599	3,456	12,812
1969	20.7	8.4	13.3	32,187	4,083	13,736
1970	22.0	37.2*	13.2	28,120	3,840	11,260
1971	22.1	9.8	12.6	25,851	3,830	10,163
1972	22.5	9.6	11.8	27,291	4,928	11,057
1973	22.6	6.8	11.1	26,592	6,385	10,305

Source: American Gas Association, American Association of Petroleum Geologists, and American Petroleum Institute (from tables in House of Representatives, Committee on Interstate and Foreign Commerce, Hearings on Natural Gas Supplies, 94th Cong., 1st sess., June, July, 1975, pp. 1043–1051).
*Represents addition of Alaskan reserves.

was only one of the advantages of the intrastate market from the producer's point of view. Other advantages included the smaller reserve requirements for pipeline sales in the producer states (fifteen as opposed to twenty years' supply), and the much shorter interval between contract negotiations and the commencement of gas deliveries. In addition, there was much greater certainty—always an important factor for the investor—about what the price and conditions of the buyer-seller relationship would be.[5] Thus, producers preferred, where possible, to sell their gas in the unregulated intrastate market.

The intrastate market expanded significantly in the 1960s as the industrial economies and populations of the gas-producing states grew more rapidly than the remainder of the country. Part of this growth may itself be attributed to fuel supply. An abundant supply and low transportation charges made gas an attractive fuel for steam generation in electric utilities, as well as other industrial uses (see Table 15). In 1970, utilities in the three major southwestern producer states burned 831.8 billion cubic feet of gas—an amount roughly equal to the total residential consumption of the states of New York, Pennsylvania, and New Jersey. Five years later, utility and industrial gas consumption in Texas, Oklahoma, and Louisiana reached 4,473 billion cubic feet, almost one-fourth of total United States marketed production.[6]

In contrast to Senator Douglas's argument that no industry would relocate to a producer state unless the price of gas were lower, some industries undoubtedly did move to, and others originated in, the producer states, because of the more favorable supply situation. Without that regulation-created advantage, the fuel position of the producer states was not particularly favorable. Domestic oil was more expensive, until 1973, than the foreign oil available to the northeastern states. The producer states have very little bituminous coal, and, in addition, transportation costs and limited railroad service make coal supply difficult and expensive in those states.

The availability of gas became more important than price in the late 1960s, as interstate pipelines began to reduce their interruptible sales to industries. By 1973–1974, most major interstate pipelines were also unable to obtain quantities sufficient to meet their firm delivery commitments, with the result that a number of states experienced factory shutdowns and school closings.[7] Pipeline curtailments totalled about one trillion cubic feet in 1970–1971; by 1976–1977, they reached 3.4 trillion cubic feet.[8] On the East Coast, most of that shortfall was replaced by expensive imported oil. Imports of natural gas also reached record highs in the early 1970s; moreover, the price of Algerian gas delivered to the East Coast was more than twice as high as that allowed for regulated domestic gas sold under new contracts.[9]

TABLE 15   INDUSTRIAL CONSUMPTION OF NATURAL GAS, 1955 AND 1975
            (MILLIONS OF CUBIC FEET)

	1955		1975	
	Quantity	Percent	Quantity	Percent
Total United States*	5,962,781	100	10,708,899	100
Six largest producing states†	3,282,364	55	5,702,843	53
Percentage of total United States marketed production used in industry		63		53
Uses				
Refineries	625,243	10	945,557	9
Carbon black	244,794	4	26,246	0
Pipeline	245,246	4	582,963	5
Cement	131,400	2	NA	
Other industrial	3,562,818	60	6,007,260	56
Utilities				
Total United States	1,153,280	19	3,146,873	29
Six largest producing states†	674,271	11	2,476,808	23

Source: Minerals Yearbook.
*"Industrial" use in this table includes gas used by electric utilities. Field uses are excluded.
†In order of production, 1975: Texas, Louisiana, Oklahoma, New Mexico, Kansas, California. Natural gas used as a pipeline fuel is not included in producer state industrial consumption.

As gas shortages began to appear in the interstate market, the issue of gas producer regulation again appeared on the congressional agenda. The producer states, of course, lost no time in proposing deregulation as a remedy for the shortage. Wyoming Senator Clifford Hansen told his Senate Interior Committee colleagues:

I cannot conceive that Congress can fail in its responsibility to take corrective actions to provide an economic climate that will encourage and assure maximum exploration for and development of domestic natural gas supplies. . . .

The economic distortion is now clear in a situation that finds our Government through the Federal Power Commission, on the one hand, holding an artificial lid on domestic natural gas prices, and, on the other hand, considering approval of imported gas substitutes, to fill the existing gap in supply, at prices two to three times the city-gate price of natural gas.

When the final chapter of this unbelievable experience is written by some historian . . . I am sure it will be put down as one of the most regrettable, counterproductive episodes in the whole history of industry-government relationships.

It is a system that dries up supplies of a product by killing investment incentives of the industry producing that product, while encouraging development of foreign supplies that will cost up to three times as much and can be denied to us at any time.[10]

As during the last severe shortage, in 1947, the producers found allies among states with low gas consumption that saw deregulation as their only hope of obtaining a greater supply of gas. Support for deregulation tended to grow in these spectator states as the gas shortage became more severe.

Representatives from areas with high residential and industrial gas usage were unwilling to accept total deregulation, but predictions of more severe curtailments during the coming winter induced some congressmen to support moderate changes in the Natural Gas Act. In 1971, the House Commerce Committee held hearings on a bill sponsored by New York Representative John Murphy and thirty other northern Democrats. The Murphy bill, HR 2513, would have exempted small producer contracts from direct price regulation and guaranteed "sanctity of contract" (that is, that prices once approved by the Federal Power Commission could not be subsequently reduced during the life of the contract). "Small" producer contracts were defined as those providing sales averaging less than ten thousand mcf a day; it was estimated that this group accounted for about 15 percent of production for interstate pipelines in 1971. In addition to the small producer exemption, the bill directed the Federal Power Commission to give "due recognition to other economic factors besides costs in setting rates for all new producer contracts."[11] Similar bills were introduced in the Senate by Ernest Hollings of South Carolina and Clifford Hansen of Wyoming; hearings were held on these bills in 1972.

Producer state representatives endorsed the Murphy bill as a "significant first step" toward easing the supply problem.[12] In a break with its past position on such legislation, the American Gas Association (AGA) also supported the bill. The AGA, representing three hundred distributor and pipeline companies, had abandoned its opposition to deregulation in 1968 and written to all five power commissioners urging them to reassess their price-setting methods in order to stimulate interstate supplies. Gas utility labor unions, finding their jobs threatened by the shortage, joined the AGA in support. In addition to gas producers and distributors, the coal industry also endorsed the Murphy proposal. National Coal Association President Carl Bagge testified in favor of the bill, and coal state senators Jennings Randolph of West Virginia and Marlow Cook of Kentucky cosponsored the legislation in the Senate. Cook told the Senate committee that "the gasification of coal promises substantial

FIGURE 10
Natural Gas Production and Value, 1938–1975

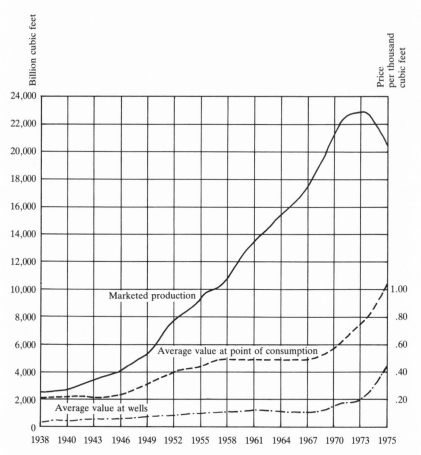

SOURCE: Based on *Minerals Yearbook* figures.

relief to the gas shortage problem. But this gas will . . . be more expensive than natural gas. . . . [I]f we are to have it, we must allow it to compete fairly and not against an artificially priced commodity."[13]

In spite of this diverse new support, the Murphy-Hollings bills were not reported. There was intense opposition to the measure on the part of some consumer spokesmen. Former Power Commission Chairman Joseph Swidler, now chairman of the New York Public Service Commission, told the House and Senate Commerce committees that the Murphy bill was "not in the interest of gas consumers" because it would frustrate effective price regulation and service guarantees.[14] California Representative John Moss, fourth-ranking member of the House Commerce

Committee, argued that the bill would "compound the advantages that the gas producers now have and in times of gas shortage, place the captive consumer at a further disadvantage."[15] Another reason for the failure of the ninety-second Congress to act on the proposed amendments to the Natural Gas Act was that the FPC, by administrative action, made such statutory change appear unnecessary to some congressional opponents of regulation.

The FPC Under Nixon

In 1969, President Nixon appointed New Hampshire Republican John Nassikas to chair the FPC. There was, however, no immediate break with past FPC policy. The Nixon administration had not yet developed a legislative program on natural gas (although an administration spokesman described HR 2513 as "consistent with our goals"), and there was no clear majority in either the House or Senate in favor of deregulation. The FPC therefore moved cautiously. In 1971, Chairman Nassikas joined Johnson Commissioners John Carver and Albert Brook in opposition to the proposal providing for small producer exemption and "sanctity of contract."[16]

However, while opposing the Murphy bill, the commission majority attempted to deflect the rising demand for regulatory change through administrative action. In 1970, the commission reopened rate proceedings in the Permian Basin and southern Louisiana areas to determine if wellhead prices should be raised to stimulate new interstate supplies. In the following year, it implemented a proposal made by an organization of large distributors to raise the southern Louisiana price ceiling by 30 to 50 percent for gas under new contracts, and to discharge producers' refund obligations in return for additional commitments to interstate pipelines. The commission also established a procedure in which producers could make short-term sales to interstate pipelines during emergencies at prices higher than the established area ceilings, and with pre-granted permission to terminate sales after a fixed period; for certificated producers, it developed an "optional pricing procedure," which allowed producers to negotiate new rates, with FPC permission.[17]

While arguing that total deregulation of small producer contracts would have "an unduly inflationary effect," the commission created, through administrative order in 1971, a certificate procedure for granting small producers, on a case by case basis, an exemption from direct price regulation.[18] Retention of some degree of regulatory control was necessary, Nassikas argued, in order to protect the public from unreasonable price increases. By way of legislative action, the most the FPC majority was willing to support in 1971–1972 was a provision that broadened and legitimated their discretion to consider economic ("non-cost") factors in determining gas prices.[19] In other words, the commission was willing to accommodate the rising demand for some supply-stimulating price increases, but wanted to control such increases on its own terms, without diminution of its regulatory jurisdiction.

Producer state representatives and their western and Republican allies soon became impatient with the commission's modest adjustments, and pressed for a legislative remedy. President Nixon's subsequent appointments to the FPC of men more amenable to deregulation than Chairman Nassikas reflected the growing agitation within his electoral constituency. Early in 1973, the administration formally proposed gradual deregulation (for new and expiring gas contracts). A bill embodying the administration proposals was introduced in the Senate by ranking Commerce Committee Republican Norris Cotton, and extensive hearings were held in 1973 and 1974 on this and other bills to amend the Natural Gas Act.[20] All four commissioners, including the chairman, testified in favor of the administration bill.[21]

As in the Eisenhower years, producer state representatives could once again count on a sympathetic president for favorable FPC appointments, and support for legislative amendment. Nevertheless, the political climate differed in important ways from the mid-1950s. Consumer area representatives now held almost 40 percent of House seats and controlled the House Interstate and Foreign Commerce Committee. In the Senate, producers and their allies were more strongly represented, but the chairman and ranking Democrats on the Commerce Committee were firmly opposed to deregulation. As a result, no action was taken on the administration's deregulation bill in the Senate committee.

Toward the end of the first session of the ninety-third Congress, during floor debate on the creation of a Federal Energy Emergency Administration, New York Conservative Senator James Buckley offered an amendment to deregulate the price of natural gas sold under new contracts. The amendment had the approval of the Nixon administration and the FPC. The Buckley proposal was narrowly defeated on a forty-five to forty-three recommittal vote in 1973.

Even though deregulation had passed the Senate fifty-three to thirty-eight in 1956, central coalition tendencies had changed little in seventeen years. Producer states still found most of their allies in western and midwestern farm states. On the other hand, opponents of deregulation were concentrated in urban industrial states with little or no production, and found allies in neighboring northeastern states. Senators from the nonproducing South were still divided on the natural gas issue but somewhat more sympathetic to deregulation than they had been in 1956.

FIGURE 11
Senate Support for Deregulation, 1973 (Percentage in Favor)*

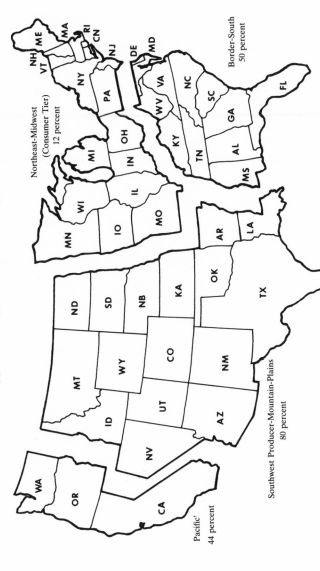

Northeast-Midwest
(Consumer Tier)
12 percent

Border-South
50 percent

Pacific†
44 percent

Southwest Producer-Mountain-Plains
80 percent

Average Gas Consumption by Region for Importing States‡

Region	Percentages
Northeast-Midwest	68
Border-South§	34
Southwest-Mountain-Plains‖	64
Pacific#	69

*Percentage of those voting or paired who opposed recommittal of Buckley amendment in 1973.

†Includes Alaska and Hawaii.

‡Consumption figures derived from tables in Bureau of Mines, *Minerals Yearbook*, 1975, and Department of Commerce, *Statistical Abstract*, 1975. The sum of all households with natural gas service is divided by the sum of all households.

§Excludes West Virginia.

‖Excludes Texas, Louisiana, Oklahoma, Kansas, New Mexico, and Wyoming.

#Excludes Alaska.

The number of states in which both senators supported deregulation had dropped from twenty to twelve. The most conspicuous among the votes "lost" to the deregulation forces were in the states of California, Iowa, and Nevada, where both senators had supported deregulation in 1956, but both were opposed in 1973. California, a major producer in the 1950s, now consumed more than three times as much gas as it produced, and its perceived interest lay with interstate regulation. In gas-importing Iowa and Nevada, the percentage of residential consumers had more than doubled since 1956. Federal regulation also picked up new support in the north central industrial states, as well as among northeastern spectator areas. Although gas consumption was not as great in New England as in the north central states, the former had become more dependent on domestic and increasingly expensive imported oil. This dependence generated growing antagonism for the petroleum industry, and brought New England into coalition with neighboring consumer states on a wide range of fuel price control and allocation issues.

Thus, a clear regional pattern formed on energy policy issues (see Figure 11). Older consumer states and their spectator neighbors supported the maintenance or strengthening of federal regulation. In the tier of seventeen states from Maine to New Jersey, west along the Ohio River, and up through Missouri, Iowa, and Minnesota—states later to form the regionally based Northeast-Midwest Economic Advancement (NEMWEA) coalition—only four of thirty-four senators supported the Buckley deregulation amendment in 1973.[22] West of the Mississippi, in the band of southwestern, plains, and mountain states extending from Louisiana to Arizona and reaching north to the Canadian border, only six of thirty-two senators opposed the amendment. Between the consumer tier and the producer belt, there existed a border region bounded by the Mason-Dixon line and the Mississippi and Ohio rivers. Exactly half the Senate votes in this twelve-state region supported the Buckley amendment. Among the Pacific states, gas-deficit California opposed deregulation, while senators from the spectator states of Oregon, Washington, and Hawaii were evenly divided. Both senators from the petroleum-producing state of Alaska supported the Buckley amendment.

Post-Embargo Politics

Events of 1973 exacerbated producer-consumer differences. During the course of the October Arab-Israeli war, Arab nations declared an embargo on oil shipments to the United States, cutting U.S. petroleum supplies about 17 percent below normal. By the end of the year, the Persian Gulf nations had doubled the price of their crude oil exports to the West; by the end of 1974, the price had doubled again. These steep oil price increases, coupled with severe interstate gas shortages in the winter of 1973, increased, rather than diminished, the consumer regions' support for federal regulation of fuel price and supply.

Domestic oil prices had been regulated prior to the embargo under general price control authority given the president in the Economic Stabilization Act of 1971. The price of newly discovered oil, however, was not controlled. In 1973, the president's Cost of Living Council set the price for "old" domestic crude oil at $5.25 a barrel. After the embargo, Congress enacted an Emergency Petroleum Allocation Act (EPAA), which directed the president to develop and implement plans for allocating scarce oil and oil products among refiners, users, and distributors. Allocations were to be made according to a congressionally mandated schedule of priorities and objectives. The EPAA also extended the oil price control authority granted the president in 1971.[23]

During the following year, congressional Democrats attempted to specify oil price levels, and extend the federal government's regulatory power to deal with the growing oil and gas shortages. In 1974, Congress passed a bill creating a Federal Energy Emergency Administration (FEEA) with power to order conversion to coal by large industries and utilities that used oil and gas for boiler fuels. The bill (entitled the Federal Energy Emergency Act) would also have reduced the federally mandated price of new and other previously exempt categories of domestic oil to $5.25, ordered increased production from oil leases on both private and federal lands, and prohibited oil and coal exports under certain conditions. President Nixon vetoed the bill in March; supporters of the FEEA failed to override the veto. A few months later, Congress approved the president's request for the establishment of a Federal Energy Administration (FEA), assigning it energy planning, allocation, pricing, and conservation authority previously scattered across a number of federal agencies. In addition, Congress in 1974 passed an Energy Supply and Environmental Coordination Act (ESECA), which again embodied a provision empowering the FEA to order electric utilities and industries to convert from oil and gas to coal, where environmental regulations, transportation facilities, and power plant equipment permitted the burning of coal as a boiler fuel.[24] While ESECA generated no significant controversy in either chamber, the institution of this modest and exemption-ridden authorization for federal control of boiler fuel use (the major and long-standing political goal of the coal industry) had far-reaching implications for United States energy policy and regional politics.

In 1975, as the price of new domestic and imported oil continued to climb, and the size of the Democratic majority expanded following the Watergate scandal, Congress enacted more stringent oil price and allocation controls. The Energy Policy and Conservation Act (EPCA) of 1975 combined expansion of the system of oil price controls with an extension of FEA authority to order conversion from oil and gas to coal.[25] The bill passed over intense opposition from oil state representatives and Republicans. President Ford signed the EPCA, although its provisions were far from the administration's preferences in energy policy. Those preferences, contained in the president's 1975 State of the Union message and subsequent legislative proposals, were clearly based on a different regulatory philosophy, and aimed at a different political constituency. The Ford proposals included decontrol of both oil and natural gas prices, and a tax on imported oil, both designed to affect conservation by price increases, as opposed to end-use regulation. In Congress, however, a new majority coalition favoring direct federal control of oil price and supply had been forged between consumer and coal area representatives; thus, the Ford proposals met with very little success. The president possessed a veto power, of course, but pressure to produce some legislative response to the nation's energy problems mitigated against its use.

Although the two issues would appear to be closely connected, the emergence of a congressional majority in support of oil price regulation did not imply similar support for continuing natural gas controls; at least, positions on price control of the two fuels were not linked in all regions of the country. Political configurations on energy issues reflected the complexity of the "energy crisis," and the existence of widely divergent proposals for dealing with it. There remained two "poles" on issues dealing with oil and gas price controls: the producer states west of the Mississippi and the energy-deficit urban areas of the Northeast and industrial Midwest. Between these poles, however, there was considerable fluidity, as representatives of coal-producing and spectator regions attempted to sort out the changing positions of their constituencies in national and international energy markets. When votes were taken on EPCA and on natural gas deregulation in 1975, it was evident that some significant shifts had taken place at the margins of the producer and consumer coalitions. Outcomes depended on the way discrete issues were combined, and, in some cases, on which energy "package" came to the floor first.

A Deregulation Majority Emerges in the Senate

In the debate on a national policy to deal with fuel shortages, price increases, and import dependence, producer state representatives faced both challenge and opportunity. On the one hand, a substantial portion of the public supported an expanded federal regulatory apparatus to cushion the impact of the "energy crisis" on consumers. On the other hand, the producer states were in a strong position to argue that federal regulation had contributed to the gas shortage and, as a result, increased dependence on imported oil.

By the mid-1970s, most economists who took public positions on the issue supported the producer arguments. Historical data on control of reserves, price-supply relationships, and comparisons of actual with simulated wellhead prices were marshaled in support of arguments that gas production was workably competitive, that gas supplies did respond to price incentives, and that the major cause of the natural gas shortage were the pricing and reserve ownership policies implemented by the Federal Power Commission in the 1960s.[26] University of Michigan economist Edward J. Mitchell told the Senate Commerce Committee in 1974:

> We . . . have extensive and profound experience with FPC regulation of interstate prices and there has developed a general consensus among economists that FPC regulations have created a massive shortage of natural gas. . . . I believe the domestic petroleum industry is essentially competitive and that competition would be a far better disciplinarian than regulation. There have been important deviations from the competitive ideal in the industry's past, but these have invariably been created by government, not by private action.[27]

In other testimony submitted during congressional hearings on natural gas shortages, MIT economist Paul MacAvoy and Harvard Law Professor Stephen Breyer argued that, "while the commission's policies were aimed at helping home consumers, . . . regulation has brought about precisely the opposite result."[28] Similarly, Edmund Kitch of the University of Chicago Law School told the Interior Committee that federal regulation of natural gas "imposes higher costs on the interstate consumer by (1) forcing him to purchase more expensive alternative fuels; (2) reducing the dependability of his gas supply; and (3) subsidizing the industrial use of natural gas in intrastate markets."[29]

The implication of this testimony was that deregulation of wellhead pricing would promote the national interest both by eliciting greater domestic fuel supplies and by producing a more efficient allocation of gas, oil, and coal. MIT economist M. A. Adelman stated the majority position bluntly: "We need a free market to encourage supply, restrict demand, and tell us what steps are advisable. . . . [F]or these reasons, I hope that the Federal Power Commission and the Congress will recognize that regulation of field prices of natural gas was a grievous mistake which has led to considerable waste and hardship to the public, and which ought to be abolished as soon as possible."[30]

The fact that major distributors and pipelines that had previously supported regulation now tended to support at least partial deregulation also strengthened the producers' argument. Armed with predictions that gas curtailments during the winter of 1975–1976 would be 30 percent greater than during the past year, the producer state representatives persuaded the Senate in October 1975 to pass an administration-backed measure calling for a gradual elimination of federal controls on "new" natural gas—the first time since 1956 that the producer coalition had succeeded in passing a deregulation bill.

The Senate vote came on an "emergency" natural gas bill (S 2310) sponsored by senators from Georgia, South Carolina, and Ohio—states expecting severe curtailments in the coming winter. S 2310 authorized the FPC to allow curtailed "priority" gas users to make purchases during a 180-day period at prices up to three times the current regulated interstate price. During floor debate on the short-term emergency bill, Senators James Pearson of Kansas and Lloyd Bentsen of Texas proposed an amendment in the form of a substitute that coupled the emergency measure with the producers' "long-term solution" to the gas shortage: gradual deregulation of wellhead prices.[31] The Senate Commerce Committee had considered numerous "long-term" solutions in 1975, which ranged from immediate deregulation to vastly expanded price and allocation controls. By a two-vote margin the committee majority had reported a bill most appropriately placed in the latter category. The bill, S 692 ("The Natural Gas Production and Conservation Act"), was scheduled for debate after the Senate disposed of S 2310. On the Commerce Committee, an alliance of consumer, spectator, and coal state senators had formed around S 692's provisions requiring boiler fuel conversion from gas to coal, and extending regulation to intrastate gas sales.[32] This coalition was thwarted (if, indeed, it had any chance of success on the Senate floor) by the introduction of the Pearson-Bentsen deregulation amendment to the emergency bill.

The Pearson-Bentsen substitute, modified by additional amendments postponing the effective date of deregulation until the following year, and narrowing the definition of "new" gas, passed the Senate by a vote of fifty-eight to thirty-two. The critical vote came when a motion to table was made by South Carolina Senator Ernest Hollings, a sponsor of the original emergency bill and a Commerce Committee supporter of S 692. The deregulation forces won this vote fifty to forty-five. Comparison of the Pearson-Bentsen vote with the 1973 vote on the Buckley deregulation amendment reveals that votes shifting to deregulation had primarily come from states experiencing significant curtailments, and from three of the four major coal-producing states (which were not among the states experiencing the most severe curtailments in the mid-1970s). Three new deregulation votes were registered in the states of Florida, Georgia, and Tennessee. These southern states, which had relatively modest household gas service ratios (ranging from 12 percent in Florida to 54 percent in Georgia), were among the fifteen states experiencing the highest curtailments in 1974–1975, and predicted to suffer the greatest percentage cutbacks in the 1975–1976 heating season.[33] In the nine nonproducer southern states, only 44 percent of the senators had supported the Buckley amendment in 1973, but two-thirds backed the Pearson-Bentsen amendment in 1975.

It should be noted that when EPCA came to the floor two months later, a majority of votes from the nine energy-deficit southern states were cast in favor of this extension of federal control over oil prices.[34] Thus, while votes on oil and gas price controls were linked in New England (which supported both), they were uncoupled in the southern spectator region.[35] Southern states were not as dependent on heating oil as New England states, but many southern utilities had been forced to convert to oil as the gas shortage worsened, and propane—widely used in the rural South—was brought into the price control system under EPCA.[36] Hence, there was substantial support in the (nonproducing) South for oil price controls. Natural gas was another matter. A minority of households in the region used natural gas, although Southerners in the fuel-deficit states would clearly have preferred gas to the far more expensive electricity and alternative fuels upon which the region's households depended.

Outside the South, the other significant shift toward deregulation occurred in the coal states. During the five-year period from 1970 to 1975, the average price of a ton of coal had tripled, and the number of men employed at the mines had reversed its long decline and begun to rise again (see Table 16). In part, the increase reflected higher labor and operating costs (resulting from the enactment of a black-lung benefits program and state environmental regulations, for example), but the spurt in coal prices was primarily a result of the heightened demand produced by shortages and price increases of gas and oil. With prosperity seemingly around the corner, some coal industry representatives began to look more favorably on legislative proposals for the decontrol of competing fuel prices.

Their reasoning was simple. Higher gas and coal prices would increase the prospects for a coal-based synthetic fuels industry, and speed the conversion of utility and industrial boilers to coal (a process already under way). The same result—conversion to coal—could also be achieved by government fiat; and, of course, federal end-use regulation had long been advocated by the industry. At the increasingly high coal price levels of the 1970s, however, some in the industry feared that forced conversion could only be won at the cost of extending price and allocation controls to coal. For this reason, the National Coal Association (NCA) under Carl Bagge opposed mandatory conversion, and supported decon-

TABLE 16   TRENDS IN COAL PRODUCTION

Year	Net Tons Produced	Average Price per Ton	Number of Men Employed
1929	535.0	$ 1.78	502,993
1935	372.4	1.77	462,403
1940	460.8	1.91	439,075
1950	516.3	4.84	415,582
1955	464.6	4.50	225,093
1960	415.5	4.69	169,400
1965	512.1	4.44	133,732
1970	602.9	6.26	140,140
1975	648.4	19.23	189,800

Source: Minerals Yearbook.

trol of natural gas prices after 1970. The coal industry was not by any means united in support of deregulation. Indeed, there were few issues that united the mine owners (represented in the National Coal Association) and mine workers (represented by the United Mine Workers Union). The competitiveness of the industry had historically made cost cutting the primary goal of management, and the bulk of coal mining costs were represented by coal miners' wages. The long and bloody history of miner-manager conflicts over wages, safety, and the right to organize made any common lobbying effort difficult. Therefore, it was not surprising that the UMW continued to oppose gas deregulation in favor of mandatory conversion, while the NCA took the opposite position.[37]

In the House, the majority of representatives from the major coal-producing districts took the position favored by the UMW. In the Senate, however, increased support for deregulation appeared in the four major coal-producing states. In 1973, only three of eight senators from Kentucky, West Virginia, Pennsylvania, and Illinois had supported the Buckley amendment. In 1975, five of eight senators backed the Pearson-Bentsen substitute on the first tabling motion, and six of eight supported the bill on final passage. As indications grew in the 1970s that the coal areas' position on the natural gas issue was changing, consumer representatives were pressed to develop an energy package that would prevent defections to the deregulation forces among representatives of coal areas. Such a package was ultimately constructed, and achieved partial success toward the end of the decade.

"Administrative Deregulation" and the Consumer Counteroffensive, 1973–1976

Two of the three political institutions on which the authority and staffing of the FPC depended—the president and the Senate—had now taken positions in favor of removing the federal controls that kept interstate natural gas prices below market levels. In the mid-1970s, the commission took administrative action that narrowed the gap between interstate and intrastate prices. These actions somewhat mitigated the demand for statutory deregulation while, at the same time, improving the supply position of regulated pipelines. Although received favorably by the president and deregulation supporters in Congress, the FPC's actions were roundly condemned in urban consumer areas, and provoked a determined counterattack by congressional opponents.

In addition to raising area rates and attempting to exempt small producers from most regulatory controls, the commission in the mid-1970s allowed producers to make "emergency" sales to interstate pipelines at market prices (and without becoming subject to federal regulation) for periods of up to six months. In 1974, the commission abandoned cost-based area pricing altogether for new gas sales. Instead, it established a nationwide ceiling price of forty-two cents per thousand cubic feet. Although still less than half the unregulated price for new intrastate contracts, the new national ceiling was almost double the maximum allowed in the 1960s. By the end of the year, the price had been raised to fifty cents. Commissioner Rush Moody protested that the new prices were still too low to elicit adequate interstate supplies; the commission majority, however, opted for a strategy that set gas prices somewhere between the preference of the producers and the core consumer blocs.

Reluctant to admit that cost-based regulation had been abandoned, the FPC described the new rate as "sufficient to allow recovery of all costs plus a return of 15 percent." In defending the increase over previous area rates, the commission argued that "the increased consumer cost attributable to higher wellhead prices [is] more than counterbalanced by the increased probability of continued service and expanded supplies." "Monitored decontrol," the commission indicated, "is a key element in [our] program to improve America's long-term natural gas supply position."[38] While the consumer majority on the Senate Commerce Committee estimated that complete deregulation of new gas prices would cost consumers almost three billion dollars between 1975 and 1980, the FPC produced a different set of estimates. Taking into account alternative fuel costs, and making very different assumptions about price-supply elasticity, the FPC estimated that deregulation would actually result in an aggregate savings of 3.5 billion dollars.[39]

In spite of its ostensible preference for statutory deregulation, the price actions of the commission in the following year were probably responsible for blunting the momentum of the deregulation drive in Congress. In July of 1976, the FPC raised the national new gas ceiling price from $.52 to $1.42. The new national ceiling remained significantly below the unregulated price for new intrastate contracts, but the sharp increase—

TABLE 17   CHRONOLOGY OF MAJOR FPC DECISIONS AND PARALLEL CONGRESSIONAL-PRESIDENTIAL ACTIONS, 1939–1976

	Congressional-Presidential Action		Action by the Federal Power Commission (FPC)
Year	*Action*	*Year*	*Action*
1938	Natural Gas Act (NGA) passed large Democratic majority in Congress	1939	Commission requires certificate for direct industrial sales (prices not regulated under 1938 Act)
		1940	FPC disclaims jurisdiction over independent producers (Columbia Fuel case)
1942	NGA amended to cover all new interstate pipeline construction	1942	Application of cost-based ("prudent investment") regulation to pipelines, including their gas-producing properties (Hope Case)
		1943	Interstate Case: FPC claims jurisdiction over sale by an interstate pipeline of gas it produces
		1944	Hope decision by Supreme Court upholds cost-based pricing for pipelines
			Memphis Case: FPC denies certificate for boiler fuel sale (end-use control)
1946	Elections produce Republican majority in House and Senate	1946	FPC asserts jurisdiction over local gas distributor (East Ohio Gas Co.) that operates a high-pressure stub line
		1946–1947	Federal courts uphold and extend FPC authority over producer sales
1947	Hearings on amendment to Natural Gas Act. House passes Rizley bill to exempt independent producers	1947	FPC supports statutory amendment exempting producers Order 139 and Finn-Kerr Case: FPC reiterates intention not to regulate independent producers
1948	Elections: Truman narrowly re-elected; Democrats regain majority in Congress Commerce committees favor producer exemption	1948	Divided report issued on natural gas investigation
1949–1950	Congress passes Kerr bill exempting independent producers December 1949: Senate defeats Leland Olds' renomination to FPC	1949	FPC in congressional testimony opposes deregulation of independent producers

Year	Legislative / Political	Year	Regulatory / Judicial
1950	President Truman vetoes Kerr bill 1950 elections: Democratic majority narrows Republicans gain 28 House seats, 5 Senate seats	1950	FPC rescinds Order 139 Supreme Court decision in East Ohio case affirms FPC jurisdiction over local distributor
1952	Eisenhower elected president; Republicans win House and Senate majority	1951	Phillips decision: FPC disclaims authority over independent producer sales
1954	Congress amends NGA to specify distributor exemption Elections: Democrats regain narrow majority in Congress House and Senate Commerce committees continue to favor deregulation of producers by narrow margin Congressional leadership and Eisenhower administration support deregulation	1954	Pipelines allowed commodity prices for gas they produce (Panhandle case) Phillips decision by Supreme Court brings independent producers under NGA 6,047 applications for certificates filed by independent producers (June 1954–June 1955) Commission does not oppose amendment specifying exemption of intrastate distributors from FPC regulation
1955–1956	Congress passes Harris-Fulbright deregulation bill Controversy over oil company action leads to Eisenhower veto	1955	FPC supports Harris-Fulbright deregulation bill
		1956	Commission issues certificate for producer sale at record price for area after producers threaten not to sell to pipeline at lower price (Catco case)
1957	Milder deregulation bill dies as result of oil company indiscretion	1959	Catco decision by Supreme Court reverses commission decision to issue unconditional certificate
1958	Elections: Democrats gain 50 House, 15 Senate seats Commerce committees oppose deregulation	1960	Commission announces decision to set area (rather than individual) prices for producers; generally maintains existing price level
1960	Elections: Kennedy elected President; Democrats maintain congressional majority	1962	FPC requests, and Congress enacts, extension of its jurisdiction Commission prohibits escalation clauses in new producer contracts
1962	NGA amended to cover suspension of industrial sales price	1963	FPC announces intention to "hold the line" on producer prices Supreme Court upholds area price method

TABLE 17 (continued)

	Congressional-Presidential Action		Action by the Federal Power Commission (FPC)
Year	Action	Year	Action
1964	Elections: President Johnson wins by landslide; Democrats hold large House and Senate majorities Consumer-state majorities on House and Senate Commerce committees support wellhead price restraint	1965	Permian Basin area prices announced Producer prices rolled back; refunds ordered
1968	Elections: Republicans win White House with election of President Nixon, but Democrats maintain control of Congress	1968	Supreme Court upholds Permian decision
		1970	FPC initiates new Permian and southern Louisiana area investigations to determine if higher rates needed to assure interstate supplies; announces it will accept applications for new sales at above-ceiling rates for areas
1971	House IFC committee holds hearings on gas shortage and bill to exempt small producer contracts from FPC regulation and guarantee contract rates	1971–1972	Commission allows increases of 30 to 50 percent in area rates to provide incentives for exploration Over four thousand small independent producers exempted from rate and certificate requirements; only indirect price surveillance (through pipeline rates) to be exercised; consumers challenge new policy in federal courts
1973	Nixon administration proposes gradual deregulation Senate narrowly defeats Buckley amendment; Senate rejects Morris nomination to FPC Senate bill 2506, introduced by consumer state senators, proposes to deregulate small producers, extend major producer regulation to the intrastate market, and set a national cost-based gas price	1972	FPC inaugurates "optional pricing procedure" allowing new producer sales at above-ceiling rates with no refund obligations
		1973–1974	FPC authorizes short-term emergency sales at unregulated prices with pre-granted abandonment

Year		Year	
1974	S371, introduced by producer state representatives, calls for immediate deregulation President Ford supports deregulation	1974	Commission announces new nationwide gas price ceilings, increases new gas price to $.42 (later $.50) Supreme Court upholds FPC power to regulate small producers indirectly but requires that standards other than market price be used to assess reasonableness
1975	Senate Commerce Committee reports bill extending regulation to intrastate market, fixing prices, and requiring coal conversion; Senate floor passes Pearson-Bentsen gradual deregulation amendment instead	1975	Federal courts overturn FPC emergency sales authorizations; FPC backs administration decontrol proposals
1976	House passes Smith amendment (similar to Senate Commerce bill); no further action taken to reconcile House-Senate approaches	1976	New gas price ceiling raised to $1.42
1976	Elections: Carter elected; Democrats maintain large majority in Congress	1977	Federal Energy Regulatory Commission absorbs FPC functions. FERC announces "prudent operator" requirement; creates Office of Enforcement to end "diversions" from interstate market
1977–1978	Congress amends Natural Gas Act, extending regulation to intrastate market while gradually deregulating new gas		

almost three times the previous year's ceiling—was immediately labeled "de facto deregulation" by consumer representatives.[40] The new FPC prices were, nevertheless, upheld by the courts.[41]

In addition to relaxing regulations and setting a sharply higher ceiling for new gas sales, the FPC under Presidents Nixon and Ford displayed a very different attitude toward producer requests for price increases under existing contracts. As can be seen in Table 18, the Johnson commission during the 1960s had refused most producer requests (in terms of dollar volume) for increases. The Nixon-Ford commission, on the other hand, allowed almost all such requests. Price increases granted for the years 1971–1975 totalled over a billion dollars.

Predictably, the commission's arguments that these pricing decisions were necessary to assure adequate interstate supplies met a hostile reception among representatives of consumer areas. The consumer reaction in Congress, which grew more hostile with each increase in the price level, took three forms: first, consumers disputed the contention that there was, in fact, a shortage of natural gas; second, they attacked the commission's personnel and procedures; and finally, the consumer alliance developed its own legislative solution for the gas shortage. This legislative remedy was designed to severely constrict FPC discretion in natural gas pricing, and to secure new interstate supplies for residential, commercial, and essential industrial uses by abolishing the intrastate-interstate distinction and prohibiting the burning of natural gas in industrial and utility boilers.

The Gas Shortage: Real or Contrived?

Before the 1970s, the American Gas Association had constituted the only accessible source of information on the size of domestic natural gas reserves. The AGA compiled its reserve estimates on the basis of confidential data submitted by the producers. After the AGA shifted its position from opposition to support for deregulation, those estimates came to be viewed with suspicion by opponents of decontrol. In addition, of course, the data were submitted to the AGA by the producers themselves; even if the AGA compilations were accurate, the suspicion remained that producers were conspiring to conceal their supplies in order to convince Congress, the FPC, and the public that price increases were necessary to encourage exploration. Once the FPC announced its intention to reexamine area rates, there appeared to be further incentives for producers to withhold supplies in anticipation of higher prices.[42]

In 1973, the Antitrust and Monopoly Subcommittee of the Senate Judiciary Committee held hearings on the degree of concentration of ownership in the petroleum industry, and the effect of market power on fuel price and supply. Subcommittee Chairman Phillip Hart of Michigan suggested that the gas shortage might well be a "hoax." The Federal

TABLE 18   FPC Disposal of Producer Requests for Price Increases, 1964–1968 and 1971–1975

Year	Total Requests Disposed of	Disallowed or Withdrawn	Total Increases Requested	Increases Allowed	Disallowed or Withdrawn
1964	1,347	NA*	$ 30,091,862	$ 14,498,000	$15,593,862
1965	1,185	796	32,409,810	17,911,531	14,498,279
1966	1,524	1,046	40,590,715	21,986,466	18,604,249
1967	999	153	5,908,949	4,875,360	1,033,589
1968	479	138	5,201,270	2,295,842	2,905,428
1971	8,980	3,674	125,777,875	94,283,690	31,494,185
1972	6,895	4,128	198,558,000	185,369,143	13,198,857
1973	8,745	2,598	153,397,551	149,076,954	4,320,793
1974	8,138	1,063	262,805,654	255,260,596	7,545,058
1975	7,511	14	797,799,694	795,447,498	2,352,196

Source: Annual Reports of the Federal Power Commission.
*NA signifies not available.

Trade Commission, at Hart's request, undertook to analyze producer records; on the basis of reports from three companies, the commission told the subcommittee that AGA reserve estimates reflected significant underreporting by the producers.[43] Federal Power Commission Chairman John Nassikas, however, contended that the shortage was real, and that gas production was sufficiently competitive to preclude a producer conspiracy to manipulate price and supply. The FPC chairman produced evidence from an FPC survey of existing gas supplies that suggested that the AGA's estimates were, in fact, too optimistic. Nassikas also disputed the consumers' contention that there was an inordinately high concentration of ownership of gas reserves, pointing out that there was considerable fluctuation in the ranks of the largest natural gas producers from year to year, and that most major industries (including the automobile industry in Senator Hart's native state) were far more concentrated, yet had not been subjected to price regulation. At any rate, Nassikas argued, the most appropriate way to deal with oligopolistic market power, if it should appear, was through antitrust proceedings and not through expanded regulation.[44]

Consumer state representatives were unconvinced. "Is it any wonder," asked Senator Hart, "with all the signals government officials have been sending out since 1969 that producers would sit on production until these prices are fulfilled?"[45] The American Public Gas Association, representing municipally owned utilities, echoed the withholding charge. "It is an indisputable fact," the Association contended in 1973, "that there is plenty of gas in the ground in the United States to preclude any of the present shortage claims."[46]

If the shortage were, indeed, contrived by the producers, then regulation must be extended to compel deliveries where contracts were in effect, or to preclude opportunities to dispose of the withheld gas at a higher price. If, on the other hand, the shortage was real, then the case for extended regulation could be made on the basis that there were no major reserves left to be discovered. In this case, price increases would be futile. While some leading economists made forceful arguments for deregulation, there were other distinguished economists who opposed it. In 1974, Alfred Kahn, a member of the New York State Public Service Commission (responsible for overseeing local gas utilities), wrote the Senate Commerce Committee to reiterate the commission's "historic opposition" to deregulation and to set forth his own reasons for taking that position. Kahn argued that gas production was "inexorably declining," and, in view of the control of production by a small number of major oil companies and high demand for the product, decontrol would only serve to transfer "tens of billions of dollars" from consumers to producers without eliciting significantly greater supplies. He added,

In these circumstances . . . deregulation of gas will surely raise price gouging opportunities; the probable windfall to the industry is a price monstrously out of proportion to the benefits that deregulation might be expected to bring. I regard simple deregulation in these circumstances as totally unthinkable, and I cannot bring myself to believe that Congress will be willing to enact it.[47]

Other economists with careers tied to utility regulation concurred with Kahn's arguments. David Schwartz, a staff economist with the FPC's Office of Economics, disputed the official FPC contention that the structure of the gas producing industry was workably competitive. The gas shortage of the 1970s, he argued before the Senate Commerce Committee, was produced by the superimposition of monopolistic constraints on a declining supply, and not by the regulatory policies of the commission in the 1960s.[48] Philadelphia public utility consultant Charles Frazier provided similar testimony before the Senate Interior Committee, concluding that the shortage of natural gas demanded that regulation be nationalized to prevent the producer states from draining the dwindling supplies to fuel their own industries. An essential question that must be addressed by those seeking a solution to the gas shortage, Frazier argued, was the following: "What are the rights of the states where the gas is produced, in contradistinction to the large gas-consuming market which was induced to switch to gas twenty years ago (by those interested in disposing of Texas, Oklahoma, and Louisiana surpluses) but now finds itself increasingly 'high and dry'?"[49] Just as the original Natural Gas Act was designed to close a regulatory gap, regulation must now be perfected by bringing the intrastate market under national control so that a dwindling resource could be managed "to the greatest advantage of the whole economy."[50] The impulse to nationalization was buttressed by the utilitarian principle: the greatest good for the greatest number of Americans could not be achieved by allowing the producer states to evade price and allocation control within their own borders. Echoes from the nationalization debate of the 1930s began to sound again in the 1970s.

The Attack on the FPC

The Senate Judiciary Committee's investigation in 1973 was only the beginning of the consumer counteroffensive against the Federal Power Commission. In the ninety-third and ninety-fourth Congresses, the House and Senate Commerce committees held a number of hearings dealing with the gas shortage and alternative legislative and administrative solutions. During the course of these hearings, the Power Commission was castigated by urban, labor, and congressional opponents for raising gas prices and failing to compel deliveries to interstate pipelines. Other agencies were called upon to assist the consumers in their inves-

TABLE 19   RESIDENTIAL NATURAL GAS CONSUMPTION, BY REGION, 1975

Region	Number of Households Using Gas (thousands)	Percentage of Households Using Gas*	Quantity (million cubic feet)	Consumption per Household (thousand cubic feet)
East North Central	9,493	70	1,524,124	160
Middle Atlantic	7,594	60	729,424	96
Pacific	6,727	67	704,889	105
West South Central	4,698	68	457,005	97
South Atlantic	3,597	32	337,533	94
West North Central	3,587	52	538,308	150
Mountain	2,227	70	286,831	129
East South Central	1,967	45	205,020	104
New England	1,626	40	140,990	87

Source: Minerals Yearbook.
*1975 Census estimates are used for numbers of households.

tigations of FPC practices. In the Senate, the Federal Trade Commission had been asked to investigate reserve and concentration data. In the House, Commerce Oversight Subcommittee Chairman John Moss of California directed the General Accounting Office to conduct "a wide-ranging probe" of the FPC's operations, and the industry ties of its personnel.[51]

The Commerce Committee Democratic majorities saw the FPC's 1973–1976 pricing decisions as clear evidence that the commission had been captured by the regulated industry. In 1976, the House Oversight Subcommittee issued a report reviewing nine federal regulatory agencies, condemning the FPC as the worst of the lot (the two Texans on the subcommittee issued a lengthy statement contesting the majority's conclusions). The report cited a survey conducted by the Congressional Reference Service among lawyers, administrative law judges, and members of the United States Administrative Conference for evaluation of regulatory agency appointees. The FPC was viewed by the regulatory professional community as significantly more favorable to industry (and less so to consumers) than it had been during the 1963–1968 period.[52] Representative Moss suggested that ownership of energy company stock by FTC personnel might be responsible for some of the agency's pro-industry bias, and warned that demonstrated conflicts of interest would invite criminal prosecution.[53]

Consumer area congressmen involved themselves directly in judicial challenges of the FPC's pricing policies. In 1972 Senators Humphrey, Mondale, and Proxmire and Representatives Moss, Aspin, Fraser, Reid, and (George) Brown joined the American Public Gas Association, the Consumer Federation, and the National League of Cities in challenging the FPC's emergency sales procedures in federal court. In 1974, House Commerce Democrats John Moss and Torbert MacDonald led court challenges of other commission rulings.

The commission's 1976 decision to raise the new gas ceiling price to $1.42 provoked outrage on the part of consumer area representatives. The pro-regulation majorities on both commerce committees conducted hearings that provided a forum for scathing criticism of the commission's actions, and a number of senators and representatives joined in the judicial appeals of the commission's orders establishing the new rates.[54] Although the federal courts upheld the Commission, citing "the national supply emergency" and the need for extraordinary steps to increase interstate gas supplies, the commerce committee outcry appeared to induce some backtracking by the commission: a few months later the FPC agreed to a rehearing and reduced the ceilings for "older" categories of "new" gas.[55] In the same year, the commission finally bowed to pressures emanating from the House Oversight Subcommittee and northeastern distributors, and commenced actions designed to compel the Gulf Oil Corporation to meet its gas delivery obligations to Texas Eastern Transmission Corporation.[56] These were, however, very modest victories for the consumer forces. It was clear that reorientation of the FPC's natural gas policy would require action more direct than lawsuits, hearings, and investigations.[57]

One of the direct alternatives available to the consumer alliance in the Senate was to exercise its veto power over commission staffing. In 1949, the Senate, on recommendation of its commerce committee, had rejected the nomination of Leland Olds because of his pro-regulation philosophy. In 1973, the Senate again exercised its veto—this time defeating a Nixon nominee on the basis of his alleged bias toward producers.

There were two vacancies on the FPC in 1973. The continuing members of the commission included one Johnson holdover who had supported the recent price increases and two Nixon appointees: Chairman Nassikas, a New England Republican who had reluctantly come to support deregulation after it was strongly endorsed by Presidents Ford and Nixon, and Rush Moody, a Texan appointed in 1971 who consistently argued for higher federal price ceilings. With the commission majority already perceived as pro-industry, consumer area representatives were wary of cementing the bias. President Nixon's post-embargo nominations were therefore closely scrutinized by consumer state senators. It became impossible to secure the appointment to the FPC of anyone connected to the petroleum industry. Late in 1973, the president sent the Senate his nomination of San Francisco attorney Robert Morris to fill one of the vacancies on the FPC. Although Morris, in his confirmation hearings before the Commerce Committee, expressed opposition to deregulation, the fact that he had represented various oil and gas companies in his legal practice was seen as evidence of a pro-producer bias.[58] With Commerce Committee Chairman Warren Magnuson leading the opposition, Morris' nomination was defeated by a vote of fifty-one to forty-two.[59]

Economic ties and state of residence were considered better cues to the voting behavior of prospective commissioners than either party or ideology. In the same year that Morris' nomination was defeated, the Senate confirmed the appointment of conservative Republican William L. Springer. Cleveland Democratic Representative Charles Vanik testified in the Senate against the Morris appointment, and in favor of the former Illinois congressman. Vanik argued that Springer came from "consumer country," whereas lawyers usually remained loyal to their clients.[60] Senate Commerce Chairman Warren Magnuson "put the White House on notice" in 1973 that his committee "would not look favorably on any FPC nominees who opposed congressional policy on the deregulation of natural gas prices." In the face of congressional hostility, Commissioner Rush

Moody resigned in 1975, saying that he found it difficult to comply with that policy.[61]

Toward a New Natural Gas Act: The Consumer Alternative

The price increases instituted by the FTC in the mid-1970s had slackened some of the producers' demand for statutory revision. The commission's action, however, had the opposite effect on the consumer forces. A highly discretionary statute had served well during the years when the consumer interest dominated both Congress and the presidency. During the 1950s, when the consumer interest was in the minority, the federal courts had overruled Republican and producer opposition with an interpretation of the statute that upheld the consumer interest. Without its judicial and presidential mainstays, however, consumers could not depend on a favorable interpretation of the ambiguous mandate of the Natural Gas Act. Not only did the Republican-dominated commission appear determined to raise the regulated interstate price to a level approaching that of the unregulated intrastate market, but the Supreme Court, with four new Republican appointees, was inclined to uphold the commission's decisions. A discretionary statute was no longer in the consumer interest.

Nor did it serve that interest to allow dual political sovereignties to divide the commerce in natural gas. The intrastate exemption was innocuous in the 1940s and 1950s, when producer state economies were too underdeveloped to threaten interstate supplies. The situation in the 1970s had clearly changed. Interstate household and industrial consumers were deprived of gas when producers "diverted" their supplies to the more lucrative intrastate markets. The federal distinction must be erased in a new Natural Gas Act if residents of the nonproducing states were to have any realistic chance of securing additional supplies.

Finally, a new statute was needed to prevent gas needed for residential and essential industrial uses from being squandered in utility and industrial boilers—particularly in the producer states where such usage was concentrated. Existing authority was inadequate to compel large-scale coal conversion. The FPC had assumed allocation authority during periods of shortage, and used this authority to direct scarce gas supplies away from utility and industrial boilers toward household, agricultural, and "essential" industrial uses. This end-use authority existed, however, only for interstate gas movements. The Federal Energy Administration had limited authority, extended by the EPCA in 1975, to order conversion to coal by large utility and industrial power plants, but there were numerous grounds on which exemptions could be granted; relatively few conversion orders actually were issued by the FEA under President Ford.

If gas prices were to be held down by federal regulation, mandatory coal conversion was necessary to achieve the redistribution of gas supplies from producer state industries to consumer state households.

An additional advantage of mandatory conversion was that it provided the basis for securing the votes of coal area representatives for gas price control proposals. Without the packaging of these two issues, some coal state congressmen might have been tempted to support deregulation—the major alternative for improving the competitive position of coal in the East, and, in addition, making coal use attractive to the growing south-western states.

There were, then, three essential components for statutory revision from the consumers' point of view. Michigan Senator Phillip Hart summarized these components in a 1974 letter to the *Washington Post*. First of all, he wrote, Congress itself must establish a set of prices for natural gas, ending the FPC's discretion over prices, and sending a clear signal to producers that "regulation is here to stay" and that withholding of reserves, therefore, is futile. Second, "the Congress should expand the FPC's authority to prohibit wasteful uses of natural gas—clearing supplies for uses that are most in the public interest." Third, "Congress should bring intrastate sales of natural gas under FPC regulation."[62] A bill embodying these three components was constructed in the Senate Commerce Committee between 1973 and 1975. The consumer package was defeated in the Senate by an alternative deregulation proposal but narrowly passed the House in 1976 and resurfaced—as the Carter administration's energy program—in 1977.

In 1973 and 1974, the Senate Commerce Committee held hearings on a bill (S 2506) that contained only two of the three components. Bill S 2506, labeled "The Consumer Energy Act," was sponsored by Commerce Committee members Adlai Stevenson of Illinois, Phillip Hart of Michigan, Hubert Humphrey of Minnesota, John Pastore of Rhode Island, and Frank Moss of Utah.[63] In its two principal features, the bill extended federal price controls to producer-state sales and established a national price range (from forty to sixty cents per mcf) within which the FPC must set new cost-based price ceilings. S 2506 exempted small producers from the price ceilings for a period of five years. Subsequent titles were added that applied price controls to oil (at this point new oil prices were not yet regulated), and created a federal corporation to drill for oil and gas on public lands. The bill was adamantly opposed by the producer states, and died in committee. Its pricing provisions apparently served as a cue to the FPC, however: during the course of the hearings the FPC raised the new national gas rate to fifty cents, squarely in the middle of the range set by S 2506. The FPC, however, opposed the bill's statutory price ceilings, along with its requirements for cost-based rate determinations and intrastate regulation.

In 1975, Senate Commerce Committee staff members developed a new version entitled "The Natural Gas Production and Conservation Act of 1975," introduced as S 692 by Chairman Warren Magnuson and Senator Ernest Hollings of South Carolina.[64] Bill S 692 packaged the three components—a statutory price range (now from forty to seventy-five cents), intrastate regulation, and a strong coal conversion requirement—and with this combination won a narrow victory on the Commerce Committee. A consumer–coal state majority of ten members reported the bill over the objections of a producer state and Republican minority.[65] In its original draft, S 692 had replaced the small producer exemption of the earlier Stevenson bill (S 2506) with a provision allowing small producers to charge up to 50 percent more than the ceiling for large producers. The bill was amended in committee, however, to exempt from price regulation the small producers not affiliated with major oil companies—a category which, it was estimated, accounted for about 10 percent of domestic production.

Before its supporters could bring S 692 to the floor, producer state Senators Pearson and Bentsen proposed their deregulation alternative as an amendment to a short-term "gas emergency" bill. In a last-ditch attempt to defeat the Pearson-Bentsen amendment, Senators Stevenson, Hollings, and Moss proposed an alternative to the decontrol proposal which would have raised the regulated price ceiling to $1.30 and—in a move probably designed to win support in the South—applied controls to oil, as well. The deregulation alliance held, however, and the Stevenson amendment failed on a forty-five to fifty-five vote. The Pearson-Bentsen substitute then passed the Senate and the consumer bill died on the calendar.[66]

Encouraged by the Senate vote, decontrol advocates in the House marshaled their forces. The House Commerce Committee reported an emergency measure (HR 9464) in December of 1975. Texas Democratic Representative Robert Krueger almost succeeded in organizing a majority coalition on the committee in favor of a seven-year "trial deregulation" of new gas. His proposal was defeated by a tie vote (twenty to twenty). As Table 20 shows, the deregulation alliance on the House Committee consisted of eleven of thirteen Republicans, and nine of twenty-eight Democrats. Most of the Democrats favoring deregulation represented districts that not only had low gas consumption, but were experiencing severe curtailments as a result of the interstate gas shortage. Committee members from areas with large (60 percent or more) household gas consumption ratios overwhelmingly opposed deregulation in both parties.

After rejection of the deregulation proposal, the House Commerce Committee reported HR 9464. In February of 1976, over the strong objections of ranking Commerce Committee Democrats, Representative

TABLE 20   HOUSE COMMITTEE ON INTERSTATE AND FOREIGN COMMERCE:
CONSTITUENCY CHARACTERISTICS AND POSITIONS ON
NATURAL GAS REGULATION, 1976

Members

Democrats

Gas Consumption Percentage in District	Name	State	Vote			
			Smith Amendment*		Deregulation†	
			In Favor	Opposed	In Favor	Opposed
(Coal)	Staggers	W.Va.	+			−
61	MacDonald	Mass.	+			−
49	Moss	Calif.	+			−
70	Dingell	Mich.	+			−
13	Rogers	Fla.	+			−
68	VanDeerlin	Calif.	+			−
39	Rooney	Pa.		−	+	
89	Murphy	N.Y.		−	+	
5	Satterfield	N.C.		−	+	
8	Adams	Wash.	+			−
31	Stuckey	Ga.	+			−
(Producer)	Eckhardt	Tex.	+			−
10	Preyer	N.C.		−	+	
60	Symington	Mo.	+			−
61	Carney	Ohio	+			−
84	Metcalf	Ill.	+			−
29	Byron	Md.		−	+	
94	Scheuer	N.Y.	+			−
75	Ottinger	N.Y.	+			−
83	Waxman	Calif.	+			−
(Producer)	Krueger	Tex.		−	+	
34	Wirth	Colo.	+			−
34	Sharp	Ind.	+			−
70	Brodhead	Mich.	+			−
6	Hefner	N.C.		−	+	
64	Florio	N.J.	+			−
31	Moffett	Conn.	+			−
26	Santini	Nev.		−	+	
Total votes			20	8	8	20
Total, high gas consumption states (≥60 percent)					1	11
Total, low gas consumption states (<40 percent)					7	5

*Smith amendment (to Krueger proposal) extending regulation to intrastate market and mandating coal conversion.
†Brown motion to recommit and report back Krueger decontrol proposal.

(in order of seniority)

Gas Consumption Percentage in District	Name	State	Republicans Vote			
			Smith Amendment		Deregulation	
			In Favor	Opposed	In Favor	Opposed
54	Devine	Ohio		−	+	
11	Broyhill	N.C.		−	+	
17	Carter	Ky.		−	+	
37	Brown	Ohio		−	+	
(Producer)	Skubitz	Kans.		−	+	
(Producer)	Collins	Tex.		−	+	
10	Frey	Fla.		−	+	
50	McCollister	Nebr.		−	+	
58	Lent	N.Y.		−	+	
76	Heinz	Pa.		−		−
58	Madigan	Ill.		−	+	
83	Moorhead	Calif.		−	+	
85	Rinaldo	N.J.	+			−
	(1 vacancy)					
Total votes			1	12	11	2
Total, high gas consumption districts					1	2
Total, low gas consumption districts					4	0

Krueger persuaded the Rules Committee to report a rule that provided for consideration of his deregulation proposal during floor debate.[67] Krueger's strategy was to offer a substitute for HR 9464 which combined the short-term emergency measure (Title I) with deregulation of new gas (Title II), as the Pearson-Bentsen substitute had done in the Senate.[68] Fearing that the Krueger proposal would prevail on the floor, Commerce Chairman Harley Staggers of West Virginia and Energy and Power Subcommittee Chairman John Dingell of Michigan quickly put together an alternative energy package that could be offered as an amendment to the Krueger substitute. Their proposal closely resembled the unsuccessful Senate Commerce Committee bill, S 692.

Iowa Representative Neal Smith offered the consumer alternative on the floor.[69] It directed the FPC to set a national ceiling price for new gas, based on average costs. The new ceiling would apply to both intrastate and interstate sales by large producers (defined as those with production of over one hundred billion cubic feet a year, a category estimated to include twenty-five to thirty producers responsible for about 75 percent of all gas production). Finally, the Smith amendment contained a strong coal conversion requirement. Existing statutes, including the conversion provision of the 1975 EPCA, granted temporary authority to the Federal Energy Administration to order power plant conversion to other fuels if certain conditions were met (for example, the plant had facilities for burning other fuels, and those fuels were readily available at a price not significantly higher than natural gas). The Smith proposal, on the other hand, put the burden of proof on the gas user to show why he should not be required to convert, and made conversion mandatory for both power plants and other boiler fuel users of natural gas. Enforcement of the expanded conversion authority was given to the FPC, a regulatory agency closer to Congress than the executive-oriented Federal Energy Administration.[70]

The Smith amendment passed the House by a four-vote margin (205 to 201).[71] It was overwhelmingly supported by representatives of coal-producing and urban consumer areas, and opposed with near unanimity in the producer states. After passage of the consumer proposal, Representative Clarence Brown of Ohio moved to recommit the bill with instructions to substitute in its place the original Krueger deregulation amendment (see Figure 12). The vote on the Brown motion provided the first direct test of House support for deregulation since 1955. Table 21 compares the two deregulation votes, and analyzes voting patterns by party and constituency interests.

For this table, household gas service ratios for congressional districts were compiled from county-level data in the 1950 and 1970 Census of Housing.[72] As the table shows, representatives from urban areas with the

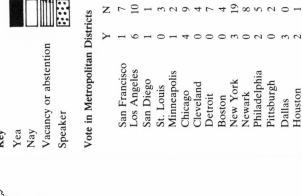

Key

Yea
Nay
Vacancy or abstention
Speaker

Vote in Metropolitan Districts

	Y	N
San Francisco	1	7
Los Angeles	6	10
San Diego	1	1
St. Louis	0	3
Minneapolis	1	2
Chicago	4	9
Cleveland	0	4
Detroit	0	7
Boston	0	4
New York	3	19
Newark	0	8
Philadelphia	2	5
Pittsburgh	0	2
Dallas	3	0
Houston	2	1

FIGURE 12

Support for Deregulation in the House of Representatives, 1976*

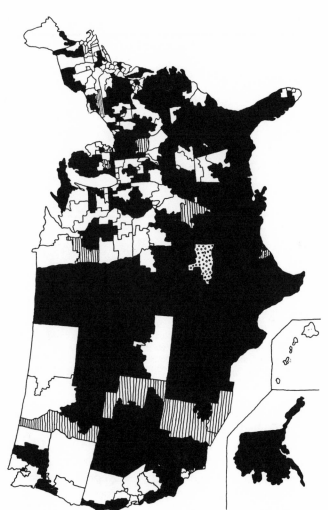

*Vote on Brown motion (see text)

160 · *The Politics of Scarcity*

TABLE 21 ANALYSIS OF SUPPORT FOR DEREGULATION OF NATURAL GAS
IN THE HOUSE OF REPRESENTATIVES, 1955 AND 1976

	Year			
	1955*		1976†	
Type of Constituency	Percentage of Members Supporting Deregulation	Number of Members	Percentage of Members Supporting Deregulation	Number of Members
Consumer districts‡	34.1	(164)	28.7	(167)
Democrats				
75.1–100	7.7	(52)	3.8	(53)
50.1–75.0	24.3	(37)	7.6	(66)
Republicans				
75.1–100	51.6	(31)	80.0	(10)
50.1–75.0	61.4	(44)	86.8	(38)
Coal districts§	28.6	(14)	41.7	(12)
Democrats	27.3	(11)	30.0	(10)
Republicans	33.3	(3)	100.0	(2)
Producer districts‖	98.5	(50)	93.3	(45)
Democrats	97.6	(41)	91.2	(34)
Republicans	100.0	(9)	100.0	(11)
Spectator districts	54.1	(196)	57.1	(196)
Democrats				
25.1–50	25.0	(28)	32.4	(68)
0 –25.0	42.6	(61)	45.3	(53)
Republicans				
25.1–50.0	73.0	(63)	85.7	(49)
0 –25.0	61.4	(44)	92.3	(26)

*Harris bill.
†Brown proposal to recommit Smith substitute and report back the Krueger deregulation substitute.
‡Figures indicate the percentage of households in the district using natural gas (for cooking).
§Major coal producing districts were identified on the basis of Bureau of Mines production and employment figures for counties. For 1955 they are: Alabama 9; Illinois 25; Kentucky 2, 7, and 8; Ohio 18; Pennsylvania 11, 12, 22, and 26; Virginia 9; and West Virginia 3, 5, and 6. For 1976, the major coal districts are: Illinois 24; Kentucky 1, 5, and 7; Ohio 18; Pennsylvania 12 and 22; Virginia 9; and all four West Virginia districts.
‖This category includes all congressional districts in Texas, Louisiana, Oklahoma, Kansas, New Mexico, Wyoming, and Alaska in 1976; in 1955, Mississippi replaces Alaska.

largest concentrations of residential gas consumers were overwhelmingly opposed to deregulation in 1976. In the 167 districts where more than half the households had gas service, over 70 percent opposed the Brown motion; in districts with consumption levels of from 75 to 100 percent, over 80 percent opposed deregulation. There was, however, great variation by political party. The relatively few Republicans who represented high-consumption districts nevertheless supported the Brown motion, whereas Democrats from such districts opposed it with near unanimity.

To some extent, these apparent partisan differences may be the result of underlying differences in constituency interest that gas consumption data cannot capture. Some Republican districts in metropolitan areas may actually have had lower gas consumption ratios, but since the available data are for counties, all congressional districts within a single county were assigned the same consumption ratio.

On the whole, however, partisan and constituency interests coincide. Most high-consumption districts are represented by Democrats; in fact, the tendency of consumer districts to elect Democrats increased between 1955 and 1976. Not only do Republican districts tend to have higher income levels (and thus less interest in controlling utility rates), but the majority of Republican congressmen represent spectator areas where only a minority of households have gas service.[73]

Natural gas shortages and oil price increases in the 1970s, together with the widespread belief that regulation had contributed to the nation's energy woes, apparently increased support for deregulation among Republicans from high-consumption districts, and among coal and spectator districts of both parties. In high-consumption urban areas represented by Democrats, however, opposition to deregulation hardened. It is among this latter group of congressmen, representing older urban industrial areas hard hit by the recession of the mid-1970s, that support for the Smith amendment was concentrated. For these congressmen, the answer to the energy crisis was to expand, not contract, the federal regulatory system.

The producer areas opposed this new consumer proposal with even greater force than they had directed against the existing system. Gas producers themselves resisted the extension of controls to the intrastate market because federal regulation would bring not only lower prices than those currently available in the producer states but also the additional costs—reporting, litigation, service requirements, and contract delays—that utility regulation entailed. Even if the smallest producers were exempted, the extension of price controls over the great majority of gas production would depress the general price level and discourage joint exploration efforts. From the point of view of gas *users* in the producer states, the existing system had several advantages over the statutory revision proposed by the Smith and similar proposals. The superiority of the unregulated intrastate market to producers had resulted in an abundance of intrastate gas that not only attracted industry (thus contributing to the development of robust producer state economies), but also provided a considerable advantage in household utility rates, as compared to the national average.[74] Complete deregulation would have erased the supply advantages for producer state residents, but would, on the other hand, have enriched their state treasuries with additional severance tax and royalty income. That development, in turn, might have lessened the tax burden and subsidized education and other social services in the producer states.

The coal conversion feature of the consumer alternative was clearly disadvantageous to the producer states. Within those states, the use of natural gas as a boiler fuel had already begun to taper off as a result of price increases, and the Texas Railroad Commission had encouraged the shift to other fuels in the interest of conservation. The consumer alternative, however, not only proposed an abrupt and economically disruptive abandonment of the native fuel, but did so in the interest of redistributing the available supply of gas to households and industries in other regions. In the view of the Texas Railroad Commission, producer state citizens had subsidized exploration by paying higher gas prices for years. To transfer the resulting supply of gas to states that had long insisted on price control and at the same time to compel the producer states to forego use of a local resource in favor of fuels produced at greater cost in other regions seemed a great injustice.[75]

Louisiana Conservation Commission Chairman Ray Sutton, testifying against the price control–coal conversion bill reported by the Senate Commerce Committee in 1975, pointed out that Louisiana had no coal and lacked transportation facilities to import it. "This dialogue," Sutton offered, "is the product of the eternal war between the haves and the have-nots." "It is not difficult to understand," he added, "why the nation is becoming regionally polarized over the energy policy being debated and formulated here in the nation's capital . . . when someone would propose that we not only give up our indigenous resource, in return for someone else's dirty coal, when the states which produce it would prefer not to consume it themselves, and then be told that they cannot pay a price for [our] indigenous commodity which [we] feel to be fair and reasonable."[76]

The conversion issue had provoked bitter opposition among producer state representatives during debate on the Energy Policy and Conservation Act in 1975. The version of EPCA that passed the House (HR 7014) in 1975 combined oil price controls with a provision for government-guaranteed loans to new underground coal mines, and a greatly expanded FEA authority to issue orders prohibiting any power plant from burning natural gas if "the order will result in making natural gas available to users who will not use it as a fuel for the production of steam." Representative Krueger tried to persuade the House to delete the conversion section during floor debate on EPCA:

> Take a State such as my own home State, Texas. There, two-thirds of the energy in the entire State is provided by natural gas. Ninety-five percent of the electricity is provided by natural gas. This two-thirds of

the total energy of the State being provided by natural gas compares, for example, with one-third of the energy in the United States generally being provided by natural gas. There is no question that over a period of time this State, like most others, will turn away from the use of natural gas as boiler fuel and go to other fuels. But this will come inevitably through the course of economic events as natural gas is over a period of time allowed to rise in price to its proper market level.

However, to give the power to mandate conversion, and prohibit the use of natural gas is really, I think, a gross misuse of Federal authority. . . .

Mr. Chairman, the capital cost of simply changing over of equipment from the burning of natural gas to other fuels would be, it has been estimated, some $18 billion in one State alone. This is not the kind of power which we on some easy afternoon here should suddenly grant to a single administrator. This involves the entire fate of a whole State and its industrial complex and its residential users.[77]

Houston Representative Bob Eckhardt, one of the few producer state representatives to support oil and gas price controls, joined Krueger in supporting deletion. The conversion requirement, Eckhardt maintained, could "shut down the entire industrial economy of my area and my state."[78] The House upheld the conversion authority, over the unanimous opposition of representatives from the major gas-producing states. However, the Senate version of EPCA (S 622) contained no such provision; the bill that emerged from conference merely extended the expiration date for the existing, exemption-ridden FEA conversion authority, and broadened somewhat the category of fuel users to which it applied.

The House votes on EPCA and the Smith proposal demonstrated the potential for a majority coalition of consumer and coal area representatives. A consumer-coal alliance faced different prospects for success in the House and the Senate, however. The composition and leadership of the House Commerce Committee favored such an alliance, and the Smith vote demonstrated that it could win, albeit by an extremely narrow margin. In the Senate, on the other hand, the intensity of producer opposition to a strong coal conversion measure (such as that represented by the House version of EPCA or the Smith amendment) and the basis of representation in the chamber made it unlikely that the consumer alternative on natural gas could muster a majority. Consumer and eastern coal states were relatively underrepresented in the Senate, while the plains and mountain states were overrepresented.[79]

The opposition of the plains and mountain states to deregulation derived from both partisan allegiance and political economy. In these twelve states, the Republican party controlled a majority of House seats and half the Senate seats. With prospering, extraction-based economies, the plains and mountain states were less affected by the urban ills and unemployment that tend to produce a greater demand for positive government. In addition, states whose economies were dependent on agriculture and mineral production could be expected to have little sympathy for the efforts of consumer areas to control the price levels of such resources. Kansas and New Mexico were major natural gas producers; Colorado contained extensive oil and coal reserves; Utah and Montana had extensive coal deposits; and Wyoming was a major producer of all three fuels in 1975.

For several reasons, the western coal states, which accounted for about a sixth of United States coal production in the mid-1970s, often took different positions on energy regulation issues than did eastern coal states. Not only were their partisan allegiances different, but eastern and western coal producers had competitive interests on such issues as scrubbing requirements (which reduce the competitive advantage of low-sulfur western coal), and reclamation regulations (including water usage).[80] In addition, the western states increasingly resented federal control of large portions of the land within their borders. Federal ownership of western lands meant control by Washington (and, ultimately, by the more populous eastern portion of the country) of such sensitive local issues as water rights, Indian land claims, and, of course, agriculture, forestry, and mineral extraction on the public domain.[81] In short, the political economy of the West increasingly brought it into alliance with other regions protesting the extent of federal economic regulation. Since the Senate overrepresented these regions, in comparison with the population-based membership of the House, consumer-sponsored proposals for the extension of federal controls over energy production generated less enthusiasm in the upper chamber.[82]

The House and Senate were spared the difficult task of trying to reconcile the Smith and Pearson-Bentsen proposals. Since the winter of 1975–1976 was milder than anticipated, gas shortages were considerably less severe than the FPC had predicted, and demand for an emergency bill evaporated. When, in July of 1976, the Federal Power Commission raised the interstate price of gas to $1.42, demand for a deregulation bill also abated. The two very different natural gas proposals, therefore, were never taken to conference. The choice between the alternatives they represented—one favored by the producer, plains, and mountain states, along with much of the South; the other, by northern cities and Appalachian coal districts—would lie with the president elected in 1976.

7 | New Policies, Old Conflicts

While former Democratic presidents had tailored their natural gas policies to the preferences of consumer regions and their commerce committee spokesmen, during the 1976 campaign candidate Jimmy Carter seemed to reverse that alignment by indicating that he supported deregulation.[1] Probably as a result of that position, he carried Texas and Louisiana. Shortly after the election, however, it became evident that the Carter administration's natural gas policy would return to the pattern of its Democratic predecessors. In the polarized politics of natural gas, President Carter was to ally himself with the interests of the northern metropolitan core of his party. On this issue, as on a variety of others, it was virtually impossible to construct a policy which would win support from both producer and gas-deficit, high-consumption areas.[2] By aligning administration policy with the urban consumer interests, a Democratic president cast his lot with traditional, reliable partisans whose electoral votes could give the incumbent president a second term.

The new administration's energy policy also tilted toward eastern coal interests. The tenuous consumer energy coalition in the House had been put together on the basis of a price control–coal conversion package that won overwhelming support in the Appalachian coal districts. In view of the fact that his Republican opponent had swept the western energy-producing states while he had carried the eastern coal and metropolitan consumer areas, it was logical that President Carter would opt for the consumer-coal package favored by the House Democratic majority rather than the Senate's deregulation alternative.

Eastern coal districts had been profoundly dissatisfied with the Nixon-Ford administration's coal policies, which favored both western and imported coal and nuclear power.[3] During the 1976 campaign, Carter appeared sympathetic to these complaints. He issued a position paper in which he promised to strongly encourage coal production and observed that energy policies which "shift job opportunities away from the industrial East and Midwest to the agricultural regions of the West" were not "in the best interests of the country."[4] On the basis of the perceived distinctions between the two candidates, coupled with the traditional Democratic leanings of the region, the major Appalachian coal districts supported Carter with a median 56 percent of the vote in 1976.

Indications of the Carter administration strategy on natural gas and coal came early in 1977, as the president:

• moved to reorganize an FPC dominated by recent Republican appointments;
• appointed to the commission chair a former House Commerce Committee staff director who had been closely linked to Energy and Power Subcommittee Chairman John Dingell;
• relied on the majority staff of the House and Senate Commerce committees in the development and management of his energy program;
• submitted to Congress new energy legislation modeled on the 1975–76 consumer alternative supported by Commerce Committee Democratic majorities; and
• pledged to promote a two-thirds increase in coal production by 1985, but insisted that all coal burning units employ the "best available control technology" to reduce sulfur emissions—a policy which greatly diminished the advantage of low-sulfur western coal.[5]

The president proposed the creation of a new Department of Energy which would absorb the functions of the FPC, Federal Energy Administration, and Energy Research and Development Administration, as well as energy programs administered by other departments. The FPC was to be abolished and its functions assigned to an Energy Regulatory Administration in the new department. The Secretary of Energy would have authority to review gas pricing and service decisions. Although Congress enacted most of these proposals, it voted to maintain an independent status for the FPC (renamed the Federal Energy Regulatory Commission). The new structure, however, did bring the commission into a much closer relationship with the administration by including the DOE secretary in natural gas policy deliberations. Congressional willingness to accept this degree of presidential control over an "independent" regulatory agency probably reflected the majority's disapproval of the Republican commission's pricing decisions, and impatience to reverse commission policy without waiting for expiration of the current members' terms. The terms of office of three Nixon-Ford commissioners would not have expired until mid-1979 or later, but for the shortening of tenure on the newly constituted Federal Energy Regulatory Commission (FERC) to four years from the five legislated for the FPC.[6]

Congress has traditionally been a major source of pressure in the regulatory appointments process, the president playing a less active role.[7] However, to the extent that recruitment to the agencies reflects the policy preferences of electoral constituencies common to both the president and congressional majority, such appointments are difficult to attribute to either predominantly presidential or congressional initiative. Shortly after his election, Carter selected House Commerce Committee staff members Charles Curtis and Robert Nordhaus and Senate Commerce Committee aide S. David Freeman to formulate an energy program on the White House transition staff. When the first vacancy occurred on the FERC, Curtis was appointed chairman. Freeman was designated to head the president's White House Energy Office, and a third member of Representative Dingell's Interstate and Foreign Commerce Committee (IFC) staff became an aide to Secretary of Energy James Schlesinger. Other Commerce Committee staff members also participated actively in the drafting of the administration's final natural gas policy proposals. This pattern of recruitment suggests extensive influence on the president's energy program by pro-regulation Commerce Committee Democrats. However, since the committee majority and the president both shared the urban Democratic constituency, this cross-fertilization cannot be characterized as congressional dominance. Rather, it simply reflects a common, electorally generated policy preference.

The president's other FERC and DOE appointments revealed a preference for persons with prior experience in regulation over persons associated with private industry. Most top policy-making positions went to individuals with prior service on state and federal energy regulatory agencies, and in Senate confirmation hearings nominees went to great lengths to disclaim any past association with, or sympathy for, oil and gas producers.[8]

The Carter Energy Program

The basic principles of the administration's energy proposals can be traced to previous legislation favored by the commerce committees—particularly the Smith amendment passed by the House in 1976, and the Natural Gas Production and Conservation bill considered by Senator Adlai Stevenson's Oil and Gas Subcommittee in the Ninety-fourth Congress. The fundamental assumption of both proposals was that, given severe physical limitations on the available supplies of oil and gas, no degree of price increase could elicit substantially greater production.[9] As a result of the irreversible decline in proven reserves, government policy must emphasize conservation and end-use control. In order to conserve rapidly diminishing oil and natural gas supplies for use by households, essential industrial uses, and boilers in areas unable to burn coal because of air pollution problems, the administration proposed "a strong regulatory program that would prohibit all new utility and industrial boilers from burning oil or gas . . . except under extraordinary conditions," and a significant diminution of oil and gas use in existing facilities.[10] Together with abolition of the intrastate-interstate distinction, conversion require- ments would end the existing "maldistribution" of domestic fuel re- sources. Although new and harder-to-find gas and oil resources would be permitted a price increase to stimulate production, the Carter plan emphasized that cost-based pricing must be maintained in order to pre- vent *"an inequitable transfer of income from the American people to the producers, whose profits* [if controls were removed] *would be excessive and would bear little relation to actual economic contribution."*[11]

Previous consumer-backed proposals had urged limitations on FPC pricing authority in order to prevent price increases of the degree im- plemented during the Nixon and Ford years. The Carter proposals went beyond earlier measures in specifying an elaborate pricing format in which each of seventeen specified categories of gas carried a fixed price ceiling and escalation formula. The national price ceiling for new gas, whether sold to intrastate or interstate pipelines, would be lifted from $1.45 (the price to which interstate gas had been allowed to rise under the Ford commission) to $1.75, with subsequent increases tied to the price of controlled domestic crude oil.[12] The administration also adopted a much more restricted definition of "new" gas. Rather than define this category by contract date, as had been done in the past, the higher incentive price would be limited to "truly new discoveries" coming at least two and one-half miles from, or one thousand feet below, an existing well.[13] The FPC would retain some discretion over flowing gas prices under renegoti- ated interstate contracts, provided that they be set no higher than $1.42 mcf. Until contract expiration, interstate gas prices would only be allowed to rise with inflation. The burden of the more expensive new gas price was to be borne disproportionately by "low priority" industrial users (through incremental pricing), thus drawing out the impact of price increases for residential consumers while discouraging industrial con- sumption.

In order to further encourage conservation and coal use, oil and gas user taxes were to be levied even on plants unable to convert to coal. The price of oil would also be increased by the imposition of a crude oil "equalization" tax (to raise the domestic price to that of imported oil without augmenting the profits of the petroleum companies). The pro- ceeds of the tax would be used for rebates to consumers and "fuel assistance payments" to welfare recipients and railroad retirees.[14]

In February, before the administration plan was submitted, Congress hurriedly passed an emergency gas bill allowing interstate pipelines to purchase gas at unregulated prices, in order to forestall shortages during an extremely cold winter. Deregulation supporters were persuaded to withhold their long-term proposals until the Carter energy plan was under consideration.

The administration's energy proposals were sent to Congress in late April. The major components were reviewed by two committees in the House (IFC and Ways and Means) and Senate (Finance and a new Energy and Natural Resources Committee that had assumed oil and gas regulatory jurisdiction) and a number of former members from the Commerce Committee.[15] Altogether, a total of five standing committees dealt with the various sections of the energy package in the House.[16]

During committee hearings there were some complaints from consumer groups about the proposed "new gas" price increase to $1.75.[17] Most of the objections, however, came from producer state congressmen, industrial users, economists, and utility groups. The producers disputed the administration's scarcity and elasticity assumptions. They argued that at least another forty years' supply remained to be discovered, and that the price increases experienced in the intrastate markets in the 1970s had dramatically increased exploration.[18] The administration plan, it was argued, would simply extend the failure of interstate regulation to the intrastate market,[19] destroy incentives for exploration, and severely penalize the producer states, with regard to both gas pricing and coal conversion requirements. Where the "new gas" definition under previous FPC rulings had relied on contract dates, the more stringent definition in the Carter bill would allow very little production to draw the ceiling price. According to Representative Hinson Moore of Louisiana, 95 percent of newly drilled gas wells in Louisiana would be "old" under the administration's definition because they were not sufficiently distant from or deeper than pre-existing wells.[20]

Passage in the House

The producers countered with a proposal for immediate deregulation of new gas (defined as gas first sold to interstate pipelines on or after January 1, 1977). The deregulation bill attracted seventy-five cosponsors in the House, where it was considered conterminously with the administration bill in the IFC Energy and Power Subcommittee. With Republican support and the votes of five Democratic members, a deregulation proposal sponsored by Texas Representative Robert Krueger carried the subcommittee. However, the subcommittee decision was then reversed on a twenty-three to twenty vote in full committee after intensive debate, procedural manipulations, and active lobbying of the few "swing votes" by both President Carter and former President Ford.[21] The full Commerce Committee upheld both the natural gas pricing and coal conversion features of the administration program.

In a rarely used procedure, the various portions of the energy program were subsequently referred (after being reported out of the original committees) to a special "Ad Hoc Energy Committee." The membership of the ad hoc committee was composed of forty senior members of those committees normally exercising jurisdiction over some aspect of the program.[22] All were appointed by the Speaker. In making the appointments, O'Neill gave some consideration to regional and partisan balance, at the same time insuring that the membership would be dominated by Democratic loyalists committed to favorable and expeditious action on the president's program.[23]

The Ad Hoc Committee made few important modifications in the Carter-IFC natural gas proposals. It did, however, approve an amendment sponsored by Texas Representatives Eckhardt and Wilson that expanded the definition of new gas by omitting the necessity to prove that a new reservoir had been tapped, as long as the new well was located more than 2.5 miles from an existing well. This amendment was designed to win support among members representing producer and spectator states on what was expected to be a close floor vote. Concerning user taxes, the Ad Hoc Committee adopted a strengthening amendment, supported by coal district representatives, which applied the oil and gas user tax to new plants that were not prohibited from burning those fuels. Provisions dealing with gas regulation, user and other taxes, credits and rebates, coal conversion and production, utility rates, and additional minor energy conservation and production incentives were then packaged together in a single "clean" bill, HR 8444. The extraordinary "ad hoc" committee procedure not only provided for an overview of the complex energy plan by a sympathetic, consumer-dominated committee, but also welded together the coal conversion and gas pricing provisions that were essential to the mobilization of a majority consumer-coal coalition in the House.

On the House floor, a natural gas deregulation amendment and an amendment deleting the crude oil equalization tax were both narrowly defeated. Leaders of the deregulation movement attributed the defeat to the handful of votes apparently won over by the expanded "new gas" definition.[24] The vote on deregulation closely followed the pattern of 1976 (see Table 21) with fewer than 10 percent of votes representing shifts from support to opposition, or vice versa. Of the forty-one vote shifts from 1976 to 1977, thirty-one represented either changes in party control of a district (for example, a Democrat opposed deregulation in 1976, a Republican from the same district supported deregulation in 1977) or, in more than half the cases, shifts in spectator districts that had no compelling economic reason to support or oppose decontrol. Most of the spectator shifts were in the South (five in Georgia alone), where southern

Democrats from areas without a large stake in the outcome could be persuaded to support the president's position.[25]

The administration's strategy had been to marshal a partisan force that would sweep through the House intact, and sustain sufficient momentum to survive an expected Senate ambush by the producer-Republican coalition. The House portion of the strategy was remarkably successful: passage of the complex and momentous energy package was achieved in record time. With Speaker Thomas O'Neill admonishing his troops to vote against "Big Oil" because "the future of America, the economy of this country, the defense of this nation, are at stake," the consumer-coal alliance defeated the producer-Republican deregulation forces by a vote of 227 to 199 on August 3.[26] Final passage of the energy bill came two days later on a 244 to 177 vote.

The voting patterns on deregulation and on final passage of HR 8444 were almost mirror images. Almost all members who supported the one opposed the other. Only 12 percent of all members who voted on both issues either supported deregulation *and* passage of the Carter plan, or opposed both. Among the small number of members casting such votes were some urban representatives (particularly from San Francisco, eastern Massachusetts, and Ohio) who opposed both deregulation and the price increases in the administration bill; but the large majority were members who supported both deregulation and the Carter program. Two-thirds of the second group came from rural and suburban spectator districts and from producer states, principally Louisiana. Interviews with Louisiana congressmen suggest that their affirmative votes on final passage were cast strategically; they voted for the bill (which now seemed assured of House passage) in exchange for the Speaker's appointment of Louisiana Representative Joe Waggoner to conference with the Senate. Producer state representatives expected a much more favorable bill to emerge from that chamber.

Rejection in the Senate

In lieu of administration proposals expanding the scope of natural gas regulation, the Senate overcame a lengthy filibuster to adopt, on October 4, a substitute proposal for deregulation.[27] The substitute was sponsored by Senators Pearson and Bentsen, who had led the deregulation forces in 1975. Other portions of the Carter energy program were also redesigned in the upper chamber. The Senate alternative on coal conversion included substantially more exemptions than the House-passed bill, and provided federal loans and grants to aid in plant conversion (see Table 22).[28] It also included a program, strongly supported by western coal states, to aid communities "impacted" by rapid development of coal and uranium resources.[29] The Finance Committee, chaired by Louisiana

TABLE 22   EVOLUTION OF THE 1978 NATIONAL ENERGY ACT IN CONGRESS:
GAS PRICING AND COAL CONVERSION PROVISIONS*

Provisions	House Version (HR 8444)*	Senate Version (S 2104 and S 977)
Natural Gas		
Pricing	Establishes a uniform national price for new gas beginning at about $1.75 per thousand cubic foot (mcf) with escalations pegged to the controlled price of domestic oil. The FPC may approve higher prices for high-cost gas. The price of old gas under existing contracts can escalate with inflation. The maximum price for old gas under new and rollover contracts is $1.45.	Eliminates federal price controls on new onshore gas in two years, new offshore gas in five years. Interim ceiling prices for new gas are fixed at the landed price of number 2 fuel oil. Old gas remains subject to FPC price determination.
Definition	"New" gas means onshore gas from a well more than 2.5 miles from an existing well, or from a new reservoir if closer than 2.5 miles. New offshore gas means gas under lease after April 20, 1977.	"New" gas means gas sold in interstate commerce for the first time after January 1, 1977, provided such gas was not "wrongfully withheld" before then (as determined by the FPC).
Designation	Classification of gas is delegated to producer state agencies if they so request, but the FPC can overturn state determination and rescind delegation.	The FPC determines whether sale dates satisfy the "new" gas requirement.
Burden of new pricing	Incremental pricing to pass on higher costs to "low priority" (industrial and utility) users until those costs equal the price of substitute fuels.	Incremental pricing to assure allocations of "old" gas to residential and other specified priority users of interstate gas.
Jurisdiction	All gas produced in the United States.	Only interstate gas subject to control.
Enforcement	Civil penalties of up to $20,000 for knowing violations of provisions relating to the production, sale,	Relies on old Natural Gas Act provision allowing FPC to bring action against violators in federal court,

	House	Senate
	transmission, or distribution of gas. Criminal penalties up to $40,000 and one-year imprisonment.	seeking mandamus or injunctive relief; available criminal penalties are $5,000 and/or two years in prison.
Conversion to other fuels	No new electric power plant or major industrial boiler may burn natural gas or oil. All existing electric power plants must cease burning natural gas by 1990. Other existing installations may be ordered to convert if they have the capability to burn other fuels. Exemptions possible primarily on grounds of (1) environmental regulations; (2) inordinate costs of other fuels (above the cost of imported oil); (3) site limitations; and (4) temporary coal supply interruptions.	New electric power plants and new major industrial users (defined as those capable of burning 100 Btu./hr. [if gas] or 300 Btu./hr. [if oil]) must use coal. Existing electric power plants must cease burning natural gas by 1990. Exemptions where: adequate and reliable coal supplies lacking; adequate coal transportation facilities not expected to be available; other fuel costs substantially exceed the cost of imported oil; environmental, physical, and legal problems cannot be overcome by good faith efforts; and for other reasons.
Taxation	For major fuel users not prohibited from burning oil and gas, those fuels would be taxed in order to speed conversion and encourage conservation.	No user taxes; contains a program of federal loans and grants to help plants convert to coal.
Financial assistance		Creates a federal assistance program for areas "impacted" by increased coal or uranium mining; authorizes $100 million for rehabilitation of railroad lines to transport coal.
Emergency purchase and allocation authority	Extends provisions of expiring Emergency Natural Gas Act of 1977, authorizing the president to allow, during temporary emergencies, purchases from producers or intrastate pipelines and authorizing the president to allocate gas between interstate pipelines; House added provision for allocating gas from intrastate pipelines, as well.	Extends provisions of ENGA (allocation authority applied to interstate pipelines only).

*In the House, the five components of the administration's energy plan were packaged in one bill. In the Senate, they were treated as separate bills.

Senator Russell Long, rejected the House-passed administration proposals for both an oil and gas users' tax and a crude oil equalization tax,
reporting instead a bill substituting tax incentives for energy conservation
and production.[30]

Once again, the different representational bases of the House and
Senate produced drastically different energy programs. The House version, closely following the Carter administration proposals, was supported by a coalition centered on urban consumer and eastern coal
interests. In the Senate, a majority coalition formed around a program
favored by producer and western states. To compromise such disparate
positions would obviously be difficult. The administration at first resisted
any weakening of the consumer position. In televised press conferences
in September and October, President Carter denounced the petroleum
industry for "profiteering in the energy crisis" and attempting through
deregulation to achieve "the biggest ripoff in history." However, faced
with the possibility of a legislative stalemate that might endanger other
parts of the energy program as well, the president ultimately threw his
support behind attempts to compromise the Senate and House natural
gas policies.

House and Senate conferees reached essential agreement on the coal
conversion, fuel conservation, and utility portions of the program in late
1977. In the case of coal conversion, the conference agreement weakened
the administration-House proposal in the direction of the multiple exemptions favored by the Senate. Finance Committee conferees, headed
by Senator Russell Long of Louisiana, refused to accede to House
provisions containing oil and gas user or crude oil equalization taxes and
delayed action on the other energy tax proposals comprising HR 8444
until the natural gas issue was settled.[31] Gas regulation had become the
lynch pin in the construction of a national energy program.

In terms of the intensity with which positions were held, and the length
of time needed to reconcile them, the gas issue proved to be one of the
most controversial pieces of legislation ever considered in the modern
Congress. Only after seven months of negotiations and persistent, mul-
tifaceted administration pressure was a compromise finally reached at the
end of May 1978.[32] As reported by the conferees, the new Natural Gas
Policy Act (NGPA) combined eventual deregulation of new gas with an
extension of controls to the intrastate market. While greatly enlarging the
scope of FERC regulation and granting it new responsibilities, such as
incremental pricing rules, the new natural gas act replaced agency price-
setting discretion with a complex tariff of prices applied to specific categories of gas. Although the classification of wells into the act's pricing
categories was left to producer state agencies (or, in the case of offshore

gas, to the United States Geological Survey), FERC could reverse the state classification within forty-five days if it found the designation not supported by available evidence. The party aggrieved by the reversal (for example, a producer or buyer) could then challenge the FERC ruling in federal court. Since it would clearly be impossible to closely scrutinize each well classification for an estimated sixteen thousand producers, FERC announced that it would rely on spot checks and stiff sanctions applied to producers who made false claims.[33]

Once the conferees had reached agreement, the administration faced the problem of selling the patchwork bill to Congress. Its cause was not helped when the director of FERC's Office of Enforcement described the gas bill as "so complex, ambiguous, and contradictory that it would be virtually impossible to enforce."[34] The statement was gleefully repeated by the bill's opponents, whose ranks swelled to encompass a diverse alliance of consumer and deregulation advocates.

Most natural gas producers strongly opposed the compromise bill. The smaller independents were particularly opposed, charging that the expansion of jurisdiction to the intrastate market and the concomitant burden of complying with federal regulation would drive many out of business.[35] The principal organization of independent producers, the International Petroleum Association of America (IPAA), lobbied against the bill throughout the summer and fall of 1978. It was joined in this campaign by the Texas Independent Producers and Royalty Owners Association, the United States Chamber of Commerce, the Farm Bureau, and the American Conservative Union, which had for some time urged immediate deregulation, and by the United Auto Workers, Consumer Federation of America, AFL-CIO, National Association of State Regulatory Commissions, and Americans for Democratic Action, all of which opposed the bill's pricing and gradual deregulation provisions.[36]

The IPAA had lost some of its allies along the way. The American Gas Association and Interstate Natural Gas Association decided to support the compromise. The bill's higher prices, phased deregulation, and single national pricing mechanism would, the distributors and pipeline companies believed, make an additional eight trillion cubic feet of gas available to the interstate market by 1985. Without a new statute, on the other hand, the new Democratic commission might well lower the existing price ceiling, greatly reducing incentives for producers to dedicate new reserves to the interstate market.[37]

The independent producers, however, were encouraged by reports that FERC Chairman Curtis had warned consumer state senators that the commission might set a new national ceiling price of $2.50–$2.60 mcf if the compromise bill was not passed.[38] The producers' association pre-

TABLE 23 CONFERENCE REPORTS: THE NATURAL GAS POLICY ACT OF 1978,
AND THE POWER PLANT AND INDUSTRIAL FUEL USE ACT OF 1978

Provisions	*Provision*
Natural gas pricing	New gas price fixed at $1.85, as of April 1977, with monthly increments based on an annual inflation index plus a specified additional increment (estimated to bring the new gas price to $1.95 in the month of passage: October 1978). New natural gas and intrastate gas selling for $1.00 mcf to be relieved of federal price controls on January 1, 1985. Four categories of high-cost gas to be deregulated within one year of passage. An additional category of gas from wells drilled after February 18, 1977, is deregulated by 1987 if the gas was not committed to interstate commerce in April of 1977.
Definition	"New" gas means (1) gas from new Outer Continental Shelf leases; (2) from old leases if discovered after July 26, 1976; (3) from reservoirs in which gas was not produced in commercial quantities before April 20, 1977; (4) gas from new onshore wells 2.5 or more miles from a "marker" well (one producing gas in commercial quantities after January 1, 1970); or (5) if closer to the marker well, one thousand feet deeper.

Pricing for "old" natural gas is specified according to its present contract price, date of drilling commencement, and whether it was dedicated to the interstate or intrastate market. Thus, "old" interstate gas can be sold at prices ranging from $.30 to $1.45, plus an inflation adjustment; when these interstate contracts are renegotiated ("rollover" contracts), the price will be "rolled up" to $.54, if it was previously below that (as the large majority of interstate gas was)* or to the applicable FERC-determined "just and reasonable" rate, if the old contract price was more than $.54. Both prices will rise with inflation. Old intrastate gas under rollover contracts will be fixed at the contract price, or $1.00, whichever is higher, plus inflation. Old intrastate gas that sold for more than $1.00 mcf will be deregulated in 1985. Gas from "stripper" wells (producing only small quantities) begins at $2.09 and rises at about the same rate as "new" gas. |
| Incremental pricing | For interstate pipelines only, under rules prescribed by the FERC. Essential agricultural uses are exempted. |
| Jurisdiction | All United States natural gas production. |

Enforcement	The FPC may assess civil penalties of $5,000/violation, except for violations of emergency provisions (for which the president may assess a $25,000 fine); criminal penalties of $5,000 and/or two years in prison (for violations of emergency provisions, $50,000). Each day counts as a "violation."
Emergency purchase and allocation authority	Authorizes the president, during a declared natural gas supply emergency, to permit purchases between interstate pipelines or distributors, and producers or intrastate pipelines. If such purchases are insufficient to protect the health and safety of high priority (residential and small commercial) users or to protect physical property, the president may allocate gas to high priority users from boiler fuel users, interstate pipeline customers, or direct industrial users.
Intervention	The Secretary of Energy is empowered to intervene in state agency proceedings relating to proration (rate of production and allocation of production rights among producers) of natural gas.
Fuel conversion	New electric power plants may not use oil or gas as a primary energy source. New major industrial boilers (capable of burning 100 million Btu./hr.) are also prohibited from using oil and gas. The Secretary of the DOE is further empowered to prohibit non-boiler uses in new major units. Existing electric power plants are required to end natural gas use (as a primary fuel) by 1990, and not to increase their natural gas use after enactment. Existing facilities can be prohibited from using oil or gas by the secretary if they have the capability to use other fuels. Exemptions can be granted by DOE if there is an inadequate or unreliable supply of coal, for compliance with environmental regulations, to prevent impairment of service, to maintain product quality control, because of physical site limitations, if alternate fuels will substantially exceed the price of imported oil, to comply with other state and local laws, and for other reasons. A "system compliance option" is provided for utilities heavily dependent on natural gas.
Financial assistance	The PIFU Act includes the Senate-passed provisions for aid to coal and uranium "impacted" areas, loans to assist plants converting to coal to install air pollution equipment, and federal aid for rail rehabilitation.

*In 1976, 11.4 trillion cubic feet of natural gas flowed interstate. Of this total, 6.4 trillion cubic feet (56 percent) sold for less than 29.5 cents per mcf; 1.7 TCF (15 percent) sold for $.52; 1.2 TCF (10.5 percent) sold for $.93; and .7 TCF (6 percent) received $1.42, the highest price allowed for new domestic gas. Gas imported from Canada (which constituted 12 percent of the total) sold for $1.80 mcf. House of Representatives, Committee on Interstate and Foreign Commerce, hearings on the National Energy Act (1977), p. 927.

ferred the status quo—even if it meant only the 1976 price with increases for inflation—to the compromise bill, and held out the hope that the Congress elected in 1978 might enact the Senate's deregulation plan.[39]

One of the most extreme denunciations of the compromise Natural Gas Policy Act came from the chairman of the Texas Railroad Commission, Mack Wallace, who charged that the NGPA institutionalized "a neocolonial policy of exploitation."[40] Wallace cited an IFC staff analysis of the compromise bill which predicted that, as a result of the bill, interstate consumers would pay six to ten billion dollars less for energy between 1978 and 1985, while producer state residents might pay up to seven billion dollars more than without the new law.[41] In Chairman Wallace's view, "Texas consumers through the higher [unregulated] prices they have paid have financed . . . a massive program of gas exploration and drilling within the state, which . . . has yielded adequate intrastate supply . . . and contributed substantially to the economic prosperity of the State in recent years." Just as the intrastate price began to drop as a result of increased supplies, the NGPA was passed, allowing interstate consumers to claim the surplus and pay artificially low prices for it. Under the provisions of the NGPA, Texas would continue to finance exploration by paying higher prices than interstate consumers, but new supplies would move into interstate pipelines. While most Texas gas sold interstate (about 70 percent, in Wallace's estimate) would be priced only up to fifty-four cents per mcf on contract expiration, gas sold intrastate would be priced in a range from $1.00 mcf up to the unregulated new gas price. Thus, Texas and other producer state residents would pay, on the average, almost six times more for a thousand cubic feet of "old" gas in 1985 than interstate consumers, while the NGPA and its companion coal conversion legislation would deny the state's utilities and industries the use of their native fuel.[42] Similar objections had been voiced by Dallas Republican Representative Jim Collins in a late August news release:

> We paid the full intrastate rates to build up our reserves, and now Washington wants to confiscate those reserves and sell them to the Northeast at fixed lower interstate rates. . . . We'll have less energy left at home and we'll have to convert all 623 of our major gas burning industrial boilers to burn coal. That alone will cost every Texas consumer between $280 and $600 in added utility costs. Why should Texans be forced to ship their gas to New York, Boston, and Chicago and then have to pay high railroad bills to bring in Wyoming coal?

For reasons like these, most producer state representatives opposed the gas compromise, although several had been involved in the marathon conference negotiations.[43] The producer congressmen, however, were no more unhappy with the compromise than representatives of urban consumer areas.

Many consumer area representatives who supported the House-administration program preferred the existing Natural Gas Act to the conference committee agreement. Democratic Senator Howard Metzenbaum of Ohio, a leading opponent of the compromise, charged that the provision for gradual deregulation would result in "a massive movement of billions of dollars from the consumers of this country to the producers." In addition, Metzenbaum charged, the provision for incremental pricing applied to interstate gas would raise energy costs for consumer state industries, encouraging them to move to the Southwest.[44]

For the consumer tier, a principal virtue of the original administration plan had been in provisions that would, it was hoped, equalize energy costs between New England, the mid-Atlantic, and Great Lakes states on the one hand, and the southwestern and mountain regions on the other. The Department of Energy had contended that the original administration program would reduce a three-to-one fuel cost advantage in the Southwest to a mere 10 percent advantage.[45] Thus, the president's energy proposals would, in the words of New York Representative Thomas Downey, "provide a measure of parity so desperately needed" to stem the flow of manufacturing jobs to the "sunbelt."[46] However, once the Senate had gutted the Carter program, omitting oil and gas user taxes and the crude oil tax and widening the array of exemptions from coal conversion mandates, its redistributive virtues were greatly diminished. It was not clear to many Northeasterners that the additional supplies to be gained from the bill's nationalized price regulation and coal conversion features were sufficient compensation for the higher gas prices it entailed.

Between the compromise version and the existing Natural Gas Act, many consumer area representatives preferred the status quo. Under present appointees (and assuming continued Democratic control of the presidency), Senator Metzenbaum argued that there would probably be no price increases of the sort experienced in the Nixon-Ford years. Furthermore, both recent federal court decisions and actions taken by the Carter-appointed commission held out the promise of a significant increase in interstate supplies through broad interpretation of the existing statute.[47]

Statutory Ambiguity and the Expansion of Regulatory Jurisdiction

In May 1978, the Supreme Court dropped a bombshell into the midst of the stalemated energy contenders. The case at hand involved Southland Royalty Company, which owned sixty-five thousand acres of land in Texas. In the 1920s, Southland had granted a fifty-year lease to the Gulf Oil Corporation, which ultimately sold the gas it produced on the land to an interstate pipeline (El Paso Natural Gas) for resale in California.

When Gulf's lease expired in 1975, the Southland owners arranged to sell the remaining gas to an intrastate buyer. El Paso then petitioned the FPC to block the intrastate sale in order to prevent a significant loss of supply to the interstate market. The Republican commission held that "once gas began to flow in interstate commerce from a field subject to a certificate of unlimited duration [in the 1950s, when Gulf secured an FPC certificate to sell gas to the El Paso pipeline, the commission was not issuing limited-term certificates], such flow could not be terminated unless the FPC authorized abandonment of service."[48]

Southland, supported by the state of Texas as amicus curiae, appealed the commission's ruling, and the Fifth Circuit Court in New Orleans overturned the FPC. The circuit court held that, since Gulf had only leased the land for a fixed number of years, and since under Texas law mineral rights reverted to the owner on expiration of the lease, Gulf could not legally dedicate what it did not own—that is, the remaining gas—to interstate commerce.

The FPC, the interstate pipeline, and the state of California petitioned the Supreme Court for review, and the high court upheld, as it had in the past, the federal agency in its assertion of jurisdiction. "The fundamental purpose of the Natural Gas Act," said the Court, "is to assure that natural gas companies furnish their interstate customers an adequate and reliable supply of gas at reasonable prices." Since producers had been held to be "natural gas companies," in the meaning of the act, Gulf could not, under section 7, "abandon all or any portion of its facilities . . . or any service rendered by means of such facilities" without the commission's consent. As to the royalty owners' claim that they, as owners of the gas, had not voluntarily taken any action that would bring them under the commission's jurisdiction (it was Gulf, the temporary leaseholder, that had applied for the FPC certificate to sell gas to El Paso), the court held that "the obligation to serve the interstate market had already attached to the *gas*," so that the royalty owners, when control of the gas reverted to them, must continue to sell it to the interstate pipeline.[49]

Not since the Phillips decision had the commission claimed, and the Court upheld, such a far-reaching expansion of its jurisdiction. In *Phillips*, national jurisdiction had expanded from pipelines to producers; in Southland, federal control reached beyond the producers and owners of the gas to the gas field itself.[50] Hailed as an important victory by pipelines, consumers, and the FPC, the Court's ruling was an unpleasant reminder to producer state representatives that the ambiguity of the original act could serve as a powerful weapon in the hands of the consumer areas. After the Southland decision, producers feared, "hungry pipelines" might produce hundreds of old contracts as evidence that gas from given fields belonged to the interstate, not intrastate, market.[51] Nor was this the only recent decision broadening the federal commission's jurisdiction to the advantage of consumer areas.

Amid persistent consumer complaints that gas producers were withholding gas from the interstate market, the commission had, in 1975, embarked on another important doctrinal innovation. First, the FPC asserted that certificates for interstate sales carried an obligation to make minimum daily deliveries to pipelines, and that it intended to enforce these delivery obligations. Then, in 1978, the new Democratic commission went a significant step further. It announced that it would henceforth apply a "prudent investor" requirement to gas producers.

A familiar concept in conventional utility regulation, the doctrine required that regulated enterprises conduct their operations efficiently so as not to impose unnecessary costs on consumers of their services. Applied to gas producers, such "prudence" seemed to imply that drilling, gathering, and processing be conducted in such a manner as to insure that enough gas was produced to meet contract obligations and that drilling operations not be abandoned while gas remained in the well, unless the FPC permitted termination of sales.[52] Earlier court decisions legitimating federal regulation of producer *sales* had affirmed that the *physical processes* of production remained in the purview of the states. Assertion of a federal "prudent operator" requirement, however, implied that the federal agency could specify the method, rate, and spacing of drilling operations, order "affirmative actions" to maintain reservoir pressure, and even direct that new wells be drilled. Such authority would clearly constitute a radical change in federal-state relationships with regard to production of natural resources, and raised the possibility that individual producers might be forced to conduct operations which, in view of the low level of some FPC-controlled prices, would not recover costs.[53] Shell and other gas producers, joined by the state of Louisiana, appealed the FERC ruling, arguing that the federal agency thereby intervened in the processes of production and gathering reserved to the states in section 1b of the Natural Gas Act.

The Fifth Circuit Court in New Orleans agreed with the producers that the proposed federal requirement of "prudent operation" encroached on an area reserved to the states, and overturned the commission's claim.[54] FERC then petitioned the Supreme Court to review the case, and it was there that matters stood during the debate on the NGPA in the fall of 1978. Since the Supreme Court had only rarely, in the past forty years, failed to uphold the federal commission's actions, consumers had reason to assume that the New Orleans decision for the producers would again be reversed by the Supreme Court on appeal.[55]

In another recent action to expand supplies available to the regulated interstate market, FERC in the spring of 1978 had announced the discontinuance of a commission policy inaugurated some years earlier to provide a stimulus for exploration on the Outer Continental Shelf (OCS). Dubbed the "Chandeleur Incentive," it allowed OCS producers to reserve varying percentages of their production either for use in their own plants or for sale in more lucrative unregulated markets. The old FPC had ruled that sales from the producers' reserves could only be made for high-priority uses in the producer states, but the new Democratic commission terminated the reserve policy altogether, requiring that all OCS gas go into interstate pipelines. The Chandeleur Incentive, it held, unfairly benefitted industries in Texas and Louisiana at the expense of those dependent on interstate gas. The volume of gas involved was estimated by the FERC to equal one-half of the quantity of all emergency gas purchases authorized for interstate pipelines in 1976.[56]

To emphasize its determination to end "unlawful diversions from certificated service" (that is, intrastate sales by producers of gas for which there is a prior interstate claim), the reconstituted FERC created in 1977 a new Office of Enforcement. The purpose of the new office was to investigate and prosecute violations of the Natural Gas Act, using all remedies available under the statute—including referral of violations to the Justice Department for criminal prosecution. During 1977 and 1978, FERC claimed to have recommended for prosecution almost as many violations as the FPC had done in forty years. In the first criminal conviction under the Natural Gas Act, Tenneco, Inc., was sentenced to pay fines totalling over a million dollars.[57]

Considerations

These and other FERC actions[58] led some consumers to view statutory change as unnecessary. In the words of one consumer lobby, Energy Action,

> For the first time in ten years, we have a commission committed to the proper enforcement of the intent and provisions of the Natural Gas Act. For the first time, the Supreme Court has affirmed the commission's authority to reclaim large amounts of gas now flowing illegally in the intrastate market. For the first time the commission has taken positive action to prohibit the diversion of huge amounts of interstate OCS (Outer Continental Shelf) gas to the intrastate market. For the first time, the commission is collecting independent, unbiased, and disaggregated data so that up-to-date and reliable price levels can be set. In short, under current law there is sufficient authority and flexibility to deal with the natural gas market in a responsible, fair, and equitable manner and to carry out the president's basic principles."[59]

Furthermore, argued Energy Action (in tones reminiscent of Senator Douglas' 1956 argument), there was presently a "glut" of gas in the producer states. Once Congress made a clear decision to maintain the existing statutory framework, "that gas will move nationally because the producer has nowhere else to sell it, and needs the cash flow to pay his creditors."[60]

In the short term, at least, this argument rang true. Rapidly escalating intrastate prices had produced an overabundance of gas in the Southwest, as a result of which the average new contract price dropped, in the first quarter of 1978, from $1.96 to $1.67 mcf.[61] The producers had hoped to reduce the glut through short-term sales to interstate pipelines, which the FPC had permitted under special limited certificates since the early 1970s. In 1978, however, the commission increasingly refused to approve such sales. This refusal was interpreted by some producers as an attempt to bring pressure on southwestern congressmen to support the NGPA.[62]

There were, of course, numerous points at which pressure could be brought to bear on producers and pipelines in order to encourage support for the administration-backed compromise. In addition to holding up short-term sales and declining to raise area rates or the national new gas ceiling, the commission could affect producer revenues in its pipeline rate determinations. For example, in the spring of 1978 the FERC announced that it would end the traditional practice by which the costs of processing and compressing gas to ready it for transmission and consumption were passed along to consumers through pipeline charges. Henceforth, the commission stated, processing costs would have to be borne by producers.[63]

Another area of regulatory discretion that aroused concern in the producer states was the allocation of pipeline supplies during times of shortage. Since the early 1970s, the FPC's assertion of authority to regulate curtailments of deliveries by interstate pipelines had led it to restrict direct sales of gas by pipelines to industrial customers, many of whom were located in the producer states. Direct sales had long been assumed to be beyond the commission's jurisdiction because of an exclusionary provision in section 1b and a Supreme Court decision in 1947 that denied the FPC rate-setting powers over direct sales.[64] However, when interstate pipelines began to experience delivery shortfalls, the commission argued that it had to supervise curtailments to all pipeline customers (including direct customers) in order to prevent discrimination in service, which was outlawed under sections 4 and 5 of the NGA. In 1972, in a case involving a direct pipeline sale to a Louisiana utility, the Court legitimated this expansion of the commission's jurisdiction, holding that it was necessary to prevent a "regulatory gap" in which the public welfare might be subverted by private interests.[65]

Producer state congressmen pressed the commission to allow industrial sales in areas where alternative fuels, such as coal, were not produced,

TABLE 24   CHRONOLOGY OF THE NATURAL GAS POLICY ACT OF 1978

Date	Action
April 20, 1977	New Natural Gas Act proposed by President Carter in address to joint session of Congress.
May 2, 1977	Administration's energy proposals introduced in the House as HR 6831 (natural gas pricing proposals are contained in Title I of the bill). In the Senate, the administration's proposals are broken into five separate bills. Natural gas pricing proposals are contained in S 2104, referred to the new Senate Committee on Energy and Natural Resources, chaired by Henry Jackson of Washington. In the House, the natural gas portion of HR 6831 is sent to the Interstate and Foreign Commerce Committee, chaired by Harley Staggers of West Virginia, and subsequently referred to the Energy and Power Subcommittee headed by John Dingell of Michigan.
June 9, 1977	House Energy and Power Subcommittee adopts (on a 12-to-10 vote) a proposal to deregulate new gas prices in place of the administration's plan.
July 14, 1977	Full Commerce Committee overrides subcommittee on a 23-to-20 vote, and reports the natural gas portion of HR 6831. Ad Hoc Committee convenes to consider all parts of HR 6831.
July 27, 1977	After a few modifications, the diverse proposals are packaged and reported to the House floor as a clean bill, HR 8444.
August 3, 1977	During floor debate in Committee of the Whole, Representative Clarence Brown (R, Ohio) proposes an amendment to HR 8444 to deregulate new natural gas prices. The amendment is defeated, 199 to 227.
August 5, 1977	House passes administration energy proposals (HR 8444) by a vote of 244 to 177.
September 15, 1977	Senate Energy Committee reports S 2104 without recommendation, since the committee is closely divided between advocates of deregulation and supporters of extended controls.

September 1977	During Senate floor debate on S 2104, a deregulation proposal is offered in lieu of the Carter plan, and a motion to table it is defeated on a 46-to-52 vote. Opponents of deregulation, led by Howard Metzenbaum (D, Ohio) and James Abourezk (D, South Dakota) begin a filibuster. Senate votes cloture (to end filibuster) on September 26, 1977.
October 4, 1977	Senate rejects administration gas proposals, passing instead a substitute plan for phased deregulation sponsored by Senators James Pearson (R, Kansas) and Lloyd Bentsen (D, Texas).
October 18, 1977	House-Senate Conference Committee convenes to reconcile diverse natural gas proposals.
July 31, 1978	Staff of Conference Committee release a draft, in legislative language, of the gas compromise. Objections by conferees produce further revisions.
August 18, 1978	Final conference report filed (as HR 5289) containing proposed new natural gas statute of sixty-six pages, to which a fifty-eight-page explanation of the proposal was appended by the conferees.
September 19, 1978	During Senate floor debate, opponents of the conference bill propose that the bill be sent back to conference with instructions that the conferees strike the natural gas pricing proposals (except for those relating to gas produced in Alaska), and report back a bill providing only for federal allocation of gas during periods of severe shortages. Recommittal motion defeated, 59 to 39.
September 27, 1978	Senate approves conference report by vote of 57 to 42.
October 13, 1978	House adopts Rules Committee motion to consider the five energy conference reports as one bill, rather than vote separately on each. Rule adopted by a vote of 207 to 206.
October 15, 1978	Five conference reports, including Natural Gas Policy Act, adopted by House as National Energy Act by vote of 231 to 168 (cleared for president's signature).

industries were not equipped to burn other fuels, and a reliable coal transportation network was lacking. In late 1977, however, a FERC hearing examiner recommended against allowing the United Gas Pipeline Company (the nation's fifth largest interstate carrier, with headquarters in Shreveport) to grant preference to Louisiana customers when it was forced to curtail deliveries. Because there was no "glut" of gas in Louisiana, and most gas produced there went into interstate pipelines, the state's congressmen strongly urged the commission to override the examiner's ruling. If upheld, Senator Bennett Johnston argued, this ruling would cause "deep unemployment, economic dislocation, and social disaster in my state." Several Louisiana congressmen hinted that, given the pressure on intrastate supplies that would result from the passage of the NGPA, they could not vote for the act unless producer states were granted priority when curtailments were necessary.[66]

By the fall of 1978, producer state congressmen felt diverse and conflicting pressures on the NGPA issue. On the one hand, passage of the new statute offered a way around both the FERC ruling on OCS gas and the Supreme Court's Southland decision. Establishment of a single national set of curtailment priorities would allow OCS gas to be sold in the producer states for high-priority uses. With regard to the Southland decision, the House and Senate conferees explicitly stated in an explanation attached to the conference report that gas from expired leases should not be considered "dedicated to interstate commerce" if the current owners were not selling the gas interstate in 1978.[67] These advantages, however, had to be juxtaposed with the disadvantages of extending regulation to the producer states—disadvantages calculated in terms of effects on local industries, job markets, and residential users.

By the fall of 1978, even the producers were split on the conference bill. A number of larger operators with new and uncommitted reserves (such as Gulf and Atlantic-Richfield, for example) supported the bill because it promised a predictable and significantly more advantageous price schedule. If the NGPA failed, there was a risk that anti-industry feelings might run stronger in the next Congress, and produce a less advantageous bill.[68] In addition, the large companies did not want to jeopardize other relationships with the administration—such as Department of Energy contracts to develop synthetic fuels, the possibility of antitrust initiatives from the Justice Department, and the regulation of crude oil prices, which the administration might allow to expire when statutory authorization for controls elapsed. For reasons such as these, the major producers' principal lobby—the Natural Gas Supply Committee—dropped its opposition to the bill. Companies that produced as well as transported gas (Tenneco, for example) openly supported the NGPA, as did the Inde-

pendent Gas Producers' Committee. The latter group represented operators who were drilling at depths below fifteen thousand feet—a category
of gas which under the NGPA would be deregulated within a year.[69]
Many producers in the Rocky Mountain states, where intrastate markets
could not absorb more than a small portion of the total production, and
owners of small-producing "stripper wells" also supported the NGPA.[70]
So did the Alaskan petroleum industry, since many believed that the
Alaskan pipeline would not be built without the bill's guaranteed price
levels. On the other hand, the small independents' major lobby group,
the Independent Petroleum Association of America, continued to
oppose the extension of controls to the intrastate market. Owners of
smaller, older reserves and low-budget "wildcat" drillers were certain
that the extension of FERC jurisdiction over their operations would bring
financially overwhelming paper work, regulatory delays, and litigation
expenses.[71]

Presidential Leverage

Whether out of sympathy for the more numerous small producers,
anticipation that a deregulation bill might yet be passed, or concern for
the bill's effect on intrastate residential consumers and industries, the
governors of the major southwestern producer states and most producer
state congressmen came to oppose the NGPA in the fall of 1978. With
committed support in the coal states, the administration, therefore,
concentrated its efforts on swaying the votes of undecided representatives from the more numerous consumer and spectator areas.

In August and September of 1978, the Carter administration mounted
one of history's most impressive executive lobbying efforts on behalf of
the natural gas compromise. All of the tools of presidential persuasion
were employed: pragmatic bargains involving tangible quid pro quos
were struck with individual congressmen; grassroots support was marshaled by lectures to visiting community opinion leaders and high-level
conferences with banking and business executives who were subtly reminded of the many ways in which executive prerogatives could be used
to help or hurt them; numerous visits and calls were made, by the
president himself or friends who were already committed; and key representatives and senators were urged to rally to their party, president, and
flag by supporting the NGPA. In return for his vote on ratification of the
compromise, Republican Senator James McClure of Idaho (a spectator
state) was, apparently, promised a four hundred million dollar breeder
reactor research project for his state.[72] It was rumored that public works
and defense contracts were promised to potential supporters and that

some congressmen, particularly "lame ducks," were offered "post-elective job opportunities," such as federal judgeships and executive branch appointments in return for their votes.[73]

During the last two weeks of August, presidential advisor Robert Strauss and Federal Reserve Board Chairman G. William Miller held White House conferences with heads of the nation's major financial institutions and executives of major industries who had previously supported deregulation and particularly objected to the NGPA's incremental pricing provisions.[74] Banking, steel, textile, and automobile executives were reminded, as one critic put it, of the realities of "doing business in a regulated environment." They were reminded of tariff negotiations presently under way, proceedings being considered at the Federal Trade and Securities and Exchange commissions, and the need to shore up the value of the dollar by curbing oil imports.[75] These appeals were apparently successful. In early September, the Department of Energy circulated a list of fifty-five major industries and banks and twenty large trade associations that now supported the NGPA.[76] Among the major corporations switching from opposition to neutrality or support were U.S. Steel, Bethlehem Steel, General Motors, the Chase Manhattan Bank, and B.F. Goodrich.[77] With the nation's major auto makers now backing the compromise, Republican Senator Robert Griffin of Michigan announced that he, too, had decided to support it.[78]

The battle was not yet won, however. Groups ranging from the AFL-CIO, the UAW, and the Consumer Federation of America on one end of the political spectrum to the Chamber of Commerce, the Farm Bureau, and the IPAA on the other, remained adamantly opposed. Democratic Senators Howard Metzenbaum of Ohio and James Abourezk of South Dakota threatened to filibuster the compromise when it reached the Senate floor. Meanwhile, they joined sixteen other senators of both parties, most of whom represented either producer or major consumer states, in a last-ditch attempt to block the compromise bill. The eighteen opponents circulated a "Dear Colleague" letter to all senators. It reiterated the major consumer and producer objections to the compromise bill:

• The compromise will not produce more gas than the status quo.
• The regulatory complexities and the restrictions placed on the free intrastate market will reduce producer incentives.
• The compromise will also mean high prices to consumers in the interstate market, without assuring additional supply.
• The incremental pricing provisions will seriously damage many industrial areas dependent on the interstate market without adequately protecting consumer interests.[79]

The strategy of the opposing coalition was to offer a motion on the floor to recommit the conference bill and report back a pared-down version containing only the emergency sales and allocation provision and a specified price for Alaskan natural gas. The latter provision, it had been argued throughout the year, was necessary for the construction of the Alaskan Pipeline from Prudhoe Bay to the midwestern states.

In spite of the absence of real enthusiasm for the NGPA compromise, the recommittal strategy failed. Senators from spectator states, who might have preferred some other set of solutions to the nation's energy problems, described the NGPA as "the best we can do."[80] New England states hoped that the bill would increase interstate supplies of natural gas (which even at the bill's higher price levels was much less expensive than imported oil or liquid natural gas). Senators from Montana and North Dakota saw the NGPA as essential to an influx of new gas supplies via the Alaskan pipeline and joined Alaskan senators in support for the bill. In the eastern coal states there was strong support for this and the other portions of the administration's energy program, since the combination of higher prices and mandatory conversion was expected to substantially increase coal production.

When the vote was taken on the recommittal motion in the Senate, eastern coal state senators supported the NGPA by seven votes to one. Senators from spectator states in New England, the Southeast, and the plains-mountain region backed it nineteen to ten, while members from the major northeastern–north central and Pacific consumer states split, nine to nine.[81] The producer states voted ten to two for recommittal. After defeating the recommittal motion, the Senate went on to pass the NGPA conference report on September 27, by a vote of fifty-seven to forty-two.

Because the opposing coalition of Republicans, producer state, and urban consumer area congressmen was stronger in the House than in the Senate, House passage was much more problematic. Unless the natural gas bill could be packaged together with the four more popular components of the Carter energy program, as the Ad Hoc bill had done in 1977, the Democratic leadership predicted defeat. Both sides concentrated their pressure on the Rules Committee, which would determine whether the five bills were considered separately or together. After intense lobbying of wavering Democrats by the president and speaker, the Rules Committee on October 13 voted nine to five to combine the bills. Later, on the same day, the House floor approved the packaging rule on a cliff-hanging 207 to 206 vote, and went on to pass the five-part National Energy Act, 231 to 168, on October 15.[82]

A cross-tabulation of the final 1977–1978 votes is presented in Table 25. As can be seen, partisanship and presidential influence were central to the approval of the original Carter program and passage of the 1978 compromise. The administration's program passed the House with overwhelming support from consumer, spectator, and coal-area Democrats.

TABLE 25   ANALYSIS OF SUPPORT FOR THE ORIGINAL CARTER PROPOSALS
AND THE COMPROMISE NATIONAL ENERGY ACT
IN THE HOUSE OF REPRESENTATIVES, 1977–1978

	1977 Carter Proposals		1978 NEA		
Type of Constituency	*Percentage for**	*Percentage against*	*Percentage for*	*Percentage against*	*Number of members*
Consumer districts†	67	30	58	39	(171)
Democrats	88	11	67	29	(124)
Republicans	13	81	34	66	(47)
Coal districts‡	67	33	75	25	(12)
Democrats	80	20	80	20	(10)
Republicans	0	100	50	50	(2)
Producer districts§	26	70	28	68	(47)
Democrats	33	64	30	67	(36)
Republicans	0	90	18	73	(11)
Spectator districts‖	54	45	58	35	(200)
Democrats	89	11	74	19	(116)
Republicans	8	91	36	57	(84)

*Percentage of all members. Announced pairs are counted for and against.
†Districts in which more than half of the households used natural gas.
‡Major coal producing districts identified on the basis of Bureau of Mines production and employment figures (aggregated county data). They are: Illinois 24; Kentucky 1, 5, and 7; Ohio 18; Pennsylvania 12 and 22; Virginia 9; and all West Virginia districts (1, 2, 3, and 4).
§This category includes all congressional districts in Texas, Louisiana, Oklahoma, Kansas, New Mexico, Wyoming, and Alaska.
‖Districts in which less than half the households used natural gas.

It was intensely opposed by Republicans and, when strategic voting is discounted, producer-state representatives of both parties.[83] The compromise National Energy Act (as the five-part package was labelled) was perceived as much less advantageous to consumer areas and lost significant blocs of support among both consumer and spectator Democrats in the northeastern and Great Lakes states. The administration was able to offset these losses by holding the eastern coal areas and southern Democratic spectator districts, and by converting a significant number of Republicans who had previously supported deregulation.[84]

Roughly the same pattern emerged in Senate voting on the natural gas compromise. Outside of Alaska, the conference bill was opposed by a two-to-one margin in the producer states. As a group, coal state senators were the bill's strongest supporters, followed by senators from spectator and consumer states. In regional terms, the president drew the most lopsided support in the South: senators from the nonproducing southern states voted twelve to five for the conference bill.

While it is tempting to attribute this regional pattern to a "native son" effect, there are several economic reasons for the popularity of the compromise energy program in the South. With a large population living at or below the poverty level and without any significant indigenous fuel source, the southeastern–south central region had little reason to oppose price controls. Since utilities and industries in the region had already begun (in the early 1970s) to substitute coal for petroleum products and to increase reliance on nuclear power, the coal conversion provisions presented no major problem for the region and promised to increase gas supplies for households and "essential" industrial uses (in the textile and fertilizer industries, for example). The new gas would carry a higher price tag than that permitted under the 1938 act, but since large areas of the South had never been supplied with gas by the interstate transmission lines that cut through the region on their way north, there was no large vested interest in maintaining low interstate prices. Thus, while deregulation proposals had won wide support in the mid-1970s as a way to increase supplies, the National Energy Act was an equally attractive alternative for the spectator South.

Winners and Losers

In the final compromise of the natural gas issue in 1978, as in the original 1938 act, all four major parties to the long controversy attained goals which, considered individually, represented significant improvements over the status quo:

1. consumer areas obtained the extension of regulation to the intrastate market, ending the supply advantage of the producer states and forcing them to diversify their fuel consumption in favor of alternative fuels produced in other regions;

2. producers gained the eventual deregulation of newly discovered gas sold interstate and higher prices for flowing gas;

3. coal interests were given long-sought protection and expansion of their utility and industrial markets through strong coal conversion requirements and gas price increases that make coal more competitive with natural gas;

4. the regulators—FERC and other units of federal energy administration—achieved wide policing powers over the petroleum industry and greatly expanded authority to manipulate industrial and utility fuel use patterns.[85]

To secure these advantages, both consumers and producers were forced to assume onerous costs. For consumers this meant higher prices without the assurance of additional supplies; for producers, the compromise extended federal controls to their home markets. Judging by the voting patterns and initial reactions, passage of the NEA was an unqualified victory only for the eastern coal region and the regulators. Consumer area congressmen shortly began to push for repeal of the incremental pricing provisions, while attorneys for Texas, Oklahoma, and Louisiana immediately filed suit in federal court to have the price control sections of the new natural gas act declared unconstitutional.

In addition to their immediate objections that the new statute deprived the producer states of tax revenues and disrupted their industrial economies, producer state politicians might have regretted the alteration in political alliances that the nationalization of regulation entailed. Not only had their southern neighbors been persuaded to support extended controls, but coal conversion threatened to disrupt the political ties that bound the energy and natural resource producing states of the nation's heartland in a laissez-faire coalition. In 1980, for example, Texas and Louisiana joined midwestern states in demanding that a national ceiling be enacted to limit the severance taxes placed on coal production by the states of Montana and Wyoming. Like the first natural gas act, the new policy sinks deep roots into the national political economy and promises to yield a variety of fruits. One inevitable result, however, will be the generation of demands both for extended regulation and for its antithesis, immediate deregulation.

8 | Conclusion

Under the broad heading of "regulation" can be grouped a wide variety of governmental activities. In every case the name implies that coercion is exercised and that individuals (or firms) are acted upon directly; their behavior is constrained to a public purpose. Yet in some instances the regulated firms cheerfully tolerate these constraints, to the point of protesting their removal, while in other cases fierce political battles ensue from regulation, sparked by the opposition of the targeted industry. Clearly, coercion can sometimes work in the interests of the regulated. Where there are "free rider" effects that can only be overcome by the imposition of high-level constraints, or where some sort of quid pro quo is attached, an individual or firm may submit voluntarily to regulation (or even request it). For example, a worker may allow a union to deduct dues from his paycheck and order him out on strike in the knowledge that from the aggregate of dues collected and strikers assembled the union may achieve benefits for its members that exceed individual costs. In another case, oil companies may decide not to protest a tax on profits in return for a promise to decontrol prices. If regulation contains no such implicit bargain, if the regulated perceive that all the costs are borne by them and all the benefits accrue to consumers of their products, then "regulation" becomes "redistribution." Add to this equation a geographical concentration of consumers and producers, in territories that coincide with political constituencies, and the stage is set for a monumental political controversy.

Regulation of the natural gas industry began as a case of the first type of regulation—a consensual regulatory bargain—but evolved into a controversy over regional redistribution of wealth. In the twists and turns of its rich history, gas regulation manages to exemplify almost every characteristic of American economic regulation. It was once considered a brilliant example of "good" regulation but, later, a prominent example of regulatory failure. It has provided for the orderly expansion of a valuable industry but also has produced waste, shortage, and distortions in regional economic growth. The original targets of regulation have prospered. However, a number of firms brought into the regulatory net at a later point were driven out of the business. Utility regulation worked disastrously for them, and also for those consumers who, as a result of regulation, were deprived of gas or the benefits of wider competition among producers.

Regulation seems inevitably to breed more regulation and to fulfill its own prophesies. Regulation of natural gas pipelines was designed to fill a "regulatory" gap. With pipelines and local gas distributors under public control, it seemed an anomaly that producers who sold gas to interstate pipelines were not regulated. Once their transactions were brought under federal regulation, new "gaps" appeared. As a result of regulation-induced interstate shortages, demands arose for the regulation of gas producers in the intrastate market as well, and for regulating fuel use by industries and utilities. At the first two junctures, when pipelines and, later, producers were brought under federal regulation, one of the arguments for regulation was the necessity to control the monopolistic tendencies of pipelines and producers. There is considerable evidence, however, that regulation itself increased concentration in both segments of the natural gas industry. A further irony is that the major petroleum companies not only control greater market shares now than they did in 1954 but are also the principal beneficiaries of federal subsidies for the development of synthetic fuels—subsidies made necessary by the fact that controls have held down the price of competing fuels.

Exemplifying another feature of American economic regulation (and bureaucratic behavior in general), the Natural Gas Act has provided a forum for a remarkable display of bureaucratic talents. On the basis of its broad "mandate," administrators have creatively expanded the scope of their jurisdiction and built a strong supportive clientele among congressmen, state regulators, and key groups in industry and the public. On the other hand, the agency has been so constrained by political pressure that it has often been forced into embarrassing reversals of policy in order to save itself from the wrath of elected officials. Finally, a selective reading of the history of gas regulation can be used to illustrate the conventional theory of regulatory "capture." It is undeniable, however, that the regulatory agency has also been an instrument for the "capture" of an industry on behalf of consumers.

In the beginning, gas regulation followed the pattern of most other economic interventions during the New Deal. It was founded on a vaguely worded, highly discretionary statute conceived in the implementing bureaucracy. The bureaucracy had every reason to prefer such a statute, and the Democratic majority in Congress, anticipating a long reign in both executive and legislative branches, had every reason to grant such discretion. As was the case with other New Deal regulatory efforts, an immediate and unusual economic crisis was the occasion for the erection of a permanent regulatory apparatus. The economy was in chaos. The major problem in the natural gas industry, as in other sectors, was overproduction. The industry could see a number of advantages in federal regulation: containment of "destructive" competition, creation of the stable market conditions necessary to attract financing for long-distance pipelines, an almost guaranteed profit margin, and the promise of federal assistance in overriding roadblocks thrown up by the states. In return for these real and anticipated advantages, the industry willingly submitted to public control.

There was, at the same time, a genuine popular demand for federal regulation. When a proposal for regulation of interstate natural gas pipelines was placed on the legislative agenda in 1938, its immediate targets were giant corporations that had managed to offend gas consumers, independent producers, and state regulatory bodies from New York to Texas. For these reasons, passage of the Natural Gas Act was consensual. Since it contained both promotional and protective features, all affected parties could see some advantage in regulation, and no overly burdensome costs were anticipated at the time of passage. The economic situation of the parties vis-à-vis each other and other sectors of the economy was bound to change in ways that could not be foreseen at the time of passage. The legal framework, however, was loose enough to permit substantial shifts in the focus and mode of regulation, and the major groups involved—urban consumers, state public utility commissions, pipeline companies, and congressional oversight committees— probably expected that they would have sufficient political clout to shape the content of regulation in beneficial ways.

At the apex of this ample statutory framework sat the Federal Power Commission, a non-elected body subject to fluctuating pressures from courts, congressmen, and presidents. Within the constraints imposed by the courts and the elected branches, the FPC acted to protect and expand the substance and importance of its jurisdiction. The Federal Power Commission and its successor agency led a revolution in utility rate making and interpreted the common phrases, "dedicated to interstate commerce" and "sales in interstate commerce," in ways that have greatly extended the reach of the national government into the production and distribution of natural resources. It is probable that no other agency has so expanded its focus of control—from pipelines to producers, from wholesales to direct sales and sales curtailments—on the basis of discretionary action. The commission was aided (and prodded) in that expansion by the Supreme Court. The fact that its actions led the FPC more frequently than other agencies into the domain of jealously exercised state regulatory powers may be responsible for the sympathy of the Court toward this regulatory aggrandizement. Both the agency and the Court, as federal actors, can be expected to uphold national claims against challenge from the states, even though the national regulatory mechanism may be in the service of various parochial interests.

When independent producers were brought under regulation against their own wishes and over the objections of state officials, the political environment of the commission changed dramatically. From this point forward, the position of congressmen and presidents on natural gas regulation depended on the importance to their electoral constituencies of gas production or consumption; the pricing decisions of the commission changed with the results of presidential and congressional elections.

The commission's original clientele, the regulated pipeline industry, has continued to thrive under controls.[1] In turn, the industry has provided a stable core of support at times when the shifting balance of power among other key groups—consumers, gas producers, and the coal industry—moved the commission, like a pendulum, from one pole to another. There is nothing in this pattern of accommodation of shifting interests that distinguishes the FPC from other "alphabet" agencies. As Samuel Huntington has written: "Successful adaptation to changing environmental circumstances is the secret of health and longevity for administrative as well as biological organisms. . . . [T]o remain viable over a period of time, an agency must adjust its sources of support so as to correspond with changes in the strength of their political pressures."[2] In the case of the FPC, however, agency "adaptation" has been an unusually dynamic and public process and has not ended in stable "capture" by gas producers.

Although regulatory issues have seldom evoked such intense and enduring regional conflicts as have occurred in natural gas regulation, all economic regulation produces differential impacts on regional economies. The potential for sectional conflict is exacerbated by the territorial basis of elections, the weakness of the party system, and a federal structure that not only encloses different political cultures and legal systems, but also supports fifty sets of elected officials sensitive to encroachments on their respective turfs. When the aggrieved consumers of a product or service are geographically distinct from the regulated industry and the latter is offered no compensatory benefit for the costs imposed by regulation, regional conflict over regulatory outcomes will understandably arise. In the 1880s, when the first federal regulatory commission (the Interstate Commerce Commission) was created, it was at the instigation of farmers, shippers, and businessmen in the Midwest, West, and South. Regulation was opposed by northeastern congressmen whose constituencies included the railroad corporations (most of which objected to federal regulation), and whose local economies benefitted from the prevailing rate structures. A regional interpretation of the subsequent "capture" of the ICC by the railroads might emphasize the dominance of the national government after 1900 by the Republican party, whose electoral base in the urban-industrial states of the East included the stockholders and financial supporters of the rail corporations. Once the financial condition of the railroads began to deteriorate, both under the burdens imposed by amendments to the original act and the emergence of competing transportation modes, the regional controversy surrounding ICC regulation was greatly diminished.

To find legislative conflicts that match those attending the natural gas issue in intensity, regionalism, partisanship, and the stability of opposing poles, one must look to the recurrent tariff and currency battles of the nineteenth and early twentieth centuries. The tariff and the gold standard were the persistent issues on which American politics revolved from the end of Reconstruction to the 1920s. Agricultural areas, particularly in the South, agitated unsuccessfully for bimetalism and protested the regional transfer of income that resulted when tariffs increased the price of imported goods to protect the markets of industry in the Northeast and Midwest, and wool growers in the West. The Republican coalition was put together with the help of logrolled tariff bills, which constituted effective political manipulation of the national economy on behalf of regionally concentrated interests.[3]

The simple economic controls of the nineteenth century gave way in the 1930s to a complex system of economic regulation, as Congress created a great variety of economic levers that could be wielded on behalf of interested groups. The authority of the Federal Power Commission was one of those levers. Its history illustrates the long struggle over control of the political economy that underlies the great regional and partisan clashes of American politics. Indeed, the design of the American constitutional system and of its extra-constitutional party system seems to produce more bitter struggles over issues of regional redistribution than over issues involving social classes.

The United States Constitution was designed with several purposes in mind, not the least of which was the creation of national fiscal institutions that would foster the development of large-scale capitalist enterprise on the eastern seaboard. The price of ratification was the maintenance of a federal structure, and federalism has at times fragmented the national market (as well as the social fabric). However, Article I, Section 8, of the Constitution (as interpreted by the federal courts since 1936) empowers Congress to override state economic controls and create national markets in the interest of regulating interstate commerce. One of the major thrusts of U.S. economic regulation in the twentieth century has been to equalize costs or prices between regions and between domestic and foreign producers. This impulse can be seen, for example, in railroad regulation, pollution standards, the minimum wage, and the tariff.

As energy costs soared in the 1970s and came to comprise a larger and larger part of the costs of production, political attention was focused on mechanisms for controlling energy prices. An elaborate system of price and allocation controls was devised for oil and gas and their products. Refineries processing controlled domestic oil were directed to write checks each month totalling millions of dollars to compensate refineries—principally in the Northeast—which utilized more expensive imported oil.[4] The regulatory apparatus for fuel price control soon grew to an impressive size. The Department of Energy, responsible for administering the controls and subsidizing the development of synthetic fuels and alternative energy sources (which were not economically feasible in a system of administered oil and gas prices), had 20,500 employees and a budget approaching twelve billion dollars in 1980.

From time to time, it has been suggested that maintenance of reasonable prices and the rational application of energy sources to their highest uses could best be achieved by nationalization of all fuel production, rather than the present mixed system of private ownership and regulation. The hope of subjecting "market" processes to systematic controls is always present among intellectuals with a social conscience, but it was particularly strong in the 1930s, when the "market," left to its own devices, had produced such dismal results.[5] A modest beginning toward federal control of fuel production and marketing was advocated by such New Deal "brain trusters" as Leland Olds and Rexford Tugwell, but never found its way into concrete legislative proposals. Given the intense objections of the natural resource producing states to centralized control, the idea was far too controversial for an administration with more mundane and immediate problems on its hands. It is possible that there existed a congressional majority in support of such a program in the 1930s, but the American political process was designed to thwart all but the largest and most determined majorities.

A Supreme Court decision in 1954 made it possible to implement a program that probably could not have been achieved through legislative means: control of the prices paid natural gas producers in the South and West on behalf of urban consumers in the Northeast, Midwest, and California. With this judicial revision of statutory content, the politics of natural gas evolved in ways that parallel the shift from regulatory to redistributive legislation in the policy typology of Theodore Lowi. Departing from the committee-centered, consensual process evoked by the original regulatory statute, legislative controversy grew, shifted to the floor, and attracted increasing attention from the president and his top advisors. The amorphous supporting coalition of 1938 give way to a polarized, regionally-based conflict between producer and urban consumer areas that was essentially a struggle over the distribution of wealth between two sets of political constituencies. That conflict was further aggravated by impending scarcity—not only the shortage of a reasonably priced domestic fuel, but the severe economic difficulties of the older industrial areas of the United States. In the 1970s these areas were suffering unemployment and outmigration to a significantly greater degree than other regions (particularly the major oil and gas producing states), and were in no mood to abandon control of an essential fuel. On the other hand, the producer states believed that their new affluence had been wrested out of the jaws of a regulatory apparatus illegitimately imposed on them, and they resented the fact that a product on which their economies depended should be controlled, while the coal and manufactured goods they imported from other states were not.

In all battles there are spectators. Just as there were some districts in the nineteenth century that, on balance, neither benefitted nor suffered significant harm from tariff levies, so there were interest-neutral areas in the natural gas controversy. Although these neutral areas do not, as a rule, generate policy alternatives, the contending interests must appeal to them in designing those alternatives. Spectators, as the name implies, are always open to the best bargain. In the natural gas controversy, these areas, particularly southern districts represented by Democrats, have vacillated between the consumer and producer poles. The same can be said of coal areas. The coal industry has favored regulation of the end uses of gas; at the same time, coal interests have resented the competition of price-controlled fuels. In the 1970s, industry spokesmen began to fear the extension of such controls to coal itself, and, as a result, became more sympathetic to arguments for deregulation of natural gas. Thus, coal area congressmen were also open to the best bargain offered by the competing poles. The irony is that when the two competing positions were compromised, the producers and a significant minority of consumers disowned the legislative result. It was the spectator and coal area congressmen whose support permitted passage of the Natural Gas Policy Act of 1978.

The patchwork bill of 1978 has been much maligned, but the new law does have several virtues. It provides for a gradual transition to deregulation, cushioning the impact on residential consumers until the new, higher price levels have a chance to elicit greater supplies. The inelasticity assumption of consumer spokesmen and the pessimistic predictions of the Carter administration appear to have been mistaken. Since passage of the NGPA, the number of drilling rigs in operation has reached an all-time high, and predictions of potential gas supplies have grown ever more optimistic.[6] With the increase in supplies available to interstate pipelines, the American Gas Association began an intensive national advertising campaign (reminiscent of the 1950s), encouraging homeowners to convert from oil to gas. To the extent that southwestern industries and utilities (which must yield gas supplies to interstate residential consumers) shift to domestically produced coal, this conversion process should bring a significant reduction in oil imports.

Another advantage in the new law is that it indicates a willingness of Congress to assert itself in economic regulation, and, reversing the pattern established in the 1930s, to specify regulated prices in legislation rather than leaving this important task to the regulatory agency. Although the NGPA and its companion legislation significantly expand the discretion of the Department of Energy and the Federal Energy Regulatory Commission to affect the fuel use practices of American industry, the trend to statutory specificity in pricing—a phenomenon observed in both oil and gas controls—runs counter to the argument that in a complex industrial economy the legislature must inevitably yield its powers to "experts" in the bureaucracy. This return to a nineteenth-century mode of regulation may create some inflexibility, but from the point of view of democratic, majoritarian control of the policy apparatus, it is an encouraging development.

There is no guarantee, however, that the 1978 statute will enjoy a long lifetime. Given the dissatisfaction of diverse groups with the compromise act and the increasing political power of the southwestern and mountain states vis-à-vis the industrial Northeast and Midwest, the NGPA cannot be viewed as a stable solution to the natural gas problem. Republican control of the legislature and the presidency might enhance the prospects for deregulation. Predictions for a victorious producer coalition are premature, however. The present expansion in household consumption will inevitably expand the consumer interest, as was the case in the 1950s. Furthermore, the southwestern-mountain alliance is already strained by the fact that the southwestern states are importing increasing amounts of coal from the mountain states for the generation of electric power. In view of this changing economic situation, it would not be surprising to find Texans proposing national regulation of coal prices, limitations on state taxing prerogatives, and federally aided construction of coal pipelines—all of which would bring Texas into conflict with Montana, Colorado, Utah, and Wyoming.

It is unreasonable to expect congressmen to forego attempts at political manipulation of the national economy on behalf of local concerns and concentrate their attention instead on the "national interest." Such an interest is usually impossible to define apart from the interests of the individuals and groups that constitute the nation. In addition, to posit a "national" interest requires that assumptions be made about the economic future in a situation of great uncertainty. As the competing economic models employed in the natural gas debate demonstrate, the choice of assumptions is, to a great extent, arbitrary and self-serving. Finally, the American political system does not encourage the sort of long-term assessment that the concept "national interest" implies. In the long term, as the wag has said, we are all dead. The short term comes around every second year.

Notes

Abbreviations

HR IFC 1934	US Congress, House, Committee on Interstate and Foreign Commerce, Petroleum Investigation, 73d Cong., recess (Sept. 1934).
HR IFC 1935	US Congress, House, Committee on Interstate and Foreign Commerce, Hearings on the Public Utility Holding Company Act, 74th Cong., 1st sess. (Feb.–March 1935).
HR IFC 1936	US Congress, House, Committee on Interstate and Foreign Commerce, Hearings on Natural Gas, 74th Cong., 2d sess. (April 1936).
HR IFC 1937	US Congress, House, Committee on Interstate and Foreign Commerce, Hearings on the Natural Gas Act, 75th Cong., 1st sess. (March 1937).
HR IFC 1939	US Congress, House, Committee on Interstate and Foreign Commerce, Petroleum Investigation, 76th Cong., 1st sess. (Nov. 1939).
HR IFC 1941	US Congress, House, Committee on Interstate and Foreign Commerce, Hearings on Natural Gas Amendments, 77th Cong., 1st sess. (July 1941).
HR IFC 1947	US Congress, House, Committee on Interstate and Foreign Commerce, Hearings on Amendments to the Natural Gas Act, 80th Cong., 1st sess. (April–May 1947).
Senate IFC 1949	US Congress, Senate, Committee on Interstate and Foreign Commerce, Hearings on the Reappointment of Leland Olds to the Federal Power Commission, 81st Cong., 1st sess. (Sept.–Oct. 1949).
HR IFC 1953	US Congress, House, Committee on Interstate and Foreign Commerce, Hearings on Natural Gas Act Amendments, 83d Cong., 1st sess. (June 1953).

HR IFC 1955   US Congress, House, Committee on Interstate and
                    Foreign Commerce, Hearings on Exemption of Natural
                    Gas Producers, 84th Cong., 1st sess. (March–April
                    1955).

Senate IFC 1955   US Congress, Senate, Committee on Interstate and
                    Foreign Commerce, Hearings on Amendments to the
                    Natural Gas Act, 84th Cong., 1st sess. (May–June
                    1955).

HR IFC 1957   US Congress, House, Committee on Interstate and
                    Foreign Commerce, Hearings on Amendments to the
                    Natural Gas Act, 85th Cong., 1st sess. (May 1957).

HR IFC 1971   US Congress, House, Committee on Interstate and
                    Foreign Commerce, Hearings on Natural Gas Amend-
                    ments of 1971, 92d Cong., 1st sess. (Sept. 1971).

Senate COC 1972   US Congress, Senate, Committee on Commerce, Hear-
                    ings on Natural Gas Regulation, 92d Cong., 2d sess.
                    (March 1972). The Senate shortened the name of this
                    committee from the older "Interstate and Foreign Com-
                    merce" form.

Senate COI 1972   US Congress, Senate, Committee on Interior and Insu-
                    lar Affairs, Hearings on Natural Gas Policy Issues, 92d
                    Cong., 2d sess. (Feb.–March 1972).

Senate COJ 1973   US Congress, Senate, Committee on the Judiciary, Sub-
                    committee on Antitrust and Monopoly, Hearings on
                    Competition in the Natural Gas Industry, 93d Cong., 1st
                    sess. (June 1973).

Senate COC 1974   US Congress, Senate, Committee on Commerce, Hear-
                    ings on the Consumer Energy Act of 1974, 4 vols., 93d
                    Cong., 1st sess., 2d sess. (Oct. 1973–March 1974).

HR IFC 1974   US Congress, House, Committee on Interstate and
                    Foreign Commerce, Special Subcommittee on Inves-
                    tigations, Hearings on Conflict of Interest, Emergency
                    Gas Sales, and Other Internal Procedures of the Federal
                    Power Commission, 93d Cong., 2d sess. (Sept.–Oct.
                    1974).

HR IFC 1975   US Congress, House, Committee on Interstate and
                    Foreign Commerce, Hearings on Natural Gas Supplies,
                    94th Cong., 1st sess. (June–July 1975).

Senate COC 1975   US Congress, Senate, Committee on Commerce, Hear-
                    ings on the Natural Gas Production and Conservation
                    Act, 94th Cong., 1st sess. (March–April 1975).

Senate COC 1976   US Congress, Senate, Committee on Commerce, Hear-
                    ings on Revised Rates for Natural Gas, 94th Cong., 2d
                    sess. (Aug. 1976).

HR IFC 1977	US Congress, House, Committee on Interstate and Foreign Commerce, Hearings on the National Energy Act, 95th Cong., 1st sess. (May 1977).
HR IFC 1978	US Congress, House, Committee on Interstate and Foreign Commerce, Energy and Power Subcommittee, Economic Analysis of HR 5289, 95th Cong., 2d sess. (Committee Print 95-62, Oct. 13, 1978).
FPC Annual Report	Annual Reports of the Federal Power Commission. Washington, D.C.: US Government Printing Office, vol. 1, 1921.
(vol.) FPC (page)	FPC Reports (opinions and decisions of the FPC). Washington, D.C.: US Government Printing Office, vol. 1, 1931.
FTC Monograph no. 36	Federal Trade Commission Monograph no. 36 on Natural Gas and Natural Gas Pipelines in USA. Published as Temporary National Economic Committee Report no. 76-3 (Senate Committee Print). Washington, D.C.: US Government Printing Office, 1940.
FTC Report	Federal Trade Commission, Report to the Senate on Public Utility Corporations, Senate Document no. 92, 70th Cong., 1st sess. (published in 96 vols.; summary recommendations in pt. 84-A, 1935).
Minerals Yearbook	United States Department of the Interior, Bureau of Mines, *Minerals Yearbook* (Washington, D.C.: US Government Printing Office); published annually (in recent years, in several volumes; the volume on fuels is indicated).
Smith-Wimberly Report and Olds-Draper Report	In 1948, the Federal Power Commission published a *Report on Natural Gas Investigation* (Docket no. G-580) in two volumes: one signed by Commissioners Nelson Smith and Harrington Wimberly, the other, by Commissioners Leland Olds and Claude Draper. The volumes are cited by the commissioners' names, with page numbers following.

Chapter 1

1. Walter Adams, "Competition, Monopoly and Countervailing Power," in Howard D. Marshall, ed., *Business and Government* (Washington, D.C.: Heath, 1970), p. 70.

2. Adams, "Competition," p. 72.

3. Marver H. Bernstein, *Regulating Business by Independent Commission* (Princeton, N.J.: Princeton University Press, 1955), p. 228.

4. Examples of the emphasis on personalities can be found in the Nader Study Group's criticism of antitrust enforcement, *The Closed Enterprise System* (New York: Grossman, 1972), p. 114, and in Robert C. Fellmeth, *The Interstate Commerce Omission* (New York: Grossman, 1970).

5. Samuel P. Huntington, "The Marasmus of the ICC," *The Yale Law Journal* 61, no. 4 (April 1952): 467–509.

6. Bernstein, *Regulating*, pp. 81–83.

7. Murray Edleman, "Symbols and Political Quiescence," *American Political Science Review* 54, no. 3 (Sept. 1960): 695–704.

8. Gabriel Kolko, *The Triumph of Conservatism* (New York: Free Press of Glencoe, 1963), and *Railroads and Regulation* (Princeton, N.J.: Princeton University Press, 1965). The establishment of the ICC, according to Kolko, represents the first of many successful efforts by industry to protect itself from the "attacks of a potentially democratic Society" (*Railroads*, p. 239).

9. George Stigler, "The Theory of Economic Regulation," *The Bell Journal of Economic and Management Science* 2, no. 1 (Spring 1971): 3–21. According to Stigler, the outcome of regulation (the degree to which the regulated industry is benefitted) is merely a function of the size, concentration, and financial resources of the regulated group.

10. Mancur Olson, *The Logic of Collective Action* (Cambridge, Mass.: Harvard University Press, 1965).

11. On the potency of coalitions composed of intense minorities, see Robert Dahl, *A Preface to Democratic Theory* (Chicago: University of Chicago Press, 1956).

12. A model of the triangular exchange of benefits can be found in Theodore Lowi, "How the Farmers Get What They Want," in *Legislative Politics, U.S.A.*, 3d ed., ed. T. J. Lowi and R. B. Ripley (Boston: Little, Brown, 1973).

13. Alan Stone, *Economic Regulation and the Public Interest* (Ithaca, N.Y.: Cornell University Press, 1977); James O. Wilson, "The Dead Hand of Regulation," *The Public Interest* 25 (Fall 1971): 46–47.

14. Stone, *Economic Regulation*, p. 257.

15. Louis L. Jaffe, *Judicial Control of Administrative Action* (Boston: Little, Brown, 1965), p. 25. See also his "The Effective Limits of the Administrative Process: A Reevaluation," *Harvard Law Review* 67, no. 7 (May 1954): 1105–1135. Jaffe makes the point that, in addition to presenting the implementing agencies with ambiguous mandates, Congress imposes on them tasks that facilitate industry participation in the regulatory process. The transportation planning and coordination functions mandated by Interstate Commerce Act amendments are cases in point. In addition, the Administrative Procedure Act and recent Magnuson-Moss amendments make the regulated groups active participants in administrative rule making, and put the "public interest," given the lesser resources of the groups claiming to represent it, on a weaker footing. Thus, regardless of the degree of "public interest" advocacy embodied in the original statute, these procedures dissipate its force.

16. Theodore J. Lowi, *The End of Liberalism*, 2d ed. (New York: Norton, 1979).

17. A recent article which investigates the conditions for passage of nondiscretionary legislation by Congress is Richard F. Bensel, "Creating the Statutory State: The Implications of a Rule of Law Standard in American Politics," *American Political Science Review* 74 (Sept. 1980): 734–744.

18. Lowi's policy typology is developed in "American Business, Public Policy, Case Studies, and Political Theory," *World Politics* 16 (July 1964): 677–715; "Four Systems of Policy, Politics, and Choice," *Public Administration Review* 32 (July/Aug. 1972): 298–310; "Decision-Making versus Policy-Making: Toward an Antidote for Technocracy," *Public Administration Review* 30 (May/June 1970): 314–325; and "Public Policy and Bureaucracy in the United States and France," paper delivered at the Edinburgh IPSA Congress, Aug. 1976.

19. Critics of Lowi's typology have pointed out that it is difficult to characterize policies as distributive or redistributive since, in the long run, almost every policy is redistributive (that is, it benefits some at the expense of others). This criticism assumes a conventional meaning for the term "redistribution." In fact, for Lowi, the word is applied as a label only to policies with certain coercive characteristics—those applying coercion at the "environmental" level (affecting broad classes of actors) and in which coercion is immediate. Some of the problems arising from Lowi's typology undoubtedly result from his use of common words like "regulation" and "redistribution" as labels with uncommon meanings. For example, some governmental activities commonly thought of as economic regulation (for example, the setting of interest rates) are "redistributive" in Lowi's scheme.

20. Lowi, *End of Liberalism*.

21. On the NRA, see Ellis Hawley, *The New Deal and the Problem of Monopoly* (Princeton, N.J.: Princeton University Press, 1966), and Bernard Bellusch, *The Failure of the NRA* (New York: Norton, 1975).

22. Lowi's approach to the study of public policy thus represents an attempt to refocus the attention of political scientists on the law and formal processes of government, concern for which was, he argues, a casualty of the behavioral revolution in the social sciences.

23. Lowi, *End of Liberalism*, pp. 146n. and 153–154.

24. Ibid., pp. 141–143.

25. See, for example, Anthony Downs, *Inside Bureaucracy* (Boston: Little, Brown, 1967); Gordon Tullock, *The Politics of Bureaucracy* (Washington, D.C.: Public Affairs Press, 1965); Aaron Wildavsky, *The Politics of the Budgetary Process* (Boston: Little, Brown, 1974); and David Braybrooke and Charles E. Lindbloom, *A Strategy of Decision* (New York: Free Press, 1963).

26. *Encyclopedia of the Social Sciences* (New York: Macmillan, 1931), p. 345.

27. Edward J. Mitchell, "The Basis of Congressional Energy Policy," *Texas Law Review* 57, no. 4 (March 1979): 592. Similarly, political scientist Pietro Nivola reports a correlation of − .74 between a measure of liberalism and support for the Krueger-Brown deregulation amendment in 1977. See his "Energy Policy and the Congress: The Politics of the Natural Gas Act of 1978," *Public Policy* 28, no. 4 (Fall 1980): 43. The measures of ideology used in both the Nivola and Mitchell studies are the scores assigned congressmen by groups like the Americans for Democratic Action. These scores are not actually measures of the underlying belief structures or attitudes of congressmen, but measures of voting patterns. ADA scores represent the percentage of time a congressman votes with the position established by congressional members of the organization, chapters of which are concentrated in large northeastern cities and the San Francisco Bay area. To a large extent, ADA votes represent issues on which there are distinct regional, social, and economic interests—for example, aid to New York City, defense spending, and deregulation of natural gas, all of which were ADA selected roll calls in the 1970s. Thus, it is not surprising that support for the ADA position would be highly correlated with support for oil and gas price controls. Support for petroleum regulation is a part of the *definition* of liberalism for the ADA.

28. For example, Representatives Long and Boggs of Louisiana.

29. Recently, however, there is a tendency among liberal congressmen to support deregulation in some sectors (airlines and trucking, for example).

30. For an argument that ideology, as embodied in the positions of groups like the ADA, rationalizes regional interests, see Richard F. Bensel, "Sectional Stress and Ideology in the U.S. House of Representatives," *Polity* (forthcoming, Spring 1982).

31. Thus, it is not surprising that a ranking of *states* by such single characteristics as consumption or curtailment levels would not predict very well the votes of congressmen, particularly in the House, on gas regulation roll calls. The Mitchell study cited above uses overall state, rather than district consumption and curtailment levels (taken separately), as measures of district economic interests. The vote on the Smith amendment in 1976 is used as a measure of opposition to deregulation. However, the Smith proposal, which is discussed in Chapter 6, was a "package" of proposals including an extension of regulation to the producer states, a fixed price range for gas, and coal conversion. Coal-producing areas thus

had an "economic" interest in the Smith bill that gas consumption and curtailment levels would not tap.

Chapter 2

1. Economist Paul Weaver goes so far as to reverse the imputation of legitimacy. Whereas the "old regulation" was frankly promotional and designed to serve its business clientele, it did encourage orderly growth within single industries. The new multi-industry regulation, according to Weaver, serves only the interests of the group of lawyers and consumer activists who make their careers by presuming to represent the public interest. Paul Weaver, "Regulation, Social Policy, and Class Conflict," in Chris Argyris et al., *Regulating Business* (San Francisco: Institute for Contemporary Studies, 1978), pp. 193–218.

2. On early mercantilist regulation see, for example, Laurence J. Friedman, *A History of American Law* (New York: Simon and Schuster, 1973), pts. I and II, William K. Jones, *Regulated Industries: Cases and Materials* (Brooklyn: Foundation Press, 1967), pp. 1–33, and Carter Goodrich, ed., *The Government and the Economy, 1783–1861* (New York: Bobbs-Merrill, 1967).

3. Gabriel Kolko, *The Triumph of Conservatism* (New York: Free Press of Glencoe, 1963), pp. 98–112.

4. Arguments for public restraint of competition are often made on the premise that unrestrained competition produces what is known as a "free rider" problem. While it is in the interest of a group of producers that production be limited and that prices significantly exceed costs, each individual producer will be tempted to cut prices and/or increase his own output. Thus the outcome will be overproduction and falling prices. Clearly, what the producers need is an agent of coercion to guarantee that no individual firm will overproduce or cut prices. If the group of producers is large, government is the obvious solution. Government regulation overcomes the free rider problem by directly setting production limits and minimum prices or by equalizing costs—for example, by requiring minimum wages and hours, setting limits on pollution and backing up, with its own coercive potential, industry price and production standards, service pooling arrangements, and so forth.

5. For a biting critique of the "natural monopoly" argument, see Walter Adams and Horace M. Gray, *Monopoly in America: The Government as Promoter* (New York: Macmillan, 1955). Gray argues elsewhere that "aside from the monopolists themselves, the most assiduous promoters of monopoly and suppressors of competition are the regulatory commissions, both state and federal." Monopolies neither "natural" nor "inevitable" were "artificially contrived" by government, Gray maintains, particularly by the federal government during the period from 1907 to 1933. Horace M. Gray, "Comment," in *Essays on Public Utility Pricing and Regulation*, ed. Harry M. Trebing (East Lansing, Mich.: State University Institute of Public Utilities, 1971), pp. 291–298.

6. The "public" nature of the enterprise is revealed by the fact that government itself has often developed and operated such services.

7. Harold Koontz and Richard Gable, *Public Control of Economic Enterprise* (New York: McGraw-Hill, 1956), p. 215.

8. On the origins and extension of the concept "affected with a public interest," see William K. Jones, *Regulated Industries*; Ford P. Hall, *The Concept of Business Affected with a Public Interest* (Bloomington, Ind.: Principia Press, 1940); Hall, *Government and Business*, 3d ed. (New York: McGraw-Hill, 1956), chap. 11; and Koontz and Gable, *Public Control*, chap. 9.

9. 94 US 113 (1877).

10. The Supreme Court's decision in the Wabash case (118 US 557) in 1886 precipitated the Interstate Commerce Act.

11. On the origins of the commission form see Marver H. Bernstein, *Regulating Business by Independent Commission* (Princeton, N.J.: Princeton University Press, 1955), and Kolko, *Triumph of Conservatism*.

12. 291 US 502 (1934). In an earlier decision (*Wolff Packing Company* v. *Kansas*, 262 US 522), the Court attempted to catalogue the set of businesses "clothed with a public interest." The major criterion for the classification was "the indispensable nature of the service," according to the Court. Most commentators are critical of the anti-competitive features of the National Recovery Administration. Horace M. Gray describes the NRA as "a haven for aspiring monopolists" in "The Passing of the Public Interest Concept," *Journal of Land and Public Utility Economics* 16, no. 1 (Feb. 1940): 8–20. For a recent critical analysis of the NRA, see Robert F. Himmelberg, *The Origins of the National Recovery Administration* (New York: Fordham University Press, 1976).

13. Elmer E. Smead, *Government Promotion and Regulation of Business* (New York: Appleton Century Crofts, 1969), pp. 400–442; Merle Fainsod, Lincoln Gordon, and Joseph C. Palamountain, Jr., *Government and the American Economy* (New York: Norton, 1959), chaps. 19 and 20.

14. Charles C. Rohlfing et al., *Business and Government* (Brooklyn: Foundation Press, 1953), p. 351. As Ellis Hawley observes in *The New Deal and the Problem of Monopoly*, "When declining demand led to excess capacity and intense competition, the transportation leaders reacted by advocating some type of cartelization" (Princeton, N.J.: Princeton University Press, 1966). In air transportation, the federal government, before 1938, had granted subsidies, both direct and in the form of lucrative mail contracts, but these subsidies were often directed to smaller lines in the interest of promoting competition. The 1938 Civil Aeronautics Act clearly had an anti-competitive thrust. The form of regulation adopted in the Merchant Marine Act of 1936 was somewhat more complicated than that imposed by the CAA. The Merchant Marine Act instituted the licensing features of utility regulation through government subsidies for shipbuilding and operation. Ship operators, in return, were subject to elaborate controls over routes, rates, and labor practices.

15. Although the trucking companies themselves supported rate and entry controls after the demise of the NRA, the railroads and the ICC had long advocated the extension of regulation to barge and motor transportation.

16. Among the most important critiques of past assumptions about economic competition were Edward H. Chamberlin, *The Theory of Monopolistic Competition* (Cambridge, Mass.: Harvard University Press, 1932); Joan Robinson, *The Economics of Imperfect Competition* (New York: Macmillan, 1933); and J. M.

Clark, "Toward a Concept of Workable Competition," *American Economic Review* 39, no. 2 (June 1940): 241–256. Influential defenders of the large corporation include Peter Drucker in *Big Business* (London: Heinemann, 1947), esp. pp. 217–226, and John Kenneth Galbraith, *American Capitalism* (Boston: Houghton-Mifflin, 1952). Adams maintains that the Depression induced a shift among leading economists to the defense of "collective" goals. To Keynesians, the structure of an industry was less important than its impact on aggregate employment and the advance of technology. Walter Adams, *The Structure of American Industry*, 3d ed. (New York: Macmillan, 1961), pp. 547–550, and Walter Adams and Horace M. Gray, *Monopoly in America*, pp. 173–175.

17. Galbraith, *American Capitalism.*

18. See, for example, Hall, *Government and Business*, p. 7.

19. The following section draws on numerous accounts of the early history of the gas industry, including particularly: Louis Stotz, *History of the Gas Industry* (Chicago: Stettiner, 1938); Alfred M. Leeston, John A. Crichton, and John C. Jacobs, *The Dynamic Natural Gas Industry* (Norman, Okla.: University of Oklahoma Press, 1963); HR IFC 1935, pp. 1788–1790 (The historical sketch included in the hearings transcript was taken from the National Association of Mutual Savings Banks [NAMSB], *History of the Natural Gas Industry*); and Ralph E. Davis, "Natural Gas Pipe Line Development During the Past Ten Years," *Natural Gas* 16, no. 12 (Dec. 1935): 3–8.

20. The first known "long-distance" pipeline was made of wood and extended twenty-five miles from a gas well at West Bloomfield to Rochester, N.Y. The first iron pipe was laid in 1872 to serve the city of Titusville, Pa. By 1910, most cities in western Pennsylvania, northern West Virginia, and Ohio had pipeline service from Appalachian fields. NAMSB, *History of the Natural Gas Industry*, HR IFC 1935, pp. 1788–1789.

21. By the late 1930s, the Panhandle and Hugoton fields were estimated to contain about half of all known United States reserves; the Appalachian fields, just over 10 percent.

22. HR IFC 1936, p. 10 (testimony of FPC solicitor Dozzier DeVane).

23. FTC Report, pt. 84-A. The most complex network was probably that of Columbia Gas and Electric, whose subsidiaries furnished gas, electricity, telephone, and water service to 1,648 communities in twenty states. James C. Bonbright and Gardner C. Means, *The Holding Company* (New York: McGraw-Hill, 1932), p. 90.

24. *Public Utility Compendium* 7, no. 1 (April 1934).

25. FTC Report, pt. 83, pp. 5–6; pt. 84-A, chap. 6; and FTC Monograph no. 36, pp. 21–30, 56–74. See also HR IFC 1936 , pp. 54–56 (testimony of William Chantland).

26. HR IFC 1936, pp. 11–12; and FTC Monograph no. 36, pp. 22–24. By 1932, three-quarters of the electricity production in the United States was controlled by eight holding companies.

27. *Public Utilities Fortnightly,* April 1934, p. 25.

28. FTC Monograph no. 36, pp. 47–50.

29. Ibid., p. 96.

30. HR IFC 1936, p. 78

31. See, for example, the account of the problems faced by the Illinois Commission in dealing with the Insull Company. HR IFC 1936, p. 157.

32. *Missouri* v. *Kansas Gas Co.*, 265 US 298 (1924); Public Utility Commission of *Rhode Island* v. *Attleboro Steam and Electric Co.*, 273 US 83 (1927).

33. FTC Report, pt. 83, pp. 27–42, 64–80, 98–100.

34. Ibid., pp. 25–26.

35. Ibid., pt. 84-A, pp. 615–616 (this is an abridged listing of the commission's recommendations).

36. Ibid., pt. 73-A, pp. 61–76; and pt. 84-A, pp. 616–617.

37. Ibid., pt. 84-A, pp. 615, 611.

38. HR IFC 1935, pt. 1. The Public Utility Holding Company bill was originally numbered HR 5423.

39. U.S. *Congressional Record* (hereafter *Cong. Rec.*), House, 1935, pp. 14622, 14623. Clair Wilcox describes the Holding Company Act as "the most stringent corrective measure ever applied to American business." *Public Policies Toward Business* (Homewood, Ill.: Irwin, 1960), p. 633.

40. HR IFC 1936, pp. 57–58 (testimony of Dr. Walter Splawn). Splawn was special counsel to the House committee and had conducted for the committee an investigation of holding companies in the transportation industry, including pipelines. The report was published as HR Report no. 2192, 72d Cong., 2d sess.

41. HR IFC 1935, pp. 57–58, 553.

42. Ibid., pp. 1721, 1802, 1867, 2282.

43. Ibid., pp. 1731, 2282.

44. Ibid., pp. 1905–1907 (testimony of a representative of Standard Gas and Electric Company).

45. Ibid., pp. 1909–1913.

46. In addition, a number of holding companies fell into bankruptcy during the Depression and were reorganized into smaller components.

47. Merle Fainsod and Lincoln Gordon, *Government and the American Economy* (New York: Norton, 1941), p. 73.

48. Thirteenth Annual Report (1947), p. 73.

49. Richard W. Hooley, *Financing the Natural Gas Industry* (New York: Columbia University Press, 1961), p. 35.

50. Rohlfing et al., *Business and Government*, pp. 257–275; see also Alfred E. Kahn, *The Economics of Regulation*, vol. 2 (New York: John Wiley and Sons, 1970), p. 71, and the fifth annual report (1939) of the SEC (the SEC regulates charges for services to companies within holding company systems).

51. HR IFC 1936, p. 141.

52. According to House Report no. 709, 75th Cong., 1st sess., $260 million of the $394 million paid for gas by consumers in 1934 went for interstate transportation.

53. HR IFC 1937, pp. 123, 134. Asked for the pipeline companies' opinion of the bill, Dougherty replied, "We think that generally it is sound regulation." This public approval contrasts, however, with negative comments made by Dougherty to a trade magazine. See *Pipeline News* (Dec. 1937), pp. 3–4.

54. HR IFC 1937, pp. 23–25, 141.

55. Ibid., p. 89.

56. Ibid., p. 55.

57. Quoted in *Oil and Gas Journal*, March 27, 1937, p. 41.

58. HR IFC 1937, pp. 62–71.

59. Ibid., p. 69. Halleck spoke in favor of the bill during floor debate.

60. Ibid., p. 82. Lea himself was a former California public utility commissioner.

61. Ibid., p. 83.

62. House Report no. 709, 75th Cong., 1st sess. A "clean bill" was reintroduced as HR 6586. The principal change from HR 4008 was the removal of a phrase exempting industrial sales from section 1b, apparently because of coal industry objections. Industrial sales were, however, still exempted from the suspension provisions of section 4c (see note 65). The Senate Commerce Committee deferred to the House report on the natural gas bill.

63. Ibid., p. 3.

64. Ibid., p. 2. In a painstaking legal analysis of the wording of the 1935, 1936, and 1937 bills, Donald J. Liebert concludes that the committee clearly intended coverage only for interstate wholesales, defined as sales at the "city gate" by transporting pipelines. See "Legislative History of the Natural Gas Act," *Georgetown Law Journal* 44, no. 4 (June 1956): 695–723.

65. Under the 1938 act, pipeline sales for resale to industries could not be suspended (and thus were not subject to refund). The price at which such sales were contracted could, however, be rolled back if the commission found them unreasonable. A 1962 amendment made industrial sales for resale subject to the suspension procedure as well. Sales for resale (by local utilities) to industries should not be confused with direct sales by pipelines to industries. Some industries run their own connector lines and purchase gas directly from the pipeline. These direct industrial sales have never been subject to price controls, although the FPC has been able to limit the quantities of gas involved in such sales by broadly interpreting its certification powers and, in the 1970s, assuming power to set priorities for pipeline curtailments.

Chapter 3

1. For a producer state endorsement, see the comments of Texas Representative Bob Poage, *Cong. Rec.*, House, pp. 1937, 6725.

2. Merle Fainsod and Lincoln Gordon, *Government and the American Economy* (New York: Norton, 1941), pp. 331–337. On the early years of the FPC, see E. Pendleton Herring, *Public Administration and the Public Interest* (New York: McGraw-Hill, 1936), pp. 139–156; and Robert E. Cushman, *The Independent Regulatory Commissions* (New York: Oxford University Press, 1941), pp. 275–296.

3. The new clientele—particularly the state commissioners and local utilities—were not likely to lapse into "quiescence," to use Edleman's term, since FPC decisions would be integrated into the work of the state commissions, and would have considerable impact on the profitability of local utility operations.

4. *Minerals Yearbook*, 1938, pp. 1042, 1047–1049.

5. The largest industrial users of natural gas in 1950 (excluding electricity generation and petroleum and natural gas production and refining) were, in order of quantities consumed: iron and steel manufacture, other metals, cement, chemicals, food processing, paper, glass, and clay products. American Gas Association, *Historical Statistics of the Gas Industry* (New York, 1956), p. 147.

6. HR IFC 1937, p. 133, and HR IFC 1941, pp. 53–54.

7. HR IFC 1941, p. 59.

8. Richard W. Hooley, *Financing the Natural Gas Industry* (New York: Columbia University Press, 1961), pp. 34–56.

9. Under the original statute, lengthy preliminary investigations were needed to ascertain whether the commission had jurisdiction over a pipeline (that is, to determine whether the area into which a new pipeline would be laid was, in fact, in a "market already served").

10. Senate Report no. 948, 77th Cong., 2d sess., p. 1. Similar wording was contained in the House report on the amendment.

11. HR IFC 1936, pp. 28–29.

12. HR IFC 1935, p. 1912. From 1929 to 1932, coal production declined 39 percent; by comparison, natural gas production dropped 22 percent, and petroleum production, 14 percent.

13. Fainsod and Gordon, *Government and the American Economy*, p. 638.

14. HR IFC 1936, p. 71.

15. HR IFC 1937, pp. 122–123.

16. *Cong. Rec.*, Senate, 1937, p. 9314.

17. The senator in question was Pat Harrison, of Gulfport, Miss. *Cong. Rec.*, Senate, 1938, p. 8347. This passage was omitted when the act was amended in 1942. Apparently both local coal interests and existing pipelines (at whose behest the act was amended) objected to encouraging new sales of low-cost gas.

18. Samuel H. Crosby, *The Natural Gas Act and Its Administration* (New York: Holly Poe, 1946), pp. 35–36; see also Crosby, *A Survey of Federal Regulation of the Natural Gas Industry* (New York: Holly Poe, 1946), pp. 42–43.

19. See the testimony of the coal and railroad spokesmen in FPC Docket no. G-230, 1943; a brief summary is provided in Crosby, *A Survey of Federal Regulation of the Natural Gas Industry*, p. 41.

20. In its 1940 annual report, for example, the FPC argued for expansion of its jurisdiction to control end uses (see p. 80). The commission also repeatedly asked Congress to grant it jurisdiction over direct industrial sales. A good discussion of the commission's interpretation of its end-use powers can be found in Jerome J. McGrath, "Federal Regulation of Producers in Relation to Conservation of Natural Gas," *Georgetown Law Journal* 44 (June 1956): 676–693.

21. *FPC v. Hope Natural Gas Co.*, 320 US 660 (1944). See also p. 612 for another reference by the Court to the commission's authority to consider conservation arguments in certificate proceedings.

22. FPC Docket no. G-522, 1944, quoted in Crosby, *A Survey of Federal Regulation of the Natural Gas Industry*, pp. 45–46. The National Coal Association argued against certification on the grounds that 88 percent of all gas sold by the pipeline was used for industrial, principally boiler fuel, purposes. The Memphis application was ultimately granted, but on the condition that there be no sales by the pipeline to new industrial customers.

23. From 1948 to 1958, the quantity of natural gas used as a boiler fuel rose from 1.3 to 4.3 trillion cubic feet. Most of this increase was registered in the producer states of Texas, California, Louisiana, Oklahoma, and Kansas, but there was also large-scale boiler fuel usage of natural gas in states within easy reach of coal supplies. One of the largest interstate industrial users of natural gas in the 1940s was the cement industry, which had previously relied on coal. Smith-Wimberly Report, 1948, pp. 373–374, and *Minerals Yearbook*, 1958.

24. HR IFC 1955, pp. 553–555.

25. The producers might have anticipated some advantage from the ability of the FPC to limit imports and to discourage pipelines from buying up gas leases for the purpose of monopolizing supply; "surplus" gas properties could not be included in pipeline costs.

26. Representative Boren of Oklahoma introduced a committee-approved "clarifying" amendment to insert the phrase "by a natural gas company" after the phrase "production and transportation of natural gas" in section 5, with the apparent understanding that a jurisdictional "natural gas company" could only be an interstate pipeline. The amendment passed by voice vote. See *Cong. Rec.*, House, 1937, p. 6728.

27. HR IFC 1936, pp. 28–42. Interstate pipelines carried substantially higher pressure than gathering lines (or local distribution mains). Thus, to exempt "gathering" lines from regulation was to exempt the nontransporting producer who sold gas at the end of his gathering lines.

28. Donald J. Liebert points out that the 1936 and 1937 hearings were considered a single process by the Commerce Committee, so that the 1937 hearings dealt only with various interest group proposals for minor changes in the bill. See "Legislative History of the Natural Gas Act," *Georgetown Law Journal* 44, no. 4 (June 1956): 711.

29. Liebert's analysis, the wording of the committee report, and the hearing and floor exchanges cited above leave little doubt of this point.

30. Such was the approach of the Bituminous Coal Conservation Act of 1937.

31. The last speaker before the House vote on the natural gas bill, Representative Faddis of Pennsylvania, made it clear that the bill was in the mainstream of New Deal regulatory policy. Said Representative Faddis, "I know the gentleman [Commerce Chairman and floor manager Clarence Lea] is in strict accord with the principles of the administration insofar as cutthroat competition shall not be encouraged. What we have been trying to do here for the past six or seven years is to prevent cutthroat competition going to the extent of destroying industry and labor engaged in the industry; and the gentleman believes this [bill] is sufficient?" Replied Representative Lea, "I believe that is sufficient." *Cong. Rec.*, House, 1938, p. 9101.

32. Computed from tables in the 1958 *Minerals Yearbook*.

33. *Minerals Yearbook*, 1945 and 1955.

34. Data on pipeline certifications are taken from the annual reports of the FPC.

35. "Natural Gas—Whoosh!" *Fortune* 40 (Dec. 1949): 108–114. According to *Fortune*, southwestern natural gas sold for about one-fourth the cost of the manufactured gas previously in use in the area. In addition, the wellhead price of southwestern gas was, at seven to eight cents per mcf, less than one-third the

wellhead price of natural gas from West Virginia and Pennsylvania. American Gas Association, *Gas Facts* (New York, 1950).

36. "Natural Gas—Whoosh!" p. 202; Smith-Wimberly Report, p. 242; FPC Annual Report, 1947, p. 99.

37. *Minerals Yearbook*, 1958. California production leveled off in 1944; production in Pennsylvania and West Virginia began to decline after 1943.

38. The number of residences using gas for heating tripled between 1945 and 1955. By 1955, 70 percent of residential gas users were using gas for house heating, which resulted in a substantial increase in gas consumption per household. American Gas Association, *Gas Facts* (New York, 1970).

39. The principal cost advantage for natural gas, as compared to coal, lay in its labor/production ratio. Not only was coal production far more labor-intensive than gas, but also a much higher percentage of coal miners were unionized, which put more upward pressure on wages.

40. In 1955, over half the households in West Virginia coal districts—and over 45 percent of households in Ohio, western Pennsylvania, and Alabama coal areas—had natural gas service: in Kentucky, Virginia, and southern Illinois coal districts, on the other hand, gas consumption was much lower. (Data aggregated into congressional districts from county data in U.S. Bureau of the Census, Census of Housing, 1950.)

41. Although it is assumed that consumers oppose entry restrictions (as, in fact, the Cities Alliance did in 1937 hearings), the price issue was much more important to them. The "consumers" considered here are gas users in nonproducing states.

42. The expansion of oil and gas sales was needed to bolster sagging producer state finances in the 1930s. Texas, for example, faced with a large deficit in its old-age pension system, raised the natural gas severance tax to 3 percent of market value. One-fourth of the state's gas tax revenues went to public schools. In 1941, Texas again raised the severance tax to support increases in school and hospital expenditures. See James R. Stockton et al., *Economics of Natural Gas in Texas* (Austin: University of Texas Press, 1952), pp. 192–193.

43. HR IFC 1939, pp. 35–36, 222.

44. Ibid., pp. 126, 176–177, 405–406, 776–782.

45. Ibid., p. 584. See also the dialogue between New Jersey Representative Charles Wolverton and Texas Railroad Commissioner Col. Ernest Thompson, pp. 586–598.

46. FTC Report, vol. 84, pt. 2, p. 2895.

47. Message to the Congress from President Roosevelt, Feb. 15, 1939.

48. National Resources Committee (NRC), *Energy Resources and National Policy*, published as House Document no. 160, 76th Cong., 1st sess. (1939). Harold Ickes chaired the committee, whose membership consisted of Frederick Delano, Harry Hopkins, Harry Woodring, Francis Harrington, Henry Wallace, Frances Perkins, and Charles E. Merriam. Leland Olds was a "special contributor" to the report.

49. HR IFC 1939, p. 169.

50. NRC, *Energy Resources and National Policy*, p. 214.

51. The governor of Oklahoma, for example, blasted the bill as potentially "despotic" and "perilous to democracy as we know it." Col. Thompson of the

Texas Railroad Commission also bitterly denounced the bill. See *Pipe Line News* (Nov. 1939), pp. 3, 10.

Chapter 4

1. Ben W. Lewis, "The Role of the FPC Regarding the Power Features of Federal Projects," *George Washington Law Review* 14, no. 1 (Dec. 1945): 105n.

2. US Senate Judiciary Committee *Report on Regulatory Agencies to the President-Elect*, 86th Cong., 2d sess. Committee Print, 1960.

3. In 1930, the FPC was reorganized from an ex officio body to an independent regulatory agency. Members henceforth were nominated by the president and confirmed by the Senate to staggered, five-year terms. The five-member body must have bipartisan membership, which means that no more than three members can be of the president's party. Members are listed in Table 8.

4. *Cong. Rec.*, Senate, 1935, pp. 1913–1914.

5. Increasingly, Congress also reserves to itself the power, through a "legislative veto" provision, to strike down particular agency decisions.

6. In 1977, Senate committees were reorganized, with a new Energy and Natural Resources Committee absorbing natural gas and other energy legislation from the Commerce and Interior committees. In 1980 the name of the House committee was changed to Energy and Commerce.

7. The jurisdiction of the House Committee on Interstate and Foreign Commerce (IFC) during this period included: federal oil, gas, and power regulation; railroads and railway labor; interstate and foreign communications; public health; inland waterways and securities exchanges; as well as other matters pertaining to interstate commerce. The committee has steadily grown to accommodate the rising demand for access to its important jurisdiction. In 1955, two of thirty-one members were from the four major southwestern oil and gas producing states; in 1963, three of thirty-four; in 1977, five of forty-three.

8. As a result of the 1946 elections, urban Democratic representatives from Illinois, Pennsylvania, New York, and Missouri were no longer counted among the committee's membership in 1947.

9. 169 US 466 (1898). On the difficulties arising from the Smyth doctrine, see Merle Fainsod, Lincoln Gordon, and Joseph C. Palamountain, Jr., *Government and the American Economy* (New York: Norton, 1959), pp. 312–324; also Alfred M. Leeston, John A. Crichton, and John C. Jacobs, *The Dynamic Natural Gas Industry* (Norman, Okla.: University of Oklahoma Press, 1963), chap. 12.

10. 169 US 546, 547.

11. Another complication is the allocation of joint production costs where the regulated company owns wells producing both oil and gas.

12. HR IFC 1935, pp. 572–575 (testimony of FPC solicitor Dozzier DeVane). DeVane argued that the most progressive state utility commissions, such as the California commission, were already following an "original cost" standard and that such a standard would inevitably become the basis for most utility regulation efforts.

13. James C. Bonbright, "Contributions of the FPC to Establishment of the Prudent Investment Doctrine of Rate Making," *George Washington Law Review* 14, no. 1 (Dec. 1945): 136–178.

218   Notes to Pages 81–88

14. 320 US 603.
15. *Colorado Interstate Gas Company* v. *FPC et al.*, 324 US 611 (1945).
16. 320 US 607, 608.
17. Ibid., p. 627.
18. 320 US 609–610. As the Court interpreted the purpose of the Natural Gas Act in its 1944 decision, the act was to regulate "the wholesale distribution to public service companies of natural gas moving interstate."
19. 2 FPC 200 (1940). An excellent summary of these early FPC decisions is found in Ralph K. Huitt, "National Regulation of the Natural Gas Industry," in *Public Administration and Policy Formation*, ed. Emmett S. Redford (New York: Greenwood, 1958), pp. 51–116.
20. 2 FPC 288 (1940).
21. *Colorado Interstate Gas Co.* v. *FPC et al.*, 324 US 581 (1945).
22. Interstate Gas Co. *v.* FPC, 331 US 682, 691–693 (1947). For a brief discussion of the significance of these cases, see Huitt, "National Regulation," pp. 82–90, and Harriet S. Daggett, ed., *Fourth Annual Institute on Mineral Law* (Baton Rouge: Louisiana State University Press, 1957), p. 45.
23. Final passage of the Moore-Rizley bill (HR 4051) was by voice vote, but a motion to substitute the more limited Priest bill was defeated on a 253 to 64 vote.
24. "The contention is," said an Ohio representative during floor debate on the Rizley bill, "that people in the South and Southwest will no longer be subject for all this terrible confusion that is causing us not to get gas in the Midwest." *Cong. Rec.*, House, 1947, p. 8743.
25. HR IFC 1953. The FPC's claim of jurisdiction over local distributors in these situations was upheld by the Supreme Court in *East Ohio Gas Company* v. *FPC*, 338 US 464 (1950). This decision was overturned by an amendment to the Natural Gas Act passed by the Republican Congress in 1954.
26. These were the Tennessee Gas and Transmission Co. and Fin-Ker Oil and Gas Production Co. cases (6 FPC 92, 94 [1947]). The dissent by Commissioner Buchanan in the Phillips Petroleum Co. case (10 FPC 284 [1951]) contains a disparaging description of the commission's retreat.
27. *Cong. Rec.*, House, July 11, 1947.
28. Smith-Wimberly Report and Olds-Draper Report.
29. Senate IFC 1949, p. 187.
30. Ibid., p. 265.
31. Ibid., testimony of Leland Olds, pp. 149–150.
32. HR IFC 1947, p. 38.
33. Senate IFC 1949, pp. 29–30.
34. Unlike the Moore-Rizley bill, the 1949 Harris bill (HR 1758) would have continued FPC regulation over pipeline-produced gas and left intact the commission's jurisdiction over interstate pipelines.
35. *Cong. Rec.*, House, Aug. 4–5, 1949, pp. 10779–10869; and *Cong. Rec.*, Senate, March 29, 1950, pp. 4275–4287 (statements of Representatives Rayburn, Harris, Dolliver, and Brooks, and Senators Connolly and McFarland).
36. *Cong. Rec.*, House, Aug. 4, 1949, pp. 10781–10849; and *Cong. Rec.*, Senate, March 29, 1950, pp. 4283–4291 (statements of Representatives Klein, Carroll, O'Sullivan, and Hesselton, and Senators Kefauver, Hendrickson, Ferguson, and Kem).

37. FPC Annual Reports, 1947–1950.

38. *Minerals Yearbook.*

39. Where there *was* heavy natural gas consumption, a number of urban Republicans opposed deregulation. Thirty Republican votes were cast against deregulation in New York, New Jersey, Illinois, Pennsylvania, Wisconsin, Minnesota, and Massachusetts in 1949.

40. The reference here is to the vote on a motion substituting the weaker Priest bill for the Rizley bill.

41. Gas consumption figures are aggregated from data supplied in the American Gas Association, *Survey of Residential Gas Use by County* (New York, 1949).

42. For example, in 1960, the average quantity of gas consumed per household ranged from 80 mcf in Alabama to 170 mcf in Ohio (computed from *Minerals Yearbook* tables). Approximately the same percentage of household gas customers in these two states used gas for house heating.

43. American Gas Association, *Gas Facts* (New York, 1952).

44. 1947 and 1949 House votes are compiled from the *Congressional Quarterly Almanac*, 1947 (pp. 518–519) and 1949 (pp. 820–821), published by Congressional Quarterly, Inc. (Washington, D.C.). Announced pairs are counted pro or con.

45. This position was exemplified by a representative from Maine who testified that his state neither produced nor consumed gas but would like to obtain it. He considered that possibility unlikely unless producers were offered sufficient incentives to produce gas for interstate sales. Such incentives would not be forthcoming under public utility regulation, he feared. See the 1949 *Congressional Quarterly Almanac*, p. 719.

46. In 1948, Alabama, Louisiana, Mississippi, and South Carolina cast their electoral votes for States Rights candidate Strom Thurmond.

47. The states affected by the "tidelands" decision were Louisiana, Texas, and California. All three cast their electoral votes for the Republican ticket in 1956.

48. The president's veto message is found in Senate Document no. 139, 81st Cong., 2d sess. (1950).

Chapter 5

1. Quoted in Clark A. Hawkins, *The Field Price Regulation of Natural Gas* (Tallahassee: Florida State University Press, 1969), p. 23.

2. 10 FPC 246 (1951); see also Ralph K. Huitt, "National Regulation of the Natural Gas Industry," in *Public Administration and Policy Formation*, ed. Emmett S. Redford (New York: Greenwood, 1958), pp. 95–100.

3. 10 FPC 284–319 (1951).

4. Hawkins, *Field Price Regulation*, p. 22.

5. *Phillips Petroleum Co.* v. *State of Wisconsin*, 347 US 672 (1954). The quoted material is taken from the Court's syllabus of the decision.

6. 347 US 688, 689 (1954). Justices Clark and Burton wrote a separate dissenting opinion.

7. FPC Orders nos. 174 and 174A, Docket no. R-138, July 16, 1954, and Aug. 6, 1954, from 13 FPC 1524 (1954).

8. Merle Fainsod, Lincoln Gordon, and Joseph C. Palamountain, Jr., *Government and the American Economy* (New York: Norton, 1959), p. 677.

9. Senate IFC 1955.

10. Testimony of mayor and city council of Baltimore, ibid., p. 345.

11. Ibid., pp. 736, 1389–1393.

12. This provision was modeled on the recommendation of the President's Advisory Committee on Energy Supplies and Resources Policy.

13. HR Report no. 992, 84th Cong., 1st sess. (1955).

14. *Letter from FPC Chairman Jerome Kuykendall*, reprinted in ibid., app., pp. 46–47.

15. The committee did, however, approve an amendment allowing the FPC to consider the reasonableness of price increases based on escalator clauses. See the 1955 *Congressional Quarterly Almanac*, p. 457.

16. HR Report no. 992, Minority Report no. 1, pp. 60–65.

17. Ibid., Minority Report no. 2, pp. 76–82.

18. Ibid., p. 15. Consolidated Edison led a major lobbying effort against the Harris deregulation bill.

19. *Congressional Quarterly Almanac*, 1955, pp. 162–163. The Harris bill was HR 6645.

20. All eleven New York City congressional representatives voted against the Harris bill. The majority of Republican representatives from New York, Connecticut, Michigan, Minnesota, and Wisconsin were also opposed.

21. Edith T. Carper, "Lobbying and the Natural Gas Bill," in *Case Studies in American Government*, ed. Edwin A. Bock and Alan K. Campbell (Englewood Cliffs, N.J.: Prentice-Hall, 1962), pp. 193–207. The Alabama League of Municipalities waged a campaign against deregulation. Petroleum industry organizations attempted to counter this sentiment with a public relations campaign emphasizing the value of new oil and gas discoveries in Alabama. A Gas and Oil Resources Committee ran ads in the state's major newspapers charging that "[a] handful of utilities led by big Eastern interests" were supporting producer regulation. The industry's campaign apparently had little effect, however, in either Alabama or other southeastern states. All six senators from Alabama, Tennessee, and Virginia voted against the Fulbright bill.

22. Energy resource production was becoming more important to the western states. For example, between 1950 and 1955, Wyoming natural gas production increased from 20 to 78 billion cubic feet, and petroleum production rose 67 percent. Wyoming Senator Joseph O'Mahoney had opposed the Kerr bill in 1950, but supported the Fulbright deregulation bill in 1956, along with the state's other senator, Frank A. Barrett.

23. Carper, "Lobbying and the Natural Gas Bill," pp. 217–219.

24. Ibid., p. 222.

25. In 1958, Louisiana Senator Russell Long introduced a bill to deregulate only small producers; the bill died in committee. Hawkins, *Field Price Regulation*, p. 35.

26. In 1945, California produced all the natural gas it consumed. By 1955, consumption exceeded production by about 20 percent; by 1974, the quantity of gas consumed was about four times the amount produced (*Minerals Yearbook*).

27. See FPC Annual Report, 1954, 1956, 1957, 1961, and HR IFC 1957, pp. 334–337.

28. Harriet S. Daggett, ed., *Fourth Annual Institute on Mineral Law* (Baton Rouge: Louisiana State University Press, 1957), p. 65 (Table B).

29. *Atlantic Richfield et al.* v. *Public Service Commission of New York et al.*, 360 U.S. 378 (1959).

30. The discussion in this paragraph is indebted to a review of the CATCO case by James H. Rempe (see under "Oil and Gas—Certificates of Public Convenience and Necessity") in the *George Washington Law Review* 27, no. 5 (June 1959): 752–760; and to Daggett, *Fourth Annual Institute*, pp. 48–57.

31. Daggett, *Fourth Annual Institute*, p. 53.

32. Rempe review, p. 757.

33. The commission's right to require unlimited certificates was upheld by the Supreme Court in *Sunray Mid Continent Oil Co.* v. *FPC*, 364 US 137.

34. Raymond W. Shibley and George B. Mickum, "The Impact of Phillips on the Interstate Pipelines," *Georgetown Law Journal* 44 (June 1956): 628–632; see also Daggett, *Fourth Annual Institute*, p. 49.

35. Shibley and Mickum, "Impact of Phillips," pp. 631–634.

36. Richard W. Hooley, *Financing the Natural Gas Industry* (New York: Columbia University Press, 1961), p. 11. The figure in the mid-1940s was 36 percent.

37. *FPC* v. *Panhandle Eastern Pipeline Co.*, 337 US 498 (1949).

38. *City of Detroit* v. *FPC et al.*, 230 F 2d 810 (1955), overturning FPC Opinion no. 269 (April 15, 1954).

39. Daggett, *Fourth Annual Institute*, p. 55.

40. It is not unusual to find the career staff members of an agency, who have often been recruited under previous administrations, holding different views on regulatory policy from the political appointees who head the agency. See no. 48, chap. 6.

41. Hawkins, *Field Price Regulation*, p. 74. See also the Supreme Court's decision in *Wisconsin* v. *FPC*, 373 US 294 (1963).

42. 24 FPC 547 (1960). The commission acknowledged, however, that "it is clear the better method would be to establish fair prices for the gas itself and for each individual producer," but, given the number of producers involved, it felt compelled to seek a "more manageable method."

43. 373 US 294 (1963).

44. The Court may well have hoped to avoid the extensive litigation that would have accompanied a case-by-case method.

45. The states of residency of commissioners were taken from a table in Hawkins, *Field Price Regulation*, app. 2, p. 219; and from *Who's Who in America*. The east north central states of Illinois, Indiana, Michigan, Ohio, and Wisconsin had by far the largest bloc of residential consumers in the 1960s and the second highest regional industrial consumption. None of Eisenhower's appointments were made from the east north central states; two of eleven Kennedy and Johnson appointments came from these states.

46. Hawkins, *Field Price Regulation*, pp. 82–83.

47. Ibid., p. 114–120.

48. Ibid., pp. 121–134.

49. Justice Douglas argued that whereas in other regulated industries "there is no constitutional guarantee that even the most inefficient will survive," individual firms may at least withdraw from a business if they are losing money. "But a producer of natural gas may not abandon his existing facilities that supply the interstate market without commission approval." See Permian Basin Area Rate Cases, 390 US 747 (1968).

50. FPC Annual Report, 1963, p. 123. See also FPC Annual Report, 1964, p. 15.

51. HR IFC 1971, pp. 166, 200.

52. HR IFC 1971, p. 281.

53. Unless otherwise attributed, the following arguments are drawn from producer testimony in congressional hearings, 1944–1977. A cogent summary of the producer position as viewed from the standpoint of a large independent (Phillips Petroleum) may be found in Rayburn F. Foster, "Natural Gas Regulation from the Producers' Standpoint," in *Georgetown Law Journal* 44, no. 4 (June 1956): 658–674.

54. Senate IFC 1955, pp. 120 ff. (testimony of Dr. John Boatwright). The percentage of gas sales made by the four largest firms increased to 24 percent in 1970; the percentage accounted for by the eight largest, to about 40 percent. The median concentration ratio for 412 manufacturing industries in the late 1960s was 48 percent (for the eight largest firms). Senate COJ 1973, p. 341 (testimony of Dr. Norman B. Ture), and Department of the Interior, Office of Economic Analysis, "Final Environmental Impact Statement—Proposed Deregulation of Natural Gas Prices" (June 1974, mimeo furnished by the Natural Gas Supply Committee). Paul MacAvoy of MIT and Stephen Breyer of Harvard Law School have argued, in an article often cited by producers, that the "power to control new contract prices probably did not exist on either side of the market, but if the scales tipped at all, then surely the balance [control over contract prices] lay with the pipeline companies rather than with the producers." See "The Natural Gas Shortage and the Regulation of Natural Gas Producers," *Harvard Law Review* 86 (1973): 947. While maintaining that their industry remains significantly more competitive than other parts of the United States economy, producer spokesmen acknowledge that the concentration ratio has increased over the past twenty years and attribute the diminished number of independent producers to the effects of regulation itself (Senate COC 1974, pt. 4, p. 1561).

55. James McKie, *The Regulation of Natural Gas* (Washington, D.C.: American Enterprise Institute, 1957), p. 32.

56. Foster, "Natural Gas Regulation," and McKie, *Regulation of Natural Gas*, pp. 30–31. McKie's analysis in the 1950s showed that only one major interstate pipeline (Michigan-Wisconsin) faced a concentrated supply situation; it paid no higher prices, on the average, than did other pipelines.

57. Senate IFC 1955, p. 1156 (testimony of a representative of the Texas Independent Producers and Royalty Owners Association).

58. Economist Leon Keyserling, testifying on a price control bill considered in Senate committee in 1975, compared trends in regulated gas pricing with other price movements. From 1953 to 1961, the wellhead price of gas increased at an

average rate of 6.4 percent. From 1961 to 1973, according to Keyserling, the rate of increase dropped to 2.9 percent, while the consumer price index increased at an average 3.4 percent a year. The average increase in the wellhead price of natural gas from 1966 to 1974 was 47 percent, compared with 178 percent for bituminous coal, 202–367 percent for oil, and 126 percent for all energy, including electricity. Senate COC 1975, p. 158.

59. According to the American Gas Association, the average retail price for natural gas to households was $1.75 per Btu. The equivalent cost for fuel oil was $2.88, and for electric space heating, $9.50. (Senate COC 1976, p. 59 [testimony of George H. Lawrence]). Imports of natural gas from Canada and liquified natural gas from Algeria typically brought prices two to three times the level allowed by the FPC for jurisdictional sales of domestic gas in the 1970s; prices allowed for synthetic gas sales were also a multiple of the regulated natural gas price. See HR IFC 1971, p. 57; FPC Annual Report, 1975, p. 34; and FPC, *Sales by Producers of Natural Gas to Interstate Pipelines*, 1972.

60. Senate IFC 1955, pp. 1403–1404, and HR IFC 1955, pp. 530–531 (testimony of the governor of New Mexico and the mayor of Tulsa, Okla.). For example, in Milwaukee, Wis. (where the Phillips case originated), residential gas users paid $1.21–1.44 mcf for natural gas in the mid-1950s. The producers received only $.087 of the delivered price. In New York City, only 3 percent of the delivered gas price represented payments to producers (HR IFC 1955, p. 521).

61. Based on John C. Jacobs, "The Gas Purchase Contract," in Alfred M. Leeston, John A. Crichton, and John C. Jacobs *The Dynamic Natural Gas Industry* (Norman, Okla.: University of Oklahoma Press, 1963), pp. 315–316.

62. According to information supplied by the state budget officials for 1979, natural gas sales generated: 13.5 percent of all state revenues in Louisiana; about 3 percent of state tax revenue in Oklahoma (leases and royalties additional); 10 percent of tax revenue in Texas; and 20 percent of state tax revenue in New Mexico (excluding rents, royalties, and local school taxes generated by gas sales). The bulk of these revenues was used to support public education in all four states.

63. Senate COC 1955, p. 1162.

64. *Georgetown Law Journal* 44, no. 4 (June 1956): 566–606.

65. Douglas, "The Case for the Consumer," p. 588. Consumer state representatives also pointed out that competition among producers was restricted by state proration practices which, in the name of conservation, served to limit production to current demand levels and thus to maintain prices. In addition, several producer states had attempted to set minimum prices at which their gas could be sold. Although the federal courts had struck down such attempts (as they affected interstate prices), Douglas argued that passage of a deregulation bill might renew such price-fixing efforts.

66. Ibid., p. 602. Douglas' calculation here is based on aggregate (industrial, residential, and commercial) national consumption.

67. Ibid., pp. 575–578.

68. McKie, *Regulation of Natural Gas*, p. 44.

69. Among the sixteen largest gas producers in 1953 were (in order of sales): Humble Oil, Phillips Petroleum, Standard Oil of California, Gulf Oil, and Atlantic Refining Co. Together these five companies owned almost 40 percent of

known reserves in that year. See Edward J. Neuner, *The Natural Gas Industry* (Norman, Okla.: University of Oklahoma Press, 1960), p. 7.

70. For a compendium of political benefits secured by the oil companies see Robert J. Engler, *The Politics of Oil* (New York: University of Chicago Press, 1960).

71. Richard B. Mancke, *The Failure of U.S. Energy Policy* (New York: Columbia University Press, 1974), p. 47. President Eisenhower's Advisory Committee on Energy Supplies and Resources Policy had urged that imports be curbed, since failure to do so would "endanger the orderly industry growth . . . necessary to the national defense."

72. Joel B. Dirlam, "Natural Gas: Cost, Conservation, and Pricing," *American Economic Review* 48, no. 2 (May 1958): 491.

73. Douglas, "The Case for the Consumer," pp. 592–593.

74. HR IFC 1971, pp. 306–307. The higher prices allowed for new interstate sales in the 1970s were, however, still lower than intrastate prices or the prices of competing fuels.

75. HR IFC 1971, p. 282.

76. Ibid., p. 209.

77. The criteria for designation of major coal districts are volumes of production and number of employees (aggregated from county data in *Minerals Yearbook*). The number of such districts varies over the period encompassed here.

78. HR 4943 and S 2001 (see the testimony of the NCA representative on these bills in Senate COC 1955, pp. 1704–1705).

Chapter 6

1. For the source of this data, see Table 15. These figures include Alaskan natural gas, which has a different (and more lucrative) pricing structure than gas in the lower forty-eight states; the tables give, therefore, a conservative picture of the decline in exploration and discoveries after the 1950s that may be attributed to the effects of regulation by the FPC.

2. Stephen A. Breyer and Paul W. MacAvoy, "Regulating Natural Gas Producers," in *Energy Supply and Government Policy*, ed. Robert J. Kalter and William A. Vogely (Ithaca, N.Y.: Cornell University Press, 1976), p. 164.

3. HR IFC 1971, p. 64. From 1970 to 1974, an annual average of 8.4 trillion cubic feet of reserves were added in intrastate markets, compared with 0.4 tcf of additional reserves allocated to interstate pipelines. House Report no. 543, vol. 2, 95th Cong., 1st sess. (data taken from Fig. 4, p. 388).

4. *Minerals Yearbook*, 1970.

5. Representative John Murphy, sponsor of a bill to lighten the regulatory burden for small producers, recounted, in 1971, the frustrations of an Amarillo gas producer who had tried for thirteen years to secure FPC approval for a one-cent increase in his gas sales contract. Even if ultimately granted, the increase might later be disallowed, and he would have to refund the additional amount. From 1962 to 1968, for example, producers were ordered by the FPC to make refunds totalling $133 million. Murphy related other examples of independent

producers who, after long delays in securing FPC approval for an interstate sale, withdrew their applications, and promptly contracted to sell their gas in Texas. HR IFC 1971, pp. 44–45, 199.

6. *Minerals Yearbook*, 1970 and 1975.

7. In January of 1970, gas shortages forced several hundred plants in Ohio to close, idling over thirty thousand workers. See HR IFC 1971, p. 74.

8. House Report no. 543 (1977), p. 90.

9. HR IFC 1971, p. 57.

10. Senate COI 1972, p. 6.

11. HR IFC 1971.

12. Ibid., p. 68.

13. Senate COC 1972, p. 39.

14. HR IFC 1971, pp. 263–269, and Senate COC 1972, pp. 142–145.

15. HR IFC 1971, p. 67.

16. Ibid., pp. 370–385.

17. Annual Reports of the Federal Power Commission, 1970–1973, and *Minerals Yearbook*, 1971.

18. Under this procedure, producers of less than ten billion cubic feet of gas a year could apply for blanket certification to cover all future sales at whatever price their contracts specified. "Unreasonably" high charges could still be disallowed in fixing pipeline charges to distributors.

19. The commission drew up such a proposal and presented it to the Commerce Committee as an alternative for HR 2313 (HR IFC 1971, pp. 23–26). Chairman Nassikas told a Senate committee in 1972 that it was his belief that natural gas producers should have been regulated since 1938. See Senate COI 1972, p. 183.

20. At the same time, four producer state senators introduced a bill for immediate deregulation.

21. There was one vacancy on the commission, which now consisted of Nassikas, Albert Brooke (a Johnson holdover), and Nixon appointees Rush Moody, a Texas lawyer, and William Springer, a former Republican congressman.

22. The coalition was organized in 1976 in the House by Massachusetts Representative Michael Harrington. Its purpose is to generate research and foster political cohesion for a regional stance on domestic economic issues. A similar but smaller and executive-dominated group is the Coalition of Northeastern Governors formed in the same year by New York Governor Hugh Carey.

23. Congressional Quarterly, Inc., *Congressional Quarterly Almanac* (Washington, D.C., 1974), p. 729.

24. Ibid., pp. 727–729.

25. EPCA extended controls to newly discovered oil. By directing that prices applied to various categories of oil result in an average price of $7.66 a barrel, the statute effected an immediate rollback of about two dollars per barrel in the price of new domestic oil, dropping domestic new oil for the first time to a level significantly below the world price. EPCA also included, as an enticement to eastern coal area representatives, a federal loan program for the opening of new underground mines. The House-passed version of EPCA set no termination date

for the price control provisions. However, because of Senate refusal to accept an open-ended law, the conference committee settled on a forty-month duration. See *Cong. Rec.*, House, Dec. 15, 1975, pp. 40681–40739.

26. A number of distributors and pipelines also blamed the FPC for the shortage. The chief executive of Consolidated Natural Gas Company, a Pittsburgh utility, argued in 1971 that the company had been unable to secure adequate supplies, "in large part because of the cumulative effects of regulation under the Natural Gas Act during the period since the Phillips decision in 1954. In my opinion, price reductions, price rollbacks, and instability have stopped exploratory operations while the resulting low rates have created an artificially high demand for natural gas." Testimony of M. D. Borger before the FPC, Docket no. AR 69-1 (quoted in Stephen Breyer and Paul MacAvoy, *Energy Regulation by the Federal Power Commission* [Washington, D.C.: Brookings Association, 1974], p. 10). By 1975, the Interstate Natural Gas Association, representing 90 percent of interstate sales, formally registered its support for new gas decontrol. Senate COC 1975, pp. 404–405.

27. Senate COC 1974, pt. 3, pp. 1350–1351.

28. Ibid., pt. 2, p. 506: abstract from "The Natural Gas Shortage and the Regulation of Natural Gas Producers," *Harvard Law Review* 86, no. 8 (April 1973). MacAvoy was one of the earliest and most prolific critics of natural gas regulation. For other statements of his position, singly and with others, see *Price Formation in Natural Gas Fields* (New Haven: Yale University Press, 1962); *The Economics of the Natural Gas Shortage*, with Robert S. Pindyck (Amsterdam: North Holland Press, 1975); and *The Regulated Industries and the Economy* (New York: Norton, 1979). Like Mitchell and Adelman, MacAvoy disputes consumer representative claims that the gas-producing industry is highly concentrated. He argues, however, that federal controls themselves distort market structure by suppressing entry, accelerating exit, and resulting in a flukish distribution of market shares, determined by fortuitous finds of new gas reserves. See his testimony before the Senate Interior Committee, 93d Cong., 1st sess. (Dec. 13, 1973), Hearings on Market Performance and Competition in the Petroleum Industry, pt. 3, p. 2.

29. The fact that the exact price-supply relationship is unknown, Kitch wrote Committee Chairman Henry Jackson, is all the more reason to deregulate natural gas production, since "in the absence of precise knowledge, a reasonably informed regulatory policy is an impossibility." See Senate COI 1972, pp. 838–840.

30. Ibid., p. 63.

31. Under the Pearson-Bentsen proposal, the price of new onshore gas (that is, gas sold under contract after Jan. 1, 1975) was to be free from federal controls immediately; controls on new offshore gas were to be gradually lifted.

32. Among the interest groups testifying against deregulation in 1975 Senate hearings were the United Auto Workers, Farmers' Union, an association of municipally owned utilities (the APGA), and the Consumer Federation of America. Supporters of deregulation, besides producer groups, included the Farm Bureau, Chamber of Commerce, pipeline and distributor associations, and the American Iron and Steel Institute. The latter, representing a class of industrial users for which natural gas is an essential process fuel, complained that the FPC

had assigned industrial users to the lowest priority during periods of curtailment, and asserted that, in general, federal regulation discouraged exploration.

33. Measured by the percentage of demand that could not be met by interstate pipelines, the Southeast was the region facing the greatest projected shortages for 1976–1977. Although overall consumption levels are modest in the South, natural gas is essential for manufacturing processes in the region's textile, fertilizer, and food-processing industries. Other states registering shifts toward deregulation in the Senate were California and Nevada, heavy gas consumers that were also among the top fifteen states in curtailment percentages for 1974–1975; and the coal-producing states of Illinois, Kentucky, and West Virginia, where 1974–1975 curtailments and 1975–1976 projected shortages were relatively modest (the range in these three states was from 0 to 19 percent, compared with 18 to 50 percent in the southeastern and western states). Federal Energy Administration, "Curtailments of Natural Gas Service," Feb. 1976; and House Report no. 94–732, 95th Cong., 1st sess.

34. The South is defined here as the eleven states of the Confederacy. Nine of seventeen votes from the nonproducing South (that is, the South minus Louisiana and Texas) were cast for EPCA in the Senate.

35. In every case, a New England senator who supported oil price regulation also opposed the Pearson-Bentsen amendment on the recommittal vote.

36. The price of propane used in the rural South doubled between 1972 and 1974. See *Cong. Rec.*, Senate, Sept. 29, 1975, p. 30707.

37. When the Senate Commerce Committee held hearings on the Stevenson bill in 1974, the United Mine Workers legislative director testified in favor of expanded controls. "The time has come," he told the committee, "to consider public ownership or nationalization of oil, which would inevitably lead to nationalization of other energy production, including coal." The UMW representative observed that most of the union's important victories had been won under federal operation of the coal mines during the long 1946 coal strike. He predicted that if all United States energy production were supervised by a National Energy Board, unions could control the board, as they dominated the National Coal Board in Great Britain (Senate COC 1974, pt. 4, pp. 1679–1680). For a brief account of the 1946–1947 UMW successes, see David H. Davis, *Energy Politics* (New York: St. Martin's Press, 1974), pp. 27–28.

38. FPC Annual Report, 1975, p. 36.

39. Ibid., p. 38.

40. HR IFC 1974, p. 6.

41. When FPC decisions are appealed there is a veritable "race" between lawyers for gas producers and those representing consumer interests. Each attempts to register the earliest filing in a favored court. Producers prefer the Fifth Circuit in New Orleans, a court with a reputation for liberalism on civil rights issues, but one that has tended to reflect regional economic interests on oil and gas regulation. Consumers, on the other hand, expect favorable rulings from the District of Columbia Appeals Court. Thus, on natural gas regulation, even the federal judiciary reflects regional competition. In the 1976 appeals, simultaneous filings were made in the Fifth and D.C. Circuits. The D.C. court claimed that in view of the simultaneous filings, the determining factor in appellate jurisdiction

should be the convenience for the parties involved. Washington was clearly more convenient for the consumer plaintiffs (which included a number of congressmen) and the producers had legal representatives in the city. The New Orleans court, on the other hand, had heard appeals from the first FPC national rate proceeding and thus could claim a jurisdictional precedent. The D.C. court ultimately decided the appeals from the 1976 decision. See US 555 F 2d, p. 852. See also "FPC's Gas Price Ruling Leaves Consumers Out in the Cold," *National Journal* 8, no. 46 (Nov. 13, 1976): 1629.

42. On the House Commerce Oversight Subcommittee, California Representative John Moss suggested a conspiracy between the producers and the AGA to falsify reserve data in order to persuade the FPC to raise prices. HR IFC 1975, vol. 1, p. 469.

43. Senate COJ 1973, p. 209.

44. Ibid., pp. 49 ff. and table, p. 44.

45. Letter to the *Washington Post*, Oct. 5, 1974.

46. American Public Gas Association, "The Deregulation of Natural Gas" (White Paper; Washington, D.C., Sept. 1973), p. 8.

47. US Congress, Senate, Committee on Commerce, Hearings on the Natural Gas Production and Conservation Act of 1974, 93d Cong., 2d sess. (Dec. 1974), pp. 260–261.

48. Senate COC 1974, pt. 1, pp. 199–223. In the early 1970s the FPC staff tended to be considerably more pro-consumer than the politically appointed commissioners; Schwartz and two other FPC staff economists on several occasions publicly criticized the agency's official positions. Appointments to commission staff vacancies are made by the chairman, although higher-level appointments must be approved by the full commission. In 1961, Kennedy-appointed Chairman Joseph Swidler, in an effort to swing the FPC away from the policies of the Eisenhower era, took firm control of staff hiring, personally interviewing all applicants for positions at the GS-7 level and above. See David M. Welborn, *Governance of the Federal Regulatory Agencies* (Knoxville: University of Tennessee Press, 1977), pp. 51, 62–76. It is not surprising that staff members recruited under Kennedy and Johnson commissions would have resisted the FPC's policy shift in the early 1970s.

49. Senate COI 1972, p. 101.

50. Ibid., p. 109.

51. The results of the investigation are discussed in the "Conflict of Interest" hearings, HR IFC 1974.

52. US Congress, House of Representatives, Committee on Interstate and Foreign Commerce, "Federal Regulation and Regulatory Reform," Report of the Subcommittee on Oversight and Investigations, 94th Cong., 2d sess. (Committee Print, 1976). See also Senate Document no. 25 (1977), app., pp. 253–256.

53. HR IFC 1974, pp. 6–7.

54. For the grounds on which the commission's decision (Opinion 770) was challenged, see Senate COC 1976, pp. 34–35.

55. *American Public Gas Association et al.* v. *FPC*, 567 F 2d, 1016. The producers, in turn, challenged this reduction, citing congressional committee interference in the regulatory process. The courts, however, continued to uphold the FPC.

56. US Congress, House of Representatives, Committee on Interstate and Foreign Commerce, Subcommittee on Oversight and Investigations, Hearings on Regulatory Reform, 94th Cong., 2d sess. (June 1976), vol. 6, pp. 771–784.

57. IFC subcommittee chairman John Moss, charging that Opinion 770 showed a "flagrant disregard" for the law, threatened to institute impeachment proceedings against the commissioners who had voted to raise the rate to $1.42 (only Commissioner Don Smith had opposed the increase). See US Congress, Senate, Committee on Rules and Administration, "Court Proceedings and Actions of Vital Interest to the Congress," 95th Cong., 2d sess. (Committee Print, May 1978), pp. 47–48.

58. US Congress, Senate, Committee on Commerce, Hearings on the Nominations of Robert H. Morris and William L. Springer to the Federal Power Commission, 93d Cong., 1st sess. (1973). The fact that Morris, described by a supporter as "a genuine, liberal San Francisco Democrat," opposed deregulation cost him several votes in producer states. See *Cong. Rec.*, 1973, pp. 19504, 19496.

59. The defeat of the Morris nomination marked the first instance since 1950 that the Senate had defeated a regulatory agency nomination. See the 1973 *Congressional Quarterly Almanac*, p. 653.

60. Ibid., pp. 86–87. Similarly, there had been no significant consumer state opposition to the appointment of Nassikas, a New Hampshire Republican who had been a public utility lawyer. After the defeat of the Morris nomination, President Nixon nominated former Arkansas Public Service Commissioner Don S. Smith, who was easily confirmed.

61. US Congress, Senate, Committee on Governmental Operation, Study on Federal Regulation, Senate Document no. 25, 95th Cong., 1st sess. (1977), pp. 171–175.

62. Letter from Senator Phillip Hart, reprinted in Senate COC 1974, p. 783.

63. Senate COC 1974.

64. Senate COC 1975.

65. Senator Adlai Stevenson of Illinois and Wendell Ford of Kentucky represented coal (and, in the former case, also consumer) states. Stevenson told the committee, "As a Senator from Illinois . . . I have for many years now been promoting coal as the major alternative source of energy for the country." See Senate COC 1974, pt. 4, p. 1685.

66. 1975 *Congressional Quarterly Almanac*, pp. 252–258.

67. *Congressional Quarterly Weekly Report*, Feb. 7, 1976, pp. 259–261. The vote to adopt the rule was 230 to 184. Speaker Carl Albert (who was, as consumer representatives pointed out, an Oklahoman) rejected Chairman Staggers' request to bring up the emergency bill under suspension of the rules—a procedure under which no amendments are permitted—and sent it instead. to the Rules Committee.

68. The Krueger amendment provided immediate deregulation for new onshore gas, but preserved the existing regulatory structure for old gas.

69. For the floor debate on the Smith amendment see *Cong. Rec.*, House, Feb. 2–4, 1976, esp. pp. 1796–1798 and 2382–2389.

70. Representative Krueger complained that the assistance of Commerce Committee staff members was denied him during floor debate as "the majority staff sat with the people offering the amendments to my proposal and I had to

assess the impact of those amendments (without staff help)." See *National Journal* 8 (Sept. 10, 1976): 965.

71. Only two of the forty-six representatives from the six gas-exporting states supported the Smith amendment: Martha Keys of Kansas and Bob Eckhardt of Texas. Eckhardt, representing a working-class Houston district, was a member of the Commerce Committee and a consistent opponent of deregulation.

72. The census enumerates household consumption for cooking and heating separately, but gives no overall figure for the number of dwellings with gas service. The figures for cooking use were employed here since they represent the larger category. While nationally, in 1975, 84 percent of gas utility customers used gas for house heating, the percentage varied by region (it was lowest in the mid-Atlantic states). The use of these census figures therefore introduces some distortion, since space heating usually results in greater gas consumption than cooking uses alone. The ideal data for measuring the consumer interest in natural gas regulation would include the total quantity of residential gas consumption by county and congressional district. Such data are not available, to the author's knowledge.

73. Of voting Republicans in 1976, forty-eight represented districts in counties where over 50 percent of households used gas; two represented coal districts; eleven, gas-producing districts, and seventy-five, "spectator" districts, where fewer than half the households had gas service.

74. In 1975, the cost of heating per million Btu. for a Dallas home was $.96 for gas, or $9.52 for electricity (much of which was generated in gas-fired boilers). Comparable prices for Atlanta, Boston, and Chicago ranged from $1.33 to $2.72 for gas, $11.46 to $14.53 for electricity, and $2.45 to $2.65 for fuel oil (data from the FPC, Office of Economics).

75. Address by Mack Wallace, Chairman, Texas Railroad Commission, to the Energy Research and Education Foundation, Houston, Tex., Oct. 24, 1978.

76. Senate COC 1975, pp. 206–207.

77. *Cong. Rec.*, House, Sept. 18, 1975, p. 29328. The House IFC version would have authorized the government to prohibit boiler fuel uses regardless of the cost of conversion as long as use of an alternative fuel was "practicable."

78. Ibid.

79. The seventeen northeast-midwest "consumer tier" states have 49 percent of House seats, but only 34 percent of Senate seats. The producer-mountain-plains belt has only 17 percent of House seats, but 32 percent of Senate votes.

80. Furthermore, a much higher percentage of western coal is strip mined. As a result, the labor force is smaller and less unionized than is the case with eastern coal.

81. Richard Bensel, "Center-Periphery Relations in the United States: The Public Domain and Federalism," paper presented at the annual meeting of the Western Political Science Association, Portland, Ore., March 21, 1978. On energy issues and western (gubernatorial) politics, see Lynton R. Hayes, *Energy, Economic Growth and Regionalism in the West* (Albuquerque, N.M.: University of New Mexico Press, 1980).

82. Evidence of the common economic interests that bind these states in a "deregulation" coalition can be found in the results of the 1980 presidential

election. The producer-mountain-plains belt identified in Figure 11 was the region that gave Republican candidate Ronald Reagan his highest vote margin— an average 59.7 percent.

Chapter 7

1. Candidate Carter pledged support for deregulation in letters to the governors of the major producer states. "I will work with the Congress," Carter wrote Governor David Boren of Oklahoma, "as the Ford administration has been unable to do, to deregulate new natural gas. The decontrol of producer prices for new natural gas would provide an incentive for new exploration and would help our nation's oil and gas operators attract needed capital . . . and lessen the prospect of shortages in the nonproducing states" (letter reprinted in the *Cong. Rec.*, Senate, Nov. 15, 1978, p. 15219).

2. Other regionally divisive issues on which the Carter administration took the position of northern urban Democrats in 1977 and 1978 include: labor law reform, common site picketing, the minimum wage, cargo preference, welfare reform, revision of federal funding formulas for community development block grants and public works jobs, water project budget cuts, and aid to New York City.

3. Appalachian coal interests particularly opposed the following policies of the Republican administration: (1) its refusal to take action reducing the level of coal imports; (2) TVA's coal purchase policies, which disadvantaged the eastern fields; (3) the FEA's stand on strip mining, which, by supporting limited reclamation requirements, failed to equalize coal-mining costs across regions; (4) the administration's efforts to encourage coal production by facilitating leasing on public (western) lands; (5) the allowance of fuel adjustment clauses for federally regulated electric utilities, permitting transportation charges to be passed on to consumers; and (6) FEA's reluctance to put into effect a small operators loan program that Congress had enacted in 1975 to promote new underground mines in the East. See West Virginia Legislature, *A Study of the West Virginia Coal Industry and Ways to Help It* (Charleston, 1977). In 1976, western states accounted for only 20 percent of United States coal production, but contained half the country's estimated reserves.

4. Quoted in West Virginia Legislature, *A Study of the West Virginia Coal Industry* (pages not numbered). Regional conflicts in the coal industry are long-standing. In the 1930s, the Roosevelt administration's coal program was undercut by southern resistance to any labor, production, and transportation provisions that minimized the competitive advantage of southern mines vis-à-vis northern coal fields. See James P. Johnson, *The Politics of Soft Coal* (Urbana: University of Illinois Press, 1979), p. 14.

5. The Best Available Control Technology (BACT) requirement was contained in Clean Air Act amendments supported by the administration in 1977. The 1977 legislation was unpopular in the West for several reasons. In addition to the BACT provision, which sharply reduced the cost advantage of burning western coal, the legislation prohibited any significant deterioration of existing air quality. Western senators complained that this provision would discourage industrial development in areas—like the mountain and plains states—with "pris-

tine" air. Another blow to western coal interests came when Senator Howard Metzenbaum of Ohio successfully offered an amendment that allowed the head of the Environmental Protection Agency to allow the burning of locally produced high sulfur coal in order to forestall serious economic dislocations in eastern coal fields. The Metzenbaum amendment was supported by all but one voting senator from the five major eastern coal states, and opposed by all but one senator in the four major western coal states. Passed by only one vote in the Senate, the amendment was invoked a few months later when an Ohio local of the United Mine Workers Union complained to the Environmental Protection Agency that a number of utilities in the state were planning to purchase non-Ohio coal. See Daniel Seligman, "The Metzenbaum Doctrine," *Fortune*, March 12, 1979, p. 77.

6. Former Federal Power Commissioner Lee White suggested in late 1976 that congressional Democrats' dissatisfaction with the present commissioners might make them more favorable to reorganization. See "FPC Gas Ruling Leaves Consumers Out in the Cold," *National Journal* 8, no. 45 (Nov. 13, 1976): 1630.

7. A study of Federal Trade Commission (FTC) and Federal Communications Commission (FCC) appointments reveals that "no less than one-third of the selections were almost entirely a result of congressional sponsorship." See Senate Document no. 25, 95th Cong., 1st sess. (1977), p. 154. It is common for regulatory appointments to reflect both patronage and presidential sensitivity to the economic interests of congressional constituencies (for example, the Johnson administration was obligated to appoint at least one New Yorker to the Securities and Exchange Commission). Under recent Democratic presidents, however, the traditional patterns have not held for appointments to the highly politicized FPC. Neither Johnson nor Carter appointed producer state residents to the commission, even though Carter won the states of Texas and Louisiana, and Johnson carried Texas in 1964.

8. US Congress, Senate, Committee on Energy and Natural Resources, Hearings on Nominations to the Federal Energy Regulatory Commission, 95th Cong., 1st sess. (Oct. 1977), pp. 28–31. Two of the five FERC appointees had previously served on state regulatory commissions, a third on an AEC licensing panel. Don S. Smith, the only commissioner to dissent from the 1976 FPC price increases, was reappointed by Carter in 1977.

9. "Market incentives," said the administration, "cannot improve on nature" (Executive Office of the President, Energy Policy and Planning Office, "The National Energy Plan," p. 11). Administration spokesman S. David Freeman told the House Commerce Committee that "by the mid and late 1980s the nation's oil and gas resources will be so scarce and so expensive and so necessary for other uses that one needs to have all segments of industry make preparations to use less and move to a coal-based source." See HR IFC 1977, p. 1129.

10. Executive Office of the President, "The National Energy Plan," p. xix. By 1990, according to the plan, "virtually no utilities would be permitted to burn natural gas." The plan noted that 60 percent of natural gas consumption took place in industries and utilities, the bulk of which were located in the producing states.

11. Ibid., p. xi (emphasis in original).

12. In addition, the FPC could set prices higher than $1.75 for specific categories of new gas discovered under difficult conditions.

13. The administration plan relied on state agencies to classify gas into the specified pricing categories, but empowered the FPC to set terms for this delegation and to rescind it, or to reverse or modify state determinations. The final statute made no provision for recision, and made commission reversals of state agency determinations subject to judicial review.

14. House Report no. 543 on the National Energy Act (Ad Hoc Committee), 95th Cong., 1st sess. (July 1977), pp. 708–746. See also the 1977 *Congressional Quarterly Almanac*, pp. 708–746. The distributional aspects of these rebates also create substantial regional disparities. In 1976, for example, Congress appropriated two hundred million dollars in fuel assistance payments for low-income households. Over half the funds went to nine midwestern and mid-Atlantic states, prompting states to the south to complain that the allocation formula was unfairly biased. *Cong. Rec.*, Senate, Oct. 6, 1977, p. 16505. In the fall of 1980, there was a protracted conflict in the House over the formula for distributing federal fuel assistance payments. Southern representatives, pointing to the large number of deaths that occurred during the heat wave of the preceding summer, argued for distribution of the funds according to the total size of residential utility bills (including air-conditioning costs). Representatives from colder areas insisted, however, that only the magnitude of heating bills be used in the formula. See "House Defeats Amendment to Give Poor, Elderly Help With Air-Conditioning Bills," *The Houston Post*, Aug. 28, 1980, p. 12A.

15. The new committee acquired energy-related jurisdiction from the former Commerce, Interior, Armed Services, Public Works, and Atomic Energy committees; it was chaired by Henry Jackson, former Interior Committee chairman. Although the new committee contained an Energy Conservation and Regulation Subcommittee headed by Bennett Johnson of Louisiana (the equivalent subcommittee on Commerce had been chaired by Adlai Stevenson III of Illinois), the balance of forces within the committee on the natural gas issue did not change significantly. The new Energy Committee contained: eight opponents of deregulation (that is, opponents of the 1975 Pearson-Bentsen admendment), eight supporters, one new senator (Spark Matzunaga of Hawaii), and one who had first opposed, then supported Pearson-Bentsen (Wendell Ford of Kentucky). Senator Jackson, like Commerce Chairman Magnuson, represented the state of Washington and took a strong pro-consumer position.

16. In addition to the natural gas, coal conversion, and taxation components, the administration program contained provisions relating to: conservation and energy efficiency for buildings, appliances, and automobiles; promotion of nonconventional energy sources; and reform of utility rates to encourage conservation among large energy consumers.

17. Among the objectors to the new gas-pricing features were representatives of municipally owned gas distributors: Lee White representing the Consumer Federation of America; James K. Flug representing Energy Action, a proconsumer organization sponsored by several people affiliated with the motion picture industry; and a representative of the Oil, Chemical, and Atomic Workers Union.

18. Senator Clifford Hansen of Wyoming claimed that, from 1971 to 1975, his state had experienced a 60 percent increase in gas supplies. Oklahoma Senator Dewey Bartlett presented evidence during floor debate that a new gas price

increase from $.30 mcf to $1.70 mcf had resulted, between 1972 and 1976, in an increase in operating drilling rigs from 103 to 192, with annual additions to reserves rising from 393 bcf to 878 bcf. See *Cong. Rec*, Senate, Sept. 19, 1977, pp. 15149–15150. According to the American Association of Petroleum Geologists, the downward trend in the total number of wells drilled for hydrocarbons in the United States was reversed in 1973. The number of wells drilled increased from 28,120 in 1970 to 37,235 in 1975, and 46,479 in 1977. See *International Petroleum Encyclopedia* (Tulsa: Petroleum Publishing Co., 1979), pp. 220–221.

19. Testimony of Edward Erickson, Department of Economics, North Carolina State University, HR IFC 1977, pp. 1110–1111.

20. Ibid., p. 1447.

21. 1977 *Congressional Quarterly Almanac*, p. 719.

22. Bruce I. Oppenheimer, "Policy Effects of US House Reform: Decentralization and the Capacity to Resolve Energy Issues," *Legislative Studies Quarterly* 1 (Feb. 1980): 5–29.

23. Representative Krueger, who was not appointed, charged that the committee was "stacked" with supporters of the Carter bill. 1977 *Congressional Quarterly Almanac*, p. 722. The Ad Hoc Committee reported the president's program by a vote of twenty-six to fourteen. All but one Democratic member voted to report the bill. Representatives Moss of California, Reuss of Wisconsin, and Moffett of Connecticut complained, however, that the bill gave too much to the producers. Since production was irreversibly declining regardless of price incentives, they argued, producers should be subjected to standard utility regulation with prices fixed to reimburse costs plus a reasonable return. See House Report no. 543, 95th Cong., 1st sess., pp. 267 ff.

24. 1977 *Congressional Quarterly Almanac*, p. 726. The deregulation proposal, offered by Representative Clarence Brown of Ohio, was defeated on a 199-to-227 vote on Aug. 3, 1977.

25. Of the forty-one shifts between 1976 and 1977, nine represented partisan changes. Twenty-two of the remaining thirty-two shifts occurred in spectator districts, fifteen of which were in the South. Three producer state representatives shifted to opposition on the 1977 deregulation amendment vote. One of these (Charles Wilson of Texas) was later appointed to the conference committee; the other two were retiring at the end of the Ninety-fifth Congress.

26. *Cong. Rec.*, House, Aug. 3, 1977, pp. 8416–8417. Almost 90 percent of House Republicans voted for the deregulation amendment and almost 75 percent of voting Democrats opposed it. Of the seventy-two Democrats who supported deregulation, only seven represented consumer districts. Thirty-three represented spectator districts, two-thirds of which were in the South; and twenty-nine represented producer state districts. Three Democratic votes for deregulation came from major coal districts. Two of the three coal district Democrats subsequently voted for the Carter plan on the final vote in 1977, however, suggesting that they found either deregulation or a combination of regulation and coal conversion equally attractive alternatives. In all, one-third of major coal district representatives supported deregulation, and two-thirds supported the Carter plan in 1977. The Ad Hoc Committee amendment to broaden the application of

the oil and gas user tax was endorsed on the floor by eleven of twelve coal district votes.

27. Deadlocked on the deregulation issue, the Energy and Natural Resources Committee had sent the administration's natural gas proposal to the floor without recommendation. The Pearson-Bentsen amendment was adopted by a vote of fifty to forty-six, the same margin by which it had survived a crucial procedural challenge in 1975.

28. Senate Report no. 36, 95th Cong, 1st sess. (1977). The Senate coal conversion bill, S 977, was less stringent as reported and was further amended on the floor to allow smaller new industrial users to continue to burn oil. The Senate floor also added provisions for federal loans to aid in coal conversion and increased financial assistance for rail rehabilitation.

29. With much of their coal reserves lying beneath arid and easily damaged federal land, western congressmen have often been more concerned about the social and environmental consequences of rapid coal development than its economic benefits.

30. An amendment was adopted on the Senate floor which added to the Finance Committee bill a provision taxing industrial oil and gas use in new and certain existing industrial and utility boilers, with a wide range of grounds for exemption. The conference committee dropped the user tax altogether. 1977 *Congressional Quarterly Almanac*, p. 742.

31. 1978 *Congressional Quarterly Almanac*, pp. 25–28.

32. The terms of the compromise were approved thirteen to twelve by House conferees, and ten to seven by the Senate negotiators. Six weeks later, after committee staff had drafted the compromise in legislative language, new opposition arose among the conferees, and majorities of the two chambers' conferees did not sign the report until Aug. 18.

33. According to Charles Curtis, the chairman of the FERC, the new law specified eleven categories of gas. Critics, however, claimed to find from thirty to thirty-three different pricing categories. The basic divisions are: (1) new onshore wells; (2) new offshore leases; (3) new onshore production wells; (4) "high cost" gas from geopressurized brine, coal seams, Devonian shale, reservoirs fifteen thousand feet below existing wells, or other high-cost situations; (5) stripper-well gas; (6) interstate gas under existing contracts ("old" or "flowing" contracts); (7) expiring interstate contracts ("rollover" contracts); (8) existing intrastate contracts; (9) expiring intrastate contracts; and (10) Alaskan natural gas (Prudhoe Bay). Several divisions (by contract price, for example) are specified within some of these categories.

34. *Wall Street Journal*, Oct. 24, 1978, p. 16.

35. *Oil and Gas Journal*, May 1, 1978, p. 25.

36. *Cong. Rec.*, Senate, Sept. 11, 1978, p. 14873. A new ally for the deregulation forces was the NAACP. The organization issued a statement opposing the Carter plan, saying, "We cannot accept the notion that our people are best served by a policy based on the inevitability of energy shortage and the need for government to allocate an ever-diminishing supply among competing interests." See *Oil and Gas Journal*, Jan. 16, 1978.

37. *Oil and Gas Journal*, April 10, 1978, p. 31.

38. "When FERC Is Better than NEP," *Oil and Gas Journal*, March 13, 1978, p. 46.

39. *Oil and Gas Journal*, April 10, 1978, p. 31. In floor debate on the compromise, producer state representatives repeatedly made the point that the Natural Gas Policy Act was not a "deregulation" bill. Under the new statute, the Department of Energy estimated, about 24 percent of gas production would be deregulated by 1985. Under the existing dual market, however, the more than 40 percent of domestic gas production consumed in the producer states was unregulated. See *Cong. Rec.*, Senate, Sept. 11, 1978, p. 14880.

40. Mack Wallace, chairman, Texas Railroad Commission, "The Natural Gas Policy Act of 1978: Pillage of the Colonies," Address to the Energy Research and Education Foundation, Houston, Tex., Oct. 24, 1978.

41. Ibid., The estimates of alternative consumer-producer benefits under the House, Senate, and Conference bills, and also the status quo is found in HR IFC 1978. These estimates, as the estimates of imported oil savings and inflationary impact, are based on a number of assumptions about demand/price elasticity, future FERC actions, and prices of uncontrolled foreign and domestic fuels. Needless to say, all such estimates are open to question. The actual range of estimates by Commerce Committee staff went from a possible six billion dollar benefit to a seven billion dollar cost for producer state residents.

42. The exemptions under the Powerplant and Industrial Fuel Use Act would, according to Wallace, allow northeastern and midwestern utilities to burn a plentiful supply of gas at old interstate prices, while Texas industrial and utility users would be forced, by higher intrastate prices and regulations for new facilities, to convert to coal.

43. The conference report was signed by Democratic Representatives Bob Eckhardt and Charles Wilson of Texas and Republican Senator Pete Dominici of New Mexico. Democratic Representative Joe Waggoner and Senator Bennett Johnston of Louisiana were conferees, but refused to approve the final agreement (as did Republican Senator Dewey Bartlett of Oklahoma). Wilson's East Texas district is served mainly by interstate pipelines, which creates an interest in regulation that most other Texas districts do not share. Eckhardt's political constituency in Houston included not only labor unions hostile to deregulation but a large utility, Houston Natural Gas, which supported the extension of regulation to intrastate sales. The House producer state conferees, although later divided on the compromise, were united on four issues of major concern to the southwestern gas states: they opposed emergency allocation from the intrastate market to interstate users, oil and gas user taxes, and incremental pricing of intrastate gas (which they felt would discourage industrial growth in the Southwest); and they strongly supported an easing of coal conversion requirements.

44. *Cong. Rec.*, Senate, Sept. 11, 1978, pp. 14873–14880. Similarly, Representative Henry Reuss released a letter from the chairman of the Wisconsin Public Service Commission warning that the compromise bill's incremental pricing provisions would be "an economic catastrophe for Wisconsin's industry, resulting in a loss of jobs . . . to gas producing states" (mimeo, Aug. 2, 1978). Opposed by pipelines, distributors, and industrial users, incremental pricing was

designed to protect interstate residential consumers from sudden increases in their utility bills by channeling high-cost gas, in effect to industrial users. However, some economists argued that residential users would reap little, if any, benefit from the method. If industrial users reacted to sharply higher prices by significantly reducing their gas consumption, residential users would have to bear a larger portion of pipeline transportation and distribution costs. See, for example, Edward W. Erickson, "Residential Consumer Impact Cost of Inefficient Use of the Natural Gas Transmission and Distribution System," published by the Natural Gas Supply Committee, Oct. 1977.

45. Steven Rattner, "Senate Energy Fight Being Lost by North," *New York Times*, Oct. 20, 1977, p. A 20.

46. Thomas Downey, *Cong. Rec.*, House, Nov. 29, 1977, E 7151. The regional implications of the Carter proposals were recognized by northeastern representatives of both parties. Said Connecticut Republican Representative Steward McKinney, a supporter of HR 8444, "The Northeast's most immediate and pressing need is to achieve energy price and supply parity between consuming regions of the nation." Quoted in Michael J. McManus, "The Northeast Needs Carter's Oil Tax," *Newsday* (reprinted in *Cong. Rec.*, House, Nov. 29, 1977, E 7151). The fuel rebates envisioned by the original Carter bill would also, according to McManus, result in a net bonus of three hundred million dollars for the Northeast.

47. During the lengthy House and Senate debate on the NGPA, there are numerous allusions to the advantages of the existing Natural Gas Act, as recently interpreted, over the new gas bill. See, for example, *Cong. Rec.*, House, Oct. 13, 1978, p. 12817, and *Cong. Rec.*, Senate, Sept. 11, 1978, p. 14871.

48. *California et al.* v. *Southland Royalty Co. et al.*, 436 US 519 (May 1978). The quote is taken from the Court's summary.

49. Ibid., p. 528 (emphasis in original). In this case, Gulf itself had also "not voluntarily taken any action that would bring [it] under the commission's jurisdiction," but was "captured" when the 1954 Phillips decision compelled all producers who were selling gas interstate to apply for FPC certificates. Justice Stevens, in dissent, argued that while Gulf was a "natural gas company," according to previous interpretations of the term, the respondents (Southland et al.) were not, since they "clearly did not transport gas and their retention of a standard, fixed royalty interest did not constitute a 'sale' of gas in interstate commerce." In addition, he argued, "the Natural Gas Act, as this Court has repeatedly stated, does not represent an exercise of Congress' full power under the Commerce clause," but applies only to interstate transactions. "Despite the Act's flexibility," Stevens concluded, "I would not stretch it to reach this case." Pp. 538–546.

50. The commission rather grandly argued that the section 7 requirement for approval of abandonment was "like an ancient covenant running with the land." See *California et al.* v. *Southland*, p. 545.

51. The *National Journal* quotes a Senate staff member as saying, "There's probably about two inches of land in Louisiana that at some time hasn't been committed to interstate sales" ("The Court Gets into the Act," Aug. 19, 1978, p. 1333).

52. Within the producer states it is generally recognized that a producer has a

responsibility to the royalty owners to continue production as long as he or she is recovering costs plus a reasonable profit. On this subject, see Kathleen Cooper Lake, "The Prudent Operator Standard and FERC Authority," *Texas Law Review* 57, no. 4 (March 1979): 662.

53. Ibid., p. 662.

54. 566 F2d (5th Cir. 1978).

55. In this instance, however, they were disappointed. The Supreme Court tied four to four, thus allowing the lower court's ruling to stand. Fortunately for the producers, they had won the FERC "appeals race" to file the case in the Fifth Circuit Court. If it had been appealed to the District of Columbia court, the decision might well have gone the other way. The Energy Policy Task Force, representing the Consumer Federation of America and several labor, farm, and public power groups, had also challenged the FERC decision on the grounds that it did not go far enough to compel deliveries.

56. "Gas Pipelines Battle FERC over Ruling on Field Costs," *Oil and Gas Journal*, March 27, 1978, p. 88.

57. Sheila S. Hollis and Phillip M. Marston, "A Review and Assessment of the FERC Natural Gas Enforcement Program," *Houston Law Review* 16, no. 5 (July 1979): 1115–1116, 1122. Hollis was the first director of the Enforcement Office.

58. For example, in another recent case, the commission had ruled that a well later drilled to a greater depth on a site once believed depleted must sell gas only to interstate pipelines if the first well had been certificated for interstate sales, and the commission had not authorized abandonment.

59. Energy Action, *Factbook on the Proposed Natural Gas Bill* (Washington, D.C., Sept. 25, 1978), p. 5.

60. Ibid., p. 51.

61. "Excess deliverability" in Texas alone was estimated at between one and three billion cfd in the summer of 1978. See "Surplus of Intrastate Gas Hits Big Producing States," *Oil and Gas Journal*, July 17, 1978, p. 19.

62. Ibid., p. 20.

63. *Oil and Gas Journal*, March 27, 1978, pp. 88–89. The pipelines opposed the ruling for fear it would discourage producers from making interstate sales.

64. The FPC had, however, successfully attempted to limit the quantities of gas involved in direct sales by denying or attaching conditions to pipeline certificates.

65. *FPC* v. *Louisiana Power and Light Co.*, 406 US 631. This case is discussed in Thomas K. Anson, "The Case for a White Market in the Allocation of Natural Gas During Shortages," *Texas Law Review* 57, no. 4 (March 1979): 619–623.

66. "Fate of Carter Energy Plan May Depend on Outcome of Louisiana Gas Firm Case," *Wall Street Journal*, Aug. 9, 1978, p. 2.

67. Section 110 of the Natural Gas Policy Act also appeared to overturn another recent FERC ruling by allowing gas processing and compression costs to be considered as an addition to, not a component of, the maximum categorical price.

68. "Gas Compromise Splits US Oil Industry," *Oil and Gas Journal*, June 9, 1978, p. 56; and "Tipro Delays Stand on Gas Compromise," *Oil and Gas Journal*, June 12, 1978, p. 34.

69. *Oil and Gas Journal*, April 10, 1978, p. 31.

70. *Oil and Gas Journal*, June 9, 1978, pp. 56–57. The *OGJ*, itself an early opponent of the extension of controls, came to support the compromise by mid-August. See "Natural Gas Stalemate Must Be Ended Promptly" (editorial), Aug. 14, 1978, p. 29. The *OGJ* saw the bill as advantageous for both interstate pipelines and producers with "a cash flow pinch from shut-in wells."

71. For example, an application to the Texas Railroad Commission for designation of a given well's production as "new" requires the producer to submit: (1) a map or plot covering a 2.5-mile radius; (2) forms W-1, A-1, or W-2, as applicable, and production records from Jan. 1, 1970, to April 20, 1977, for all wells within the 2.5-mile radius; (3) any directional survey required to be filed on the subject well; plus (4) required oaths and certificates of service. Intervenors may protest any categorization requested by the producer, delaying his application at the state level. At the federal level, if FERC has not acted on the request for price categorization within forty-five days, the producer may charge the requested price subject to refund if the designation is later overturned. Opponents frequently pointed out that in 1978 FERC already had a backlog of from fifteen to twenty thousand cases under its old NGA jurisdiction.

72. McClure rather forthrightly announced at a press conference the presumably connected events: he had changed his position from insistence on the Senate's earlier deregulation program to support for the compromise, and the administration had agreed to fund the breeder reactor research (even though the president had earlier insisted on ending the program for fear that nuclear wastes could fall into the hands of terrorists). The McClure deal generated some bad feelings in Congress, among both breeder reactor opponents and Tennessee congressmen who resented the earlier loss of funding for the Clinch River, Tenn., reactor project. See 1978 *Congressional Quarterly Almanac*, pp. 656–657, and "White House Lobbyists Employ the Hard Sell to Win Senate Support for the Natural Gas Bill," *Congressional Quarterly Weekly Report*, Sept. 16, 1978, pp. 2452–2453.

73. Representative Clarence J. Brown, "The Servility of Business," *Wall Street Journal*, Nov. 29, 1978, p. 22.

74. *Congressional Quarterly*, "White House Lobbyists."

75. Brown, "Servility of Business," p. 22.

76. *Congressional Quarterly*, "White House Lobbyists."

77. "Gas Pricing Battle at Standoff," *Houston Post*, Sept. 8, 1978, p. 19A.

78. *Congressional Quarterly*, "White House Lobbyists."

79. US Senate, Aug. 23, 1978.

80. See, for example *Cong. Rec.*, Senate, Sept. 13, 1978, pp. 15011–15013.

81. Spectator states are defined here as those with natural gas service in fewer than 50 percent of households in 1975, using *Minerals Yearbook* gas service data and census estimates of the number of households in states. Alaska is omitted from the producer state support pattern reported here because of the NGPA's special relevance to the proposed Alaskan pipeline. The recommittal motion described here is the second motion on Sept. 26, 1978. An earlier recommittal motion was defeated on a roll call vote of thirty-nine to fifty-nine on Sept. 19.

82. 1978 *Congressional Quarterly Almanac*, pp. 660–662.

83. Several producer state representatives who later opposed even the com-

promise bill voted for the Ad Hoc bill in 1977, in order to secure the appointment
to conference of several producer state representatives.

84. There were approximately equal numbers of Democratic spectator representatives in the "Consumer Tier" and the "Border-South" regions. In the
former, spectator Democratic support for the energy package dropped from 93
percent in 1977 to 69 percent in 1978. In the Border-South, however, support held
steady at 80 percent in both years.

85. In anticipation of the passage of the NGPA, the FERC requested three
hundred new employees and a significant expansion of its budget. See *Wall Street
Journal*, Oct. 24, 1978.

Chapter 8

1. Paul MacAvoy reports that in the 1960s, even as it kept a tight lid on
producer prices, the FPC allowed high returns in almost all pipeline rate cases. In
general, according to MacAvoy, the commission exercised "no systematic regulatory restraints on profit-making by the pipelines." Interstate electric power
projects, another part of the FPC's original jurisdiction, have also fared
extremely well, MacAvoy finds. See "The Formal Work Product of the Federal
Power Commissioners," *Bell Journal of Economics and Management Science* 2
(Spring 1971): 379–395.

2. Samuel P. Huntington, "The Marasmus of the ICC," *The Yale Law Journal*
61, no. 4 (April 1952): 470.

3. On this tariff-based Republican Coalition, see E. E. Schattschneider, *Politics, Pressures and the Tariff* (New York: Prentice-Hall, 1935), and David
Mayhew, *Party Loyalty Among Congressmen* (Cambridge, Mass.: Harvard University Press, 1966).

4. In a recent article entitled "The Energy Crisis—Moral Equivalent of Civil
War," Joseph Kalt and Peter Navarro conclude from an analysis of petroleum
regulatory policy in the mid-1970s that "regulation of the petroleum industry has
been explicitly designed in Congress as a mechanism to redistribute wealth." See
Regulation 4 (Jan./Feb. 1980): 43.

5. For a generalized and richly historical argument for social control of market
processes, see Karl Polanyi, *The Great Transformation* (Boston: Beacon Press,
1957).

6. According to *Oil and Gas Journal*, the average number of rigs active in 1980
surpassed by several hundred the previous record set in 1955 and represented a
200 percent increase over 1971 drilling activity. See *Oil and Gas Journal* 79 (Jan.
12, 1981): 24. Although it seems reasonable to interpret this increase as a result of
new discoveries in response to price increases, an argument might be made (in
line with the consumer contention in the late 1970s) that producers had neglected
to produce known reserves in anticipation of higher prices and that it was price
certainty, not a price increase per se, that elicited the "new" supplies.

Glossary

Additions to reserves	Confirmed gas discoveries (new "proven reserves").
Area rate	A methodology employed by the Federal Power Commission, beginning in the 1960s, to fix allowable prices for gas producers in specified gas-producing areas based on average costs for producers in the area.
Arm's length transactions	Transactions between unaffiliated companies, for example, sales by a gas producer to a separate pipeline company.
Bcf	Billion cubic feet. A standard measure of natural gas volume. A pressure of 14.7 psia and temperature of sixty degrees are assumed. Lesser quantities are usually measured in mcf (thousand cubic feet); greater quantities, in tcf (trillion cubic feet).
Capture rule	The practice, applied in the law, of granting free exploitation of a mineral resource to its finder.
Certificate	A license to operate granted by a regulatory agency where entry into the regulated business is restricted. Those approved to do business under the aegis of the agency are described as "certificated." The certificate specifies the firm's obligations to the agency and the public, the area in which it is allowed to operate, and so forth.
Common carrier	A transporter (for example, a pipeline or railroad firm) that is obligated by law to accept products for transmission without discriminating among shippers.
Cost-based rate	In utility regulation this concept implies that a public agency fixes prices for the regulated industry based on a determination of their "actual, legitimate costs"—that is, the justifiable costs they have incurred in providing the required service—plus a "reasonable" return (for example, 10 percent) on investment.

241

Deregulation	In natural gas policy, the specification in law that sales of gas by independent producers are exempt from regulation by the FPC (FERC).
Dry hole	A well drilled in search of hydrocarbons that yields no appreciable quantities.
End-use control	The regulation of the uses of natural gas, typically in order to conserve gas for its highest priority uses (in households and industrial processes) and prohibit its use for steam generation in utility and industrial boilers.
Escalator clauses	Clauses inserted in gas sales contracts, particularly during the 1950s, which allowed the sales price to be adjusted upward during the life of the contract.
FPC/FERC	Federal Power Commission until 1977; Federal Energy Regulatory Commission thereafter. The agency charged with administering the Natural Gas Act of 1938 and the Natural Gas Policy Act of 1978. Its principal functions are certification, price and service regulation of interstate natural gas sales by producers and pipelines, and the licensing, service, and sales price regulation (for interstate sales) of hydroelectric power plants on navigable waters.
Gathering	The collecting of gas from one or more wells in order to channel it to a central place for processing or sale.
Holding company	A firm that controls other companies by ownership of a sufficient block of their common stock. Stock transactions and other practices of these companies are regulated by the SEC.
"Hot" oil	Oil produced and sold above that allowed by state "conservation" agencies responsible for setting production quotas.
Independent producer	In natural gas regulation, a gas producer not affiliated with a pipeline company or local gas-distributing utility.
Intervenor	One who participates in a regulatory proceeding to offer evidence and argument, but who is not directly involved in the case at hand.
Market price	The price that prevails (or would prevail) in an unregulated exchange between unaffiliated buyers and sellers.
Natural monopoly	An enterprise in which, because of high capitalization costs and economies of scale (once a certain size is reached, its market can be extended at declining marginal costs), a monopoly can operate more efficiently than competitive enterprises within a given territory or market.
New gas	Newly discovered or newly marketed gas, according to statutory or administrative specification; the upper

	"tier" of gas has been granted, since the 1960s, a higher price than "old" (or "flowing") gas in order to encourage exploration.
Proven reserves	The quantity of gas in a known reservoir, according to best available methods of estimation.
Prudent investment	The "legitimate" costs incurred by a regulated utility; the point is not to "give credit," in fixing rates, to unnecessary or "imprudent" expenditures by the company, in order to encourage sound business practices.
Recommittal vote	The vote on a motion, made on the House or Senate floor toward the conclusion of debate, to send a bill back to the committee of jurisdiction (which usually kills the bill for that session).
Rollover contracts	Contracts between sellers (gas producers) and buyers (usually transporting pipelines) that represent renewals after an original sale (as, for example, when a twenty-year contract expires and is renewed for another twenty years). Once "certificated," gas producers are required by the FERC to continue to sell gas from a given field to interstate pipelines unless the agency permits "abandonment" of deliveries. However, a rollover contract may specify a new sale price, subject to statutory (formerly agency-determined) ceilings.
Spectator area	In this study, a state or congressional district in which fewer than 50 percent of households have natural gas service.
Stripper wells	Wells capable of producing only small quantities (specified in the law) of oil or gas.
Stub lines	Short pipelines used to transport gas to or from a major pipeline.
Wellhead price	The price paid to the producer of natural gas, the "wellhead" being the point at which the gas comes out of the ground.
Wildcat well	A well drilled in an area where there have, as yet, been no confirmed, significant discoveries. One who drills such wells is a "wildcatter."

Index